GHOSTS OF THE FIREGROUND

GHOSTS OF THE FIREGROUND

Echoes of the Great Peshtigo

Fire and the Calling

of a Wildland

Firefighter

PETER M. LESCHAK

HarperSanFrancisco

A Division of HarperCollinsPublishers

363.379   8/29/02   FIRST EDITION
Les   Designed by Joseph Rutt

Library of Congress Cataloging-in-Publication Data has been ordered.
ISBN 0–06–251777–5
02 03 04 05 06 ❖/RRD 10 9 8 7 6 5 4 3 2 1

TO ALL WHO HAUNT THE FIREGROUND—
LIVING AND DEAD.

Then the angel took the censer, filled it with fire from the altar, and poured it on the earth; there followed peels of thunder, loud blasts, flashes of lightning, and an earthquake.

REVELATION 8:5

Beloved, think it not strange concerning the firey trial which is to try you, as though some strange thing happened to you: But rejoice. . . .

I PETER 4:12-13

Fire is power.

STEPHEN J. PYNE

CONTENTS

GLEAMING EVERYWHERE

Mike was first to spot the smoke.

"There," he said, and swung the nose of the helicopter a few degrees southeast.

A lazy white plume curled out of a pine stand near the crest of a ridge. Fanned by treetop wind, it quickly dispersed to haze. I keyed the radio.

"Flathead Dispatch, this is helicopter Alpha-Hotel-Romeo. We have the smoke in sight. Stand by for a size-up."

We were close to Blacktail Mountain, in the Salish range, a dozen miles south of Kalispell, Montana. The crystalline expanse of Flathead Lake was two ridgelines to the east. It was August 26, 2000, and wildfires had been rampaging throughout the northern Rockies since mid-July.

In a minute we were over the newest one, Mike banking steeply to the left so I could gaze straight down into the trees. The fire was still small, partially hidden by the forest canopy and shielded from wind. A timely attack would catch it. Since it was near the top of the slope, there wasn't much room for it to run. Ground forces were rolling from Boorman Station at Little Bitterroot Lake but were nearly an hour away.

I had three crew members in the backseats, and over the intercom I offered a benediction: "This one is ours."

Doug responded with a terse, emphatic, "Yes!"

As Mike swung the Bell 212 north to search for a landing zone—or *helispot*—I radioed a brief report to Flathead Dispatch, then pointed to a clearing about 200 yards below the fire.

"What about that, Mike?"

He'd seen it but wasn't impressed. The wind was unfavorable for an easy landing—the air on the lee side of the ridge might be "squirrelly," with troublesome eddies on the downslope. And the ground looked rough. As Mike eased us in for a better look, we saw it really wasn't ground at all but a thick mat of old logging slash. Still, it was ideal in reference to the fire—unusually close and safely below.

"Okay. Let's give it a try," he said, deadpan, as usual. To call Mike taciturn was an understatement. In nearly two months of fire and flying, I'd yet to witness him agitated. He was forty-five years old and had 13,000 hours at the controls of a helicopter. He was cool to the point of cadaverous.

He brought Alpha-Hotel-Romeo in slowly, and I cracked open my door to gain a clear view of the left skid. The crew did the same in back, leaning out to scan for the best spot in the tangle of limbs and logs.

"Looks good on this side," I said.

But in the rear Doug saw a protruding stump. "A foot to the right!"

Mike jiggled the cyclic stick a fraction of an inch.

"Okay."

I could see he was struggling a little.

The ship settled and for a moment felt spongy. Mike lifted us a foot, crabbed left, and settled again. We were tilted slightly to the right, but it felt firm enough.

Just before I unplugged my avionics, Mike turned and said, deadpan of course, "That was fun. I won't be picking you up here."

I grinned. "Ten-four."

The thing was, we were here, now. At a fire. We'd worry about the pickup later.

I doffed my flight helmet, stowed it between the seats, and grabbed my fireground hard hat on the way out the door. Doug and the crew were muscling the 150-pound, 320-gallon Bambi Bucket from a cargo compartment, and I positioned myself forty feet in front of the ship so I could monitor the operation, acting as safety officer and, I thought, as a kind of priest.

Since June 1 we'd practiced this bucket deployment in dry runs and "wet" runs, refining the sequence to the point of ritual. I once mused—only half in jest—that crew members were like altar boys or vestal virgins, precisely performing a sacred rite. We honed it to fine detail, knowing which hand would be used by what person to manipulate a given buckle, latch, or handle. The task was to hook the bucket to the belly of the ship and test it, then transform ourselves from air crew to fire crew. The goal was rapid perfection, speed without stumbling.

One of our training manuals asserts that fireground air operations, like maritime activities, are not inherently dangerous, it's just that they unfold in a tenaciously unforgiving environment, intolerant of mistakes. One miscue can court disaster. I count this drill a ritual because it can kill you. I know of a colleague who, during such a procedure, made a mistake. A few seconds later, a helicopter was trashed, a pilot injured, and the colleague decapitated by a tail rotor. That was a sacrifice we wished to avoid.

One of the relief pilots called our crew a well-oiled machine. I preferred to think of us as ceremonial dancers, preparing for the next baptism of fire with careful choreography. Because the stakes are high and final. All summer we'd been stationed in northeastern Minnesota, prepared for initial attack in the Blowdown—25 million broken, uprooted trees, the biggest fuel load in North America. A July 4, 1999, megastorm had flattened 477,000 acres of the Superior National Forest, mostly in the Boundary Waters Canoe Area Wilderness, and in 2000 there was acute potential for magnificent, dangerous fires in remote and rugged terrain. We trained and drilled with that in mind. Sooner or later the Blowdown would burn—big-time. Meanwhile, there was Montana.

When the bucket was ready, our flight gear stowed, and our hand tools and fireline packs secured on the ground, the crew gathered behind me. I scanned earth and sky, searching for any defects—another aircraft, a control head cable draped over a skid, a loose item in the rotorwash. Satisfied the scene was righteous, I gave Mike a jubilant thumbs-up. Alpha-Hotel-Romeo powered away for a nearby lake. Pulling my earplugs, I briefly surveyed the bright, open faces of the crew.

"Shall we go?" I asked.

A chorus of boyish hoots.

We donned our packs, picked up our *pulaskis* (a combination ax and grub hoe) and chain saw, and headed upslope for the fire, a happy band of brothers eagerly hiking toward the drudgery and perils of the fireground.

But this joyful anticipation of struggle is not the only face of fire. A happy band is not the only congregation to frequent smoky

4

woods. The minions of terror and death are also illuminated by torching trees. And never with such an awful brightness than was seen in Peshtigo, Wisconsin, on an October day 130 years ago.

On September 22, 1871, the Reverend Peter Pernin, age forty-six, a Catholic priest in northeastern Wisconsin, was on a routine ministerial mission at the Sugar Bush, a collection of farms near the town of Peshtigo. The twelve-year-old son of a local parishioner offered to guide him on a pheasant hunt, and they ventured into surrounding woods. The Reverend recorded no kills, and a few hours later, near sundown, he suggested the boy lead him back to the homestead. Soon it was apparent they were lost. Darkness was settling, and the autumn forest was quiet except for "the crackling of a tiny tongue of fire that ran along the ground, in and out, among the trunks of the trees, leaving them unscathed but devouring the dry leaves. . . ."

The summer of 1871 had been uncommonly arid, with only two rainfalls from July through September. Local farmers seized the opportunity to expand their fields, felling dense forest and burning the residue of limbs, foliage, and stumps. This was standard practice, slash-and-burn agriculture—what we now consider Third World land mis-management. As historian Stephen Pyne has written, "Gilded Age America was the burning Brazil of its day." In 1831, Gustave Beaumont, a companion of Alexis de Tocqueville, observed the pioneers of the young nation hacking farms out of forest. He noted there was "in America a general hatred of trees." The autumn fires of northeast Wisconsin were no remarkable event, and Father Pernin wrote, "In this way the woods, particularly in the fall, are gleaming everywhere with fires lighted by man. . . ."

As he and his young companion wandered through the woods, a rising breeze swayed the canopy, and the innocent, creeping flames in the leaf litter and duff began to lengthen, some tongues licking up the tree trunks. Alarmed, they shouted for help, and when no reply was heard, Pernin fired his gun several times as a distress signal.

Eventually they heard answering shouts. The boy's parents and their farmhands had mounted a search and homed in on the gunshots. By then Pernin and the boy were circled by fire, and their rescuers wielded conifer boughs to beat a narrow passage through the flames.

A few days later Pernin was returning to Peshtigo after a visit to an outlying parish on the banks of the Menominee River. He was driving his horse and buggy along a forest road when fire burgeoned on both sides. Gagging on smoke, he urged his horse forward. The animal balked, but the priest persisted, and they burrowed into an orange-tinted tunnel of smoke. Five or six minutes later they burst into clear air, facing a dozen wagons halted by the fire.

"Can we pass?" asked a driver.

"Yes," replied Pernin, "since I've just done so, but loosen your reins and urge on your horses or you may be suffocated." Though being strangled by unconfined wildfire smoke isn't a likely scenario, and some drivers did rush forward, most turned back to town.

All this was ominous preamble. Scattered, unextinguished fires, coupled with drought, and the strong winds of a massive cold front, birthed disaster.

On October 8, 1871, a wildfire of staggering immensity transformed the lumbering town of Peshtigo, Wisconsin (population 2000), into a literal, burning hell. It was the deadliest forest fire in North American history. At least 1200 people died, and the actual number of fatalities is unknown. Eighteen hundred square miles of woods, fields, and settlements were burned. By cruel coincidence, it was the very day and hour of the Great Chicago Fire, the famous conflagration supposedly ignited by Mrs. O'Leary's lantern-kicking cow.

Chicago grabbed the first headlines, delaying aid to the bedeviled victims of Peshtigo, some of whom were driven mad by the terror of their catastrophe. The unlucky simultaneity of the two infernos has rendered Peshtigo unknown to most Americans.

But the details of that horrific autumn day are unforgettable: a hogshead of nails fused into an iron glob by unimaginable heat; an oxygen-sucking firestorm that was probably unequaled in power until the incendiary bombing of Dresden or the destruction of Hiroshima; a panicked mother plunging into the frigid Peshtigo River with a bundled infant, only to discover the wrappings were empty; a man running to relative safety with his wife on his back, realizing too late that he had the wrong woman; a distraught father cutting the throats of his children to spare them the inevitable death by fire.

Father Pernin survived the firestorm by taking refuge in the river, and he later published an account of his living nightmare. During the remarkable fire season of 2000, I studied his book and other stories of the Peshtigo disaster, realizing that in that Wisconsin hecatomb of calcined human bones there was a telling counterpoint to the joyful demeanor of my initial attack helicopter crew. As much as study, imagination, and my experience would allow, I joined the priest in the river, trying to learn more about this enemy/friend, adversary/mentor—good and evil fire.

As a professional firefighter, I long for flame, smoke, and stress. On its face, this is strange stuff. Sometimes, usually in winter when I'm laid off and the northern forest is choked with snow, I muse on how I got here. I wonder why sucking smoke and blowing black snot has evolved into a transcendent experience. Some might say I became a firefighter by accident. I say it was synchronicity.

In the summer of 1973 I toiled as a high-side chaser on a logging crew in the Oregon Cascades. It was a mad, gritty job reeking

of bar oil and blood. Two percent of us got killed every year—
crushed by logs, beheaded by steel cable, mangled by chain saws or
bulldozers. The goal was plywood.

I was green and hungry and broke, and our boss—the Hook—
paid us well for the risk, though I once heard him lament, "I can't
afford to bury you."

July and August were dry, the trail dust six inches deep. It
plugged our nostrils and seasoned our sandwiches. Lightning
ignited forest fires. The Forest Service cut back our hours in the
woods and hinted we might be drafted for the firelines. I knew nothing of fire except movie images, and it seemed romantic.

One afternoon, when my mind would've been better focused on
the singing steel cables, I spun a vivid daydream: I was clad in the
yellow shirt of a wildland firefighter, a hefty McCulloch Super Pro
81 chain saw balanced on my left shoulder, and behind me, strung
out in a sinuous line down a mountainside, was a column of firefighters. We were returning from "the battle," and I imagined the
scene framed by the red borders of a *Time* magazine cover.
Vainglorious adolescent wish perhaps, but it was a powerful image.

Even so, it faded by the end of the summer, and I returned to my
theological studies at a Bible college in Texas. I was going to be a
minister. I was passionate about God.

But fourteen years later I awoke as if from long hibernation and
found myself on a mountainside in Oregon with a McCulloch chain
saw riding my left shoulder. Nineteen firefighters walked behind
me. My face was streaked with soot, like slashes of war paint. I
stopped dead in my tracks and sucked a deep, wondering breath.
The guy behind almost bumped into me.

"What's up?" he asked.

"Oh, nothing," I replied. "I just remembered something."

Ever since I've been trying to figure out what the hell happened.

But that day I knew I was in a place—a mind-set, a discipline, a mission, a vocation—where I indisputably belonged. I resisted the thought of destiny, because what sort of wretch would actually be destined to the sublime craziness of the fireground? I'd planned on the ministry, for godssake—had studied Hebrew and biblical Greek; had fasted, prayed, and meditated about my "calling"; had taken eight semesters of homiletics. Had ended up in the smoke with a chain saw slung over my shoulder. And I was glad.

In 1999 I worked a fire in Montana that was torching lodgepole pine adjacent to a Federal Job Corps camp. Some of the young enrollees had received basic fire training and were geared up and dispatched to the line. I happened to eavesdrop on an argument between the camp superintendent and one of his counselors. The counselor was vehemently opposed to her students being sent to the fire. She rested her case by spitting: "We're training these students to get jobs, not to be firefighters!"

I almost choked, stifling a guffaw. She'd nailed it! Wildland firefighting is not a job. Anyone who does it for the money is either a desperate derelict or requires remedial arithmetic.

Each year I train rookies and tell them the truth: wildland firefighting is mostly dirt and drudgery. You do it for the 5 percent of the time when it's the best gig in the world; for the peak experience moments when all other vocations are as ashes beneath your boots; for the days when you feel sorry for the poor saps who opted for law school, med school, or Silicon Valley; for the brutal hours when the pain is so intense it shades into a kind of ecstasy; for the dreadful/wonderful moments when fear makes you so alive you simply cannot die. Though we do—about 700 since 1910. I know some of the names.

But the adventure, fellowship, and challenges are only the veneer—the thin and perishable tinsel and glitter. They will not sustain you over the long haul of twenty seasons and may not sustain you for even five minutes when the fire howls and snatches the day. What I understand is this: I've weathered twenty-one seasons—560 fires in eleven states and one Canadian province—because I've tapped into the spiritual aspects of working fire.

There is a core of mystery and faith that has guided not only my career but also my life. To me, the fireground is a sacred locale, a place of power that is rich not only in tradition, history, and ecological imperatives, but also in sources of emotion and meditations that I can only describe in terms of reverence and awe. In the past few seasons it's dawned on me that I've become a minister after all; that I did not forsake a religious vocation but merely discovered a different way to express it. I'm no longer an apologist for Judeo-Christian theology, but I've struck a wellspring of spiritual inspiration and practice.

One of my colleagues, Kevin Malley, wrote in a fire service journal:

> Firefighting is an inherently dangerous occupation. As a matter of standard operating procedures, individuals routinely perform arduous physical tasks with a sense of urgency, at times for extended periods, in environments that are largely unfamiliar, uncontrolled, and uninhabitable. This presents those who pursue this line of work with an extraordinary potential for job-related illness, injury, and death.

But also an exceptional opportunity for growth in mind and spirit.

A Buddhist proverb: "If you meet the Buddha on the road, kill him."

A passage from the New Testament: "Work out your own salvation with fear and trembling."

They are congruent. They say: Sooner or later it is you who must blaze the trail. My path has been through fire, but we all share a similar route. Join me on the line, and I'll show you what I've learned. That line stretches across the continent from Minnesota to Wisconsin, Ontario, Montana, Idaho, and to other locales where my colleagues and I have both battled and nurtured fire. It encompasses the historical roots of our complex relationship with wildland fire—from Native American practices to the challenges of 2000. My personal struggles as a firefighter, from rookie to veteran, will provide a framework. There is much to reveal, but I can offer you only part of the story. The rest will issue from Father Peter Pernin and the ashes of Peshtigo.

ONE

A FIERCE, SATISFIED LIGHT

The snow was only seven inches deep. On February 9. In northern Minnesota. Our septic system had frozen twelve days earlier, ensuring a long winter even without blizzards. There wasn't enough snow to insulate the drainfield. We were locked in drought, and I checked my phenology records to glean some perspective: in early February the year before, we enjoyed a fourteen-inch blanket; in 1997 it was twenty-eight inches. But in the first months of the new century our forest was parchment dry. No significant precipitation had fallen since mid-October. A local newspaper reported that Death Valley, California, was having a wetter season.

This was exciting data, the major topic of conversation during occasional phone calls to my wildland firefighting colleagues. Like me, most were laid off for the winter and keenly interested in prospects for the coming spring and summer. We never tired of chattering about the awe-inspiring potential of fire in the Blowdown.

Not since the turn of the previous century, when entire sections in the vast pineries of the Upper Midwest were buried in logging slash, had there been such a massive concentration of wildland fuel. In 1871, a citizen of Port Huron, Michigan, reportedly walked for a mile on fallen tree trunks. But now, in the Boundary Waters Canoe Area Wilderness of northeastern Minnesota, there existed a swath of downed timber five to twelve miles wide and thirty miles long. The havoc wreaked by 90-mile-per-hour winds was apocalyptic in scale, like a twisted vision from the book of Revelation. Forest Service calculations pegged a normal fuel load for such boreal forest at about 15 to 20 tons per acre. After the violent July 4 storm, the load was estimated at 50 to 100 tons per acre. If arid conditions lingered into spring and summer . . . well, we might witness *the* fire of the new century, and it would be uncommonly dangerous. There was no fire behavior model to adequately predict the nature of a fire in such a glut of fuel.

On this relatively balmy February 9, I received a phone call from the Minnesota Interagency Fire Center (MIFC), a coordination hub for emergency operations. Out of the blue, I was thrust into the center of the messy, seductive scenario. Because of the fresh surplus of hazard, the Minnesota Department of Natural Resources Division of Forestry (DNR) decided to fund a Type-II initial attack helicopter to be based at Grand Marais, on the eastern periphery of the Blowdown. If I so desired, I could be the manager of that Bell 212 and its crew.

When I heard the offer, the nape of my neck pulsed and tingled, as if I'd backed into a live wire. I was both thrilled and flattered, but also pinched by dread. Even while hearing myself posing prudent questions and ostensibly weighing a decision, an inner voice (perhaps resident in the reptilian portion of the brain) was bellowing, "Yes! Yes! Hell, yes!"

In my charge would be eight to ten people and a four-million-dollar aircraft. We'd be an elite, high-profile resource, expected to be on ten-minute readiness, seven days a week, and to be one of the first, if not the first, to arrive at any fire or other emergency, including blazes in the Blowdown. The assignment would last a minimum of three months and probably be extended. My outer voice said, "Okay. I'll commit for ninety days."

It would begin on June 1, and thus my summer income—always an iffy proposition—was assured. I rushed downstairs to tell Pam, and in that telling, with the spoken words actually breathing life into what until then had been an abstraction, my neck tingled again. What had I gotten myself into? Could it be I was in over my head? For the next several months, the Assignment, as I called it, was ever haunting my thoughts. Was it more than I could do?

That night I had a flying dream. I'm not a pilot, but I've spent enough intense time in the left front seat of a helicopter to decorate such dreams with special lucidity. I was at the controls of a small Type-III helicopter, perhaps a Bell 206 Jet Ranger. My left hand grasped the collective stick and I slowly raised it, increasing the pitch of the main rotor blades to lift the ship off the ground. My right hand—sweating—clutched the cyclic stick between my knees. I pushed it forward, tilting the entire rotor disk toward the nose of the helicopter, and it jumped ahead for a tree line of tall aspens. My feet were lightly pressing on the two antitorque pedals that control the pitch of the tail rotor, and I struggled to keep the tail boom from swerving back and forth. I surged over the trees, joyful and soaring, but saw a mountain range ahead. The controls suddenly seemed leaden and unresponsive, and I couldn't compensate. It was painfully obvious I wasn't going to clear the ridges.

I believe, as did psychoanalyst Carl Jung, that there is no sharp divide between dreams and waking reality. Dreams are a natural process and don't fool us. In his autobiography Jung wrote, "To me dreams are a part of nature, which harbors no intention to deceive, but expresses something as best it can. . . ." Why should the machinations of our wakeful mind be considered more potent, more "real," than those of our "sleeping" mind? No compelling reason occurs to me.

So I understood the dream to be a manifestation of fear. The inner voice had shouted "Yes!" but it was tinged with whistling bravado. I was afraid. Not of death or injury, but of failure.

It brought to mind an episode from a fire in northwest Ontario in June 1996. Our squad of Minnesotans was working a remote flank of a large fire, laying down hundreds of feet of hose and advancing a nozzle along the perimeter. At the end of the shift we were to be extracted via helicopter, and we waited for the ship in an opening in a small spruce bog. Squadrons of mosquitoes enthusiastically fed on our faces, so we were glad to hear the distinctive *thump-thump* of a Bell 204 "Huey."

We recognized the pilot from the day before. He was a brash New Zealander we'd already dubbed "Cowboy" because of his flamboyant, sometimes frightening, style of flying. We quickly piled into the back of the copter, and I slipped on a headset. In the left front seat was a voluble Canadian firefighter, the equivalent of our American helicopter manager, who talked incessantly. As Cowboy lifted, the Canadian half-turned toward us, jabbering away.

From the left side rear I had a clear view out the windscreen. The solid conifer tree line was uncomfortably close, and I thought Cowboy should be gaining altitude a bit more quickly. At that elevation and temperature he surely had enough power. The spires of black spruce seemed to grow taller as we approached, looming before us like a stockade. Shit! We weren't going to clear the trees!

I started to crouch into the crash position—bent over at the waist, arms tucked under the thighs behind the knees—and the Canadian manager spun forward and shut up. My sphincter actually clenched as I imagined spruce tops spearing through the belly of the ship like giant pungi sticks. Five supercharged seconds passed, then all I saw out the front was sky and horizon. We must've cleared the canopy by mere inches.

The Canadian turned toward us again, grinning.

"Sorry for the interruption, lads, but I didn't think we were going to clear the trees, eh, and I wouldn't want to miss that."

Yes, the Assignment was burly and intimidating, demanding a range of skills. I'd have the chance to fail as a leader, as a tactician, as a firefighter, as a contract administrator. Sins would be simple to commit. I might not clear the trees. But I sure wouldn't want to miss it.

Miss what? Let's slice to the core: miss the chance to die. My Canadian colleague spoke only half in jest. True, it was a neat bit of bravado, a movie clip, for godsake. But there's usually a kernel of truth in a throwaway line. I accepted the Assignment—and my fire career in general—because it might kill me. There's history here.

In August 1910, the American West was blasted by wildfire. The siege became known as the Big Blowup, and over five million acres burned in the national forests. Seventy-eight firefighters perished. That same month, at Harvard University, philosopher and pacifist William James published his famous essay *On the Moral Equivalent of War*. Distressed by the rampant militarism of the day, he suggested that such energy and fervor be redirected. Why not draft youth into an army of laborers to further tame nature? That idealistic conscription did not transpire in 1910, and four years later the ever-popular militarism spiraled into the monstrous carnage of World War I.

But James's phrase—"moral equivalent of war"—resonated in the fledgling U. S. Forest Service, established in 1905. Was not wildfire an enemy to be fought? Historian Stephen J. Pyne has written, "Revealingly, Forest Service archival records on fire begin with the body count of the 1910 conflagration." War was declared on wildland fire. Not until three decades later would the Forest Service deem fire as anything but an adversary to be battled. In short, firefighters were soldiers. And soldiers die. James wrote, "The martial type of character can be bred without war." Yes, but it cannot be bred without blood.

During rookie training we emphasize the dangers of the fireground and, in a course titled "Standards for Survival," provide a basic code of conduct to encourage safety. The finale of the class is a practice *fire shelter* deployment. A fire shelter is an aluminum foil pup tent designed to reflect radiant heat. It's folded compactly into a plastic case that firefighters carry on their belts or in a field pack. If you're about to be overrun by fire, you rip the shelter from its case, shake it open into the tent shape, and scoot underneath. Unless the shelter suffers direct flame impingement, you may survive in a relatively small open area away from heavy fuels, though it will probably became painfully hot inside the tent, and difficult to breathe. At 500 degrees Fahrenheit—not outrageously hot in a fire environment— the shelter begins to delaminate and seriously weaken. Violent convection currents or wind could tear it open. Though it has saved lives, we stress that it's a last resort, like a parachute. A firefighter might be forced to remain in a shelter for fifteen to ninety minutes, or longer, essentially being tortured in a claustrophobic environment. The government booklet *Your Fire Shelter* therefore advises intense concentration on "an object, person, or religious symbol that is very meaningful to you." In other words, pray. It's startling and sobering to read that in a federal publication.

We line out the sober rookies for the deployment drill. While they adjust their web gear and practice reaching behind for the shelter, I indicate the direction from which the flame front is approaching. When they're in the shelters, their boots should be pointing that way because if worse comes to worst, *it's better to burn your feet than your head.* The standard for deployment is twenty-five seconds. I hold up my watch.

"On your mark . . . go!"

Then the instructors are yelling.

"Hurry up! Let's go! The fire is right here! Come on, faster!"

They struggle and fumble, and though it's a harmless exercise, they're nervous and a little scared, and we keep on shouting.

"Twenty seconds gone! You're running out of time! You're going to burn!"

A few make it. Most take forty seconds or longer, and about 20 percent get it wrong, with a boot or an elbow sticking out. When they're all deployed I say, "Stay underneath. Think about a half hour, an hour." Even in the practice shelters it's hot and uncomfortable.

We weave through the cluster of tents and tug on the front and rear of each, simulating an unforgiving wind. Some of the shelters come off easily, and I grab an exposed boot and snap, "Foot's burning!"

Then we just let them lie there and in silence, thinking. After a few minutes I say, "Okay, your crew boss says it's all right to come out."

That's a trick. They've been taught there's no definitive way to know when it's safe to emerge. It depends—on how hot the inside surface of the shelter is (feel it with the back of your hand), whether or not there's decent air to inhale outside (carefully lift a corner of the shelter for a sample). And though the roar of the fire has abated, latent radiant heat might still burn you or a dense pall of smoke poison you with carbon monoxide.

A few respond to the "crew boss" and start to rise without performing the checks. I mock them. "Well, there's a trusting soul. And maybe dead in a few minutes!" They redden and crawl back in.

Finally, we tell them all to get up, and I watch. There are grins and kidding, and on some faces I see what I'm looking for—a kind of fierce, satisfied light, like radiant heat itself. For these, it wasn't merely a drill but a rite, and they'll celebrate it often if they stick around. The fire shelter demonstrates this is a game played for keeps. This is a job where your bosses teach that prayer might be a tool and urge you to consider the grim logic of losing your feet instead of your head. This is a vocation where it's assumed that colleagues and perhaps buddies will be injured and killed.

After the horrific fires of 1910, one survivor, a Wallace, Idaho, resident named Mrs. Swain, said, "It was a terrible ordeal, but I wouldn't have missed it for anything." Ordeal. I think of it in terms of the primitive method of determining guilt or innocence and, by extension, worthiness. One method was a trial by fire, and the medieval Saxon version had a defendant grasp a red-hot iron. If the person was innocent, God would heal the burn in three days.

Ordeal is a powerful lure. This is not fast food or MTV. It's not retail sales or software hype. It's probably not promoted on career day at the local high school. Wildland firefighting is a path to pain and not to a fat stock portfolio. There is mystery here—the romantic attraction of hardship and hazard amid a corpulent society obsessed with mammon. I understand the flinty joy of acknowledging that I'd better serve and be served by my congregation (crew), because the world (fire) doesn't care about me at all, at all. I accepted the Assignment because of the welcome danger but also for the same reason I once matriculated at a Bible school—to be a minister in a church. To scratch a line to salvation. To grasp the hot iron.

It's curious that a life of action, and occasionally turmoil, was birthed by a quiet season of reading. During the summer of 1963 (between sixth and seventh grades), I read forty books—about three per week. I passed hundreds of hours leafing pages in my room or out on the lawn in the backyard. Most were novels of adventure, intrigue, science fiction, and battle. I portaged armloads of books to and from the public library and bought fifty-cent paperbacks at a local newsstand. I didn't totally neglect baseball, swimming, and forays into the woods, but that summer is evoked not by Harmon Killebrew's signature on a Louisville Slugger, but by the aroma of the library stacks. Every summer after that I held a job, and '63 was an idyll of sorts. I remember it fondly.

I was especially fascinated by one book in particular. I don't remember the title, author, or cover, but the story is with me still: in a small town not unlike the one I lived in, a gang of friends about my age discover a large fallen tree—an oak or maple—whose trunk curves slightly up from the ground. To them it suggests the hull of a ship, and they commandeer it as a pirate vessel, sailing off to imaginary exploits—the kind of youthful make-believe that transcends mundane reality and becomes adventure in itself. They forget and I forgot that it was only a tree.

As fortune would have it, an old elm on our block—a victim of Dutch elm disease—was felled that very week. The limbs were cut and hauled off, but the massive trunk remained in the boulevard for a few days. It too curved up from the grass to mimic the prow of a ship, and I boarded it as soon as the city maintenance crew drove away. It was life imitating art imitating life, and the tales and fantasies engendered by dozens of books inspired me. I felt that old elm running with the wind on a following sea and heard Jolly Roger snapping in a zephyr. Overhead, cliffs of cumulus billowed into a blue dome now revealed by the fallen canopy of hardwood leaves. It was like I'd never seen the blue before. The freshly sawed stump exuded the pungent odor of elm sap, and to this day a whiff of that distinctive smell transports me to the furrowed bark of that "pitching" trunk. Which soon transformed from schooner to airship, bound for the flattened summits of nascent thunderheads. One reason I love helicopters is that they deliver me to the sky.

That season was more semester than summer, and those books plotted a course and a story. The many thousands of silent words made me believe in risk—convinced me that life was supposed to brandish a keenly dangerous edge, and I was meant to live the narratives of my fantasies. Beyond the biology of existence and the formidable structure of culture, life was drama. A good story. The kind of tale to keep a kid up late with a book. I imagined and assumed I would live such a story. I craved adventure.

But there was also a strand of darkness that twined through those months. It was embodied by an Act of Contrition, the formulaic, Roman Catholic prayer of the confessional: "O my God, I am heartily sorry for having offended Thee, and I detest all my sins. . . ." A single recitation of the prayer, requiring about fifteen seconds, was good for three years off a sentence to Purgatory, which made me wonder about the scale of such a sentence. If a simple prayer was worth three years, would a typical penalty in Purgatory be thousands of years? Were my sins that serious? They must be. I was zealously religious and thus wracked by guilt and fear of divine retribution. The local priests conducted confession every Saturday, and I was there, fervently and shamefully admitting to white lies, anger with my siblings, selfishness, and "impure thoughts"—the stirrings of puberty I didn't even fully understand. I've wondered since what the priests must've thought as they listened through the shadowy screen to those tallies of universal petty misdemeanors from the lips of an innocent child. Did they know how scared I was? Did they understand the love-hate relationship I had with confession and penance? If I committed a sin during the week—for example, yelled at my brother—I often felt burdened and depressed until I could recite my mistakes to a priest. Then I relished the flash of warmth and release when he absolved me—clean and whole again, worthy to receive the Eucharist next morning. The walk home from the church was light and delicious, but the feeling was doomed. The first new blemishes on my immortal soul were only hours or even minutes away. The cycle of self-recrimination and absolution would be renewed.

As I followed Father Peter Pernin into the hellfire of Peshtigo, I disassociated him from the priests of my childhood. He was a leader, not a shrouded confessor—or so I wished to anoint him. Though I pictured him in a black cassock, I faintly resented his priesthood, his assumed detestation of my sins. But I cheered for his escape and gradually forgot he was an arbiter of the cycles of penance.

The books of 1963 transported me from that cycle, and perhaps it was one reason I escaped to them so often. I cannot say I openly resisted the power of the priests, for I was too much in their thrall, but the stories I read presented views of the universe that kindled an imaginative blaze destined to scorch my childish beliefs and fears. The confessional was too small to contain me. There was too much contrast between the heroes who crackled the pages and my own life of timid hand-wringing.

And stark also the contrast of buccaneers, astronauts, and knights with the lives of adults I knew. My father returned home from the iron mine with dirty overalls and a battered aluminum lunch pail. He spoke little, and nothing about his job, which, though it seemed to be the focus of his life, remained a joyless mystery. I didn't inquire. My mother abhorred dirt, so the trademark overalls took on a seamy aspect. The only thing of my father's "uniform" that intrigued me was his round, wide-brimmed hard hat, adorned with a decal bearing the logo of United States Steel. It appeared vaguely military, and I was fond of placing it on my head.

Most wildland firefighters wear the cap-style hard hat popular with construction and factory workers. I believe it's no coincidence that mine is round and full brimmed. It's not government issue; I had to buy that style myself. The ostensible reason for the purchase was that it offered better protection, but the first time I donned it I understood the real reason. It was even the same color as my father's, and I hadn't thought about that at all. I hadn't even thought about his helmet for thirty years, but now I owned one exactly like it. I wondered how much conscious control I had over destiny.

In 2000, I was slated to return to my Department of Natural Resources (DNR) fire engine on April 1, in time for the usual spring wildfire season in northeastern Minnesota. But by February 26, what little snow we had lay in puddles, and I was called back early. On March 3, a time when we are normally still skiing and feeding insatiable woodstoves, my partner Richard and I ran on our first blaze of the year.

A smoke was reported only a few miles from our Side Lake work station, and we headed south and east on a network of backcountry gravel roads. As I drove, Richard flipped open our plat book to get a fix on the location. Over the radio we heard a local volunteer fire department was also dispatched, but we figured to be first in—about eight to ten minutes en route.

Being en route to a fire is usually the most stressful period of the operation. You're never certain what you're facing until you arrive, and early reports—especially if they're from the public—are often suspect. I once responded to what was described as a "grass and brush fire" and was surprised and a tad dismayed to discover five buildings ablaze. Sure, it began as a brush fire. Actually, some genius had dumped ashes and coals from his sauna stove into dry grass. It burst into flame. Go figure.

Richard and I heard the county dispatcher mention that a structure was threatened by this first fire of the season, so we had reason to hurry. But minutes seem to dilate when you're en route, and though I happened to know that our Ford 350—weighing six tons, with water—would easily top eighty miles per hour, it's fool-hardy to bully narrow, winding dirt roads. I kept it at fifty or under and let the minutes stretch. It's better to get there a bit later than not at all.

To pass the time we chatted about books. We'd both recently read the best-selling memoirs of Frank McCourt and agreed that from now on our preferred workaday expletive would be "Jaysus, Frankie!" Since we often find cause to employ expletives, we like to keep them fresh.

The smoke wasn't visible until we were a half-mile out. Through a screen of naked aspens we spied a medium-sized column, grayish white in color. A good sign. Burning structures usually emit magnificent black billows.

I turned east on a dead-end road and in a few seconds we saw flames. The fire had started in tall, golden grass at the edge of the road and was spreading briskly across a field toward the woods. The flame lengths were four to five feet, impressive for the first week of March, especially since there wasn't much wind. The structure, a ramshackle trailer house probably serving as a hunting shack, was protected by a modest circle of lawn, and that line of fire had mostly burned itself out. Our strategy was clear—kill the flames before they slammed into the woods.

The ground looked firm, so I wheeled off the road and into the black, charging the running fire from behind. I halted partway up the left flank, and we hopped out into the smoke. As Richard yanked hose off the reel, I started the pump and set the eductor to provide a small dosage of *class-A foam*—a surfactant that breaks the surface tension of water, thus making it "wetter"—and effectively extending our 200-gallon water supply.

Richard energetically worked the line with the nozzle, knocking down flames. I surveyed the fireground to make sure we weren't missing something important, then followed behind him, mopping up with a five-gallon backpack pump, or "piss can"—basically an industrial strength squirt gun linked to a water can by a small hose.

Our plan was to flank the fire until we reached the *head*—the driving, expanding front of the blaze—then pinch it off and work down the right flank back to the road to finish the job. It was a standard, uncomplicated tactic for an early-spring grass fire, but we soon understood we weren't going to win the race to the woods. With so little snow over the winter, the grass had not been compacted. It was tall tinder, fully exposed to oxygen. The heat was intense. Occasionally wind and convection currents, influenced by the combustion, whirled flames into our faces, forcing us to back off.

A forty-foot jack pine snag, long dead and cured, stood at the edge of the aspen woods, but I didn't expect it to burn hard. Early fires are not typically that aggressive. Latent moisture from the snowmelt, cool temperatures, and relatively short days conspire to temper the first blazes. But when the headfire pushed past the old pine, it fairly erupted into flames, fire quickly laddering up the gnarled trunk and spindly limbs. In moments the tree was a resinous torch, fiercely burning from top to bottom and casting embers into the sky.

Now that, I thought, is pretty special for March 3. If there was any doubt the fuels were dry . . .

"Hey, Richard! Check that out."

He glanced up from his nozzle work, and bemusement fluttered across his face.

"Jaysus, Frankie!" he said.

Two fire department trucks appeared on the road, and I pointed to the right flank. They'd handle it.

We had all the hose off our reel, so I advanced the engine another hundred fifty feet, supplying enough slack to reach the head. The fire slowed when it hit the trees and shorter grass, and I could see we'd nail the last of the running fire in a few minutes. But that jack pine had to fall.

I pulled a chain saw off the engine. It was my personal favorite, a Stihl 044 with a twenty-inch bar—wickedly powerful but deceptively light. I'd freshly honed the chain only an hour before, carefully filing each cutter to the desired pitch, like tuning the strings of a mountain dulcimer.

Felling a burning snag fits neatly into the category "don't try this at home." Further weakened by fire, the dead tree is even more prone to drop widow-makers, and I waited until Richard had the leisure to watch the top of the tree. I wrapped a Nomex shroud over my nose and mouth, kicked aside some burning bark and limbs, and made the undercut.

The chain spewed sparks and black sawdust, and every several seconds heat and smoke pushed me away. Almost a minute passed before I was able to kick a half-moon slab out of the trunk. As I started the backcut, Richard was ready with a wedge, and the instant there was room, he shoved it into the kerf and tapped it with the blunt side of a faller's ax. One branch fell from above, but it was small and bounced off my helmet.

I withdrew the saw and stepped back to watch the top lean as he hammered the wedge. In a few moments the snag toppled, and I waded into the hot tangle to buck it into manageable chunks that we rolled around and doused with water and foam.

The fire was over, but on the drive back to the station we agreed that neither of us had ever seen such snappy fire behavior so early in the year. It was a harbinger and a warning. Heads up.

During that spring, I first focused on the Great Peshtigo Fire and the Reverend Peter Pernin. I approached him as a postulant to a prophet. Though he was not a firefighter, he was thrust into a horrible, marvelous locus where I had never been—the center of a firestorm. I was rigorously trained to avoid the situation he survived, because it's usually not survivable. But as a firefighter, you prepare for the worst, hoping that if you're trapped in hell you'll have the stamina and presence of mind to obey Standard Fire Order #10: *Stay alert, keep calm, think clearly, act decisively.* It seems that Peter Pernin did. In an environment where other humans went drooling mad with terror, this man was a conscious servant and leader. And I was intrigued that the most vivid account of Peshtigo was written by him, a Catholic priest.

When I was in the eighth grade our parish priest—a man for whom I felt a blend of affection and fear (and a hidden resentment for the confessional time)—suggested I should leave home for a seminary and pursue the vocation of the priesthood. I demurred, also eschewing his invitation to be an altar boy. But four years later I spent two semesters at the College of St. Thomas in St. Paul. Though I was no longer Catholic, and would soon decamp for the ministerial program at fundamentalist Ambassador College, I was influenced by another priest. He taught freshman English, and I took his poetry class. He guided us, quite passionately, on a survey of prominent poets, one of whom was Wilfred Owen, the young British army officer who won the Victoria Cross in World War I and died in battle a week before the Armistice. One of my classmates was a Vietnam veteran who'd been wounded in combat. I remember his vivid, forgivable cynicism. The priest had the temerity to tell the embittered vet that he would learn something about war from Owen's poetry. The man was skeptical, almost contemptuous. But by the time we finished reading Owen's work, the young soldier was astonished. The war had numbed him, but Owen wrote potent, terribly beautiful verse in the trenches. The poetry helped my classmate to crystallize his Vietnam experience, transforming emotion into thought and thoughts into emotion. I was amazed the priest had known this would happen, that he had such confidence in the vigor of poetry.

As I read Father Pernin's story, one of the lines of Wilfred Owen came forcefully to mind. In a poem titled "Greater Love," he addresses a woman, a lover representing all the civilians who cannot even imagine the trials of the Western Front. The final line is, "Weep, you may weep, for you may touch them not."

How close could Pernin bring me to the awful wonder of Peshtigo? Could I touch the clarity of mind and purpose that lifted him beyond survival to an almost heroic awareness? Or could I merely weep, unable to share the firestorm? Despite my training and experience, and a basic affinity for the fireground, could I ever perform as he did in the face of such stress and ordeal? Better, perhaps, to be never trapped in hell—to keep the trials manageable. Nevertheless, even in hell I'd be expected to meet the challenge of Standard Fire Order #10. I studied the priest's every move and recorded thought.

In late September 1871, Father Pernin's two close brushes with fire planted a seed of foreboding in the mind of the priest, which not all his neighbors shared—at least not until the last horrifying minutes of their lives. Pernin would subsequently invest his dread with deep religious significance, and his belief would later spur the declaration of a postfire miracle.

Meanwhile, on the night of Saturday, September 23, Peshtigo was assaulted by fire. From the north a howling *crown fire*—a violent, sustained fire run through the treetops that can devour forest at a rate of five miles per hour—drove thousands of birds from their roosts, and they clamored over the town. It's common for a wildfire to "lie down" in the evening, as temperatures drop, humidity rises, and daytime winds slacken. Modern firefighters often take advantage of this daily cycle to gain ground on a fire during a night shift, when fire behavior is usually less volatile and dangerous. A crown fire at night speaks to the dryness of the Peshtigo region that season, with low fuel moisture overcoming the tempering effect of night.

A reporter for the *Green Bay Advocate*, sporting the florid journalistic style of the day, described the fire as a "grand sight . . . and it burned to the tops of the tallest trees, enveloped them in a mantle of flames, or, winding itself about them like a huge serpent, crept to their summits, out upon the branches, and wound its huge folds about them. Hissing and glaring it lapped out its myriad firey tongues while its fierce breath swept off the green leaves and roared through the forest like a tempest."

Occasionally an old pine *snag*, or standing dead tree, would burn off and crash to the ground, ejecting a spume of sparks and embers. These firebrands were sucked into the convection column of heated smoke and cast out over the river.

Even today, the majority of houses destroyed by wildfires are ignited not by direct flame impingement but by showers of embers raining from above or by intense radiant heat. Experience in Australia and southern California indicates that a noncombustible roof is a significant contributing factor to a structure's survival.

That night at Peshtigo, a crew of townsfolk stationed themselves on the riverbank near the woodenware factory of Chicago millionaire William B. Ogden. Forty percent of the 2000 inhabitants of the town were employed by the timber and milling industry. They were frontier folk, accustomed to hard labor and self-sufficiency, and there existed no force of state or federal firefighters to come to their aid. Ogden's was then the largest such facility in the nation, daily producing 1060 pails, 370 tubs, 5000 broom handles, 45,000 shingles, and numerous other items out of logs floated in on the Peshtigo River, which bisected the town. A nearby sawmill, also owned by Ogden, supported 97 saws and cut an average of 150,000 feet of lumber a day.

These two facilities were the heart and lifeblood of the community, and physically at its center. The checkerboard plat of Peshtigo spread east and west from the river and the mills, pushing into surrounding forest and fields. East Front Street and West Front Street bracketed the river, with the inevitable Ogden Avenue directly serving the mill complex on the east bank. Father Pernin's church was in the northwest corner of town, near a creek that fed the Peshtigo River and served as a village boundary. Its north bank was heavily wooded, posing one of the threats on September 23. As the blizzard of firebrands landed in sawdust and heaps of dried slab wood, citizens rushed to each new curl of smoke and snuffed them with water from the prepositioned hogsheads. All the while a dark pillar of pungent smoke, backlit by flame, arched overhead. In an editorial flourish the journalist reported that "all earnestly hoped and many hearts fervently prayed for rain."

By Sunday morning the fire had quieted, and the latest threat was past. Local churches filled, and normal routine seemed to be reestablished. But around 11:00 A.M. the steam whistle at the factory shrieked a warning, and the churches emptied in a rush. The sawdust had caught fire again—most likely the rekindle of a spot fire from the night before. Heat can enjoy a surprisingly long life span in tightly arranged fuels such as sawdust, hay, forest duff, or peat. In some cases, such *sleepers* (pockets of latent fire) have survived for a year or more in peat and deep duff. It's common for a lightning-struck snag to quietly smolder unnoticed for days before bursting into flame.

The spot was quickly doused, but a gale arose from the north-west and a fresh wall of flame again peppered the town with air-borne embers. The local fire engine was deployed, and hundreds of new wooden pails were commandeered from the factory. People scattered like dogs after birds, splashing water on each fresh start, shouting and coughing. Dense smoke and whirls of ash and dust brought tears to their eyes, aggravated by rivulets of sweat. Teams of horses hauled water from the river, and over three hundred people labored through the day. Buildings on the outskirts were evacuated, their furniture and other goods shifted toward the center of town. Wet blankets were draped over roofs, and smoldering trees were felled and slapped with water.

At sundown the wind tapered off; by Monday morning it shifted to the south and the smoke cleared. Amazingly, not a single building was lost. On Wednesday, September 27, the town was "quiet and going on as usual."

But this was merely a skirmish, not the war.

Reverend Pernin ascribed the events to God—a divine warning. The Almighty was directing natural means to display His will. Pernin wrote that "these various signs were but forerunners of the great tragedy for which He wished us to be in some degree prepared."

But the ensuing tragedy was largely instigated by humans, and few of them were prepared.

TWO

THE ACCELERATION
OF JOY

Preparation. That concept was my beacon in spring 2000, and first priority for the Assignment was selecting the *helitack* crew, my airborne firefighters. Sheldon Mack, helicopter operations specialist for the Department of Natural Resources, called a meeting at the Minnesota Interagency Fire Center in Grand Rapids. His three assistants and I gathered in what one of them referred to as a "smoke-filled room" to make relatively weighty decisions about other people's lives. As Sheldon read names from a list of sixty-seven carded helicopter crew members, we responded in a chorus of ayes or nays. We knew most of these people, and snap judgments were the rule. Discussion was limited to one-liners like "He's not a team player" or "She can't commit for three months." Sheldon reserved the power of final approval or veto. In the end, about twenty people were slated to receive written invitations to join my crew for the summer.

My criteria for choice were: at least five years of fire experience and a worthy record in the helitack organization, a gregarious personality, and a demonstrated skill for "doing time." We'd be together for a long tour, and our duty wouldn't all be sound and fury. No matter what the weather delivered, we'd undoubtedly have to endure periods of inactivity. It's easy to be cheerful and engaged when you're ripping along in the midst of emergency—challenged and busy and tallying overtime pay. What distinguishes the professionals from the dilettantes is the ability to maintain high morale and high readiness when nothing interesting has happened for several days. Anybody can be happy on the fireline; it's standby—all keyed up with nothing to fight—that will sap your strength and will.

A facet of my personal preparation was prayer. Not the traditional entreaty to a deity, but a process and state of mind I call meditative action.

When I was a ministerial student at Ambassador College, we had "prayer closets" in the dormitories—tiny, private rooms where students retreated to pray. I spent many hours in the closets, intently talking to my perceptions of Jehovah and Jesus or just thinking. Over the course of time and study, I gradually detoured past Christianity, but I've retained respect for prayer and the closets. Because whether a deity is actually listening or not, there is value in formally announcing your needs, desires, worries, sins, and goals in a focused, prayerful attitude. Only when you are aware can you take action. As a believer, I often asked for help, guidance, and even miracles, professing to trust that God would handle it but also affirming the old saw that "God helps those who help themselves"—a brand of benevolent Christian cynicism.

Now when I pray, the closet may be my office, the backseat of our canoe, a lawn chair beside the garden, any quiet, peaceful place. The entreaties are often presented as questions. Not to a god, but to myself. Prayer is an inner dialogue about the outer world, with a blurred boundary between.

Concerning the Assignment, my pressing question was, How do I mold a crew that remains effective and content under pressure for three months away from home, and likely longer? Having the right people to begin with was important but not enough.

In mid-April my nine crew members were selected—a compromise between desirability and availability. I scanned the final list and was more or less satisfied. But seeing the names in black and white also triggered anxiety. These were the individuals who must coalesce into a crew, a family, a congregation.

One morning I sat at my desk and stared at the wall where years ago I had taped up a map of the Superior National Forest, the region where we'd probably spend most of our time—from Lake Superior on the east to Nett Lake on the west; from the Canadian border to the Mesabi Iron Range. I beseeched my mind for answers, as I had once supplicated God. Heresy, in the old days. But I submit that delving into personal mind—as opposed to the mind of God, or some numinous realm—is what I was really doing in the prayer closet anyway. Pondering the map, I imagined flying over lakes and forest toward a burgeoning column of smoke and scrolled through a list of hazards and tasks. I experienced a stab of fear and thought, "Please don't let me make a bad mistake, but if I do, let me be the first to die."

It was a selfish thought. But I recalled the story of the Mann Gulch fire in Montana in 1949. Fifteen smokejumpers parachuted from a C-47 to a lightning-sparked blaze north of Helena near the Gates of the Mountains on the Missouri River. As are most initial attacks, it was considered more or less routine, though record high temperatures had baked the forest fuels. The U.S. Forest Service smokejumper operation was only nine years old that year, and the spotter on the plane that day was one of the two men who'd made the first ever fire jump in 1940. A smokejumper had never been killed on a fire, and in his 1992 book *Young Men and Fire,* Norman Maclean wrote, "They were still so young they hadn't learned to count the odds and to sense they might owe the universe a tragedy."

After landing and regrouping, crew boss Wag Dodge led his outfit toward the fire, hoping to aggressively engage it and have it contained with a hand-dug control line by the next morning. But the fire crossed the gulch into cured grass, and the crew was caught on a steep sidehill with a wall of fire roaring upslope from below. They dropped their tools and ran, but Dodge realized it was hopeless; the flames would catch them before they reached the top of the ridge and relative safety on the other side. In a stroke of genius, he struck a match to the surrounding waist-high grass, lighting an escape fire that would roll upslope before them, creating a black zone where they could lie flat and survive. Today, this is a standard survival tactic taught to rookies, who are encouraged to pack *fusees,* ignition devices similar to highway flares. Dodge shouted for the crew to follow him into the burned ground, but they didn't comprehend—thought he was nuts to be starting another fire. All but two of them died. Dodge chased his fire uphill and lay down in the black. He lived to help carry bodies down to the Missouri River. A helicopter was dispatched to evacuate the injured—the first time one was used on a wildfire.

This was a nightmare scenario, a Peshtigo-Pernin situation. I was deeply moved by Maclean's phrase "owe the universe a tragedy." It fed my firefighter's sense of fatalism—tempt Fate for too long and she'll eventually crush you. She's merciless, aloof to life dreams. How wretched, I thought, to survive my crew, especially if they died because I made a mistake. And in the midst of that meditation I accepted an answer. A single word sprang to mind: perfection.

I immediately drafted a letter to my prospective crew. I understood that expectations generate results, and I established our code: the professional performance of all duties, an attitude of courtesy and service to all our colleagues (no "helidonnas"), and a commitment to superior physical fitness (no "helislugs"). I advised them we'd be under agency and public scrutiny.

It's an unfortunate fact of life that one mistake, on the job or off, can overshadow a ton of good work. Aircraft accidents were the #2 killer of wildland firefighters from 1990 to 1998, and fireground helicopter operations unfold in a tenaciously unforgiving environment. . . . Perfection may not be possible, but that will be our goal.

I resisted the temptation to affix Amen.

On May 3, a wildfire of suspicious origin blew up in the heavily forested country north of Lake Vermilion. It rapidly swelled into a full-fledged crown fire, running northeast in the general direction of the Boundary Waters Canoe Area Wilderness (BWCAW). The southwest wind was ferocious. I scaled the fire tower at Side Lake, and even from thirty miles away the smoke was huge, like a pregnant thunderhead.

I restlessly monitored the radio traffic as helicopters and air tankers were requested from Ely and Hibbing in Minnesota and from Dryden, Ontario. We were an hour away by road, so our engine could conceivably be dispatched, but not long after, my fire department pager squealed and the county dispatcher announced that a furniture delivery van was burning in a residential driveway on Boldt Road. Since I was the local volunteer fire chief, this was my responsibility. Matt, my Department of Natural Resources engine partner that day, also belonged to the department, so I dropped him off at the fire hall to grab our big pumper, and I rushed to Boldt Road in the wildland engine. Such a fire could easily spread to the woods and threaten neighboring houses.

The rear of the van was a rolling boil of flame and pitch-black smoke. It was parked fifteen feet from an open garage door. The wind was howling from across Little Sturgeon Lake, driving the flames nearly parallel to the building. Good. But if the wind shifted even a few degrees west, the garage would ignite almost instantly.

I reported "on scene" to dispatch and parked seventy-five feet back. The small pump and hose on my wildland rig was no match for this fire, but I hoped to soften it and help protect the garage until the fire department truck arrived.

I started the pump and dialed in a high dosage of foam, then jogged toward the rear of the van and crouched low. My lightweight wildland clothing didn't allow me to approach closer than twenty feet. My nozzle stream had some effect, at least enough for me to scramble over to the garage, quickly stand, and pull the door closed.

Matt arrived with the big pumper and three more firefighters, and a concentrated blast from an inch-and-three-quarter hoseline knocked down the fire in the cargo compartment. I hustled to the pumper to don some heavy structure fire turnout gear, and by then the flames in the cab and engine compartment had also been cooled.

We could now see the real problem. The van's fuel line had separated, and a steady stream of gasoline the diameter of a pencil was splashing onto the ground, spreading out in an explosive, rainbow-colored film. The rear tires were still smoldering, and the gas vapors ignited, fire flashing beneath the vehicle and lapping up the sides, menacing the garage again.

We swept the flames away with bursts from our nozzles, but in a minute fire exploded anew. Another sweep, resoaking the tires, and the flames snapped out but reignited as fresh gasoline flowed from the tank. I asked the driver—haplessly staring at the black hulk of his van—how much fuel there was, and he figured the tank was about half full when he'd arrived. This battle could drag on. It would be nice to halt the hemorrhage of gasoline.

I had the crew work the tires until they seemed to be extinguished, then with two nozzles playing a continuous curtain of water on the ground, diluting and cooling the gas, I crawled beneath the truck with locking pliers. Gasoline dribbled onto my gloves and sleeves, and the crew soaked them with water. I established a grip on the fuel line and tried to crimp it shut but couldn't completely crush it. I rolled back out. We had no choice but to keep water flowing until the fuel tank was empty.

That evening, when I told Pam the story, she erupted.

"That's crazy! Under the truck? In gasoline?"

I hadn't considered it stupid. I judged that with constant flushing and the tires cooled, there was minimal risk. On the other hand, I'd gone under there myself because I wasn't comfortable asking someone else to take the chance of being burned. And for what? At most, probably, to save a garage. The van was already junk.

Yes, I could understand Pam's point of view, but after years in the fire service a certain level of hazard becomes routine. The concept is called risk homeostasis. It indicates the way that most people will consciously or unconsciously behave to maintain an acceptable threshold of risk. For example, a study in Germany demonstrated that after acquiring antilock brakes, a sample of cab drivers eventually drove more aggressively. Initially, their accident rate declined with the introduction of the brakes, but over time it rose to its original level. The new safety device encouraged riskier behavior.

Similarly, over the past fifteen years the personal protective clothing issued to structural firefighters has dramatically improved, offering extraordinary protection from heat. A positive development, right? Yes, except for the fact that so armored, firefighters are able to readily penetrate farther into burning buildings (or beneath furniture vans), for longer periods of time, thus exposing themselves to more acute danger. Risk homeostasis, coupled with the often critical need for decisive action, is why firefighters will continue to be injured and killed.

The editor of a fire service journal recently wrote that safety is a state of mind, and to reduce the hazards of the vocation, "the only answer lies in changing the culture, that is, in lowering the level of risk that firefighters are willing to accept under the majority of fireground conditions."

Well, I suppose we could just let more stuff burn. In some wildland settings, that's actually an option. But how much do we want to change the culture and code of the fire service? For example, our volunteer fire department in Side Lake, Minnesota, has a written set of standard operating guidelines, designed to format our behavior on the fireground. One of the most sacred tenets is that "full personal protective gear will be worn at all incidents." In other words, if you aren't dressed to play, stay in the bleachers. It's a fundamental rule of safety and common sense. But one early spring morning a few years ago, we were paged to a fire in a lakeside home. A teenager awoke to see flames around a fireplace chimney. She dialed 911 and fled the house. Our first member on scene was Arden, a fifteen-year veteran, who arrived in his personal vehicle and had not yet donned his turnout gear. But he quickly assessed the situation, grabbed a snow shovel that was leaning against the porch, and scooped up a load. He rushed into the house in street clothes and snuffed the nascent fire with a well-aimed blast of snow.

When I arrived a few minutes later, he sheepishly told the story, acknowledging that yes, he'd violated one of our most basic precepts. I silently surveyed the scene. The fire was out and the home saved. Arden was uninjured, though he'd ostensibly set an extremely poor example for our younger firefighters. What to say?

I said, "Good job."

Yes, he'd sinned, but saving homes from fire is one of our primary missions. He'd done it. It was impossible to denigrate success. At our debriefing I repeated the old dictum that if your plan is going to break the rules, then it damn well better work. Arden's had. As we'll see, Father Peter Pernin chose a course of action that on its face was foolhardy. But it led him to an almost mystical plane of awareness that allowed him to save the lives of others. He worked out his own salvation.

Consider this from William James: "It's only by risking our persons from one hour to another that we live at all." Religious seers have long recognized this human peculiarity. In the New Testament, for example, Jesus says, "No man is worthy of me who does not take up his cross and walk in my footsteps. By gaining his life a man will lose it; by losing his life for my sake, he will gain it." Taking up a cross is nothing if not risky. Assuming risk is a means of tapping into an essential human energy that promises a chance at survival. This is what we don't want to miss—the spike of vitality and meaning arising from shared hazard and hardship. Perhaps what our modern Western culture regards as peculiar is a remnant of the ethos enjoyed by our hunter-gatherer ancestors who lived in a far tougher world, directly depending on a close community to shoulder the labor and danger. We are much safer than they, at least on a daily basis, and if absolute safety were possible, I imagine we'd be enervated to the point of terminal ennui. The old saying goes, "There is no atheist in a foxhole." I'd argue that many atheists were created in war. But I'd also argue there is no bored, self-absorbed, antisocial hermit in a foxhole. Crawling under the van was a validation of faith in the community, the crew. Besides, no matter what you may or may not do in life, the end result is the same: death. Given that, it makes little sense to live timidly.

Of course, I also crawled under that van with pliers because it was fun. It was better to do it than not to do it.

But hazard isn't the only siren song of fire. Like all meritorious disciplines, it exposes devotees to raw beauty, and to the pleasant shock of accidental wonder. I've seen and experienced charms and refinements on the fireground that I could encounter nowhere else. Or if I did, they'd probably lack the sinewy zip engendered by a flame-induced mind-set. For instance, a few days later, in the midst of an evening social gathering at our house—my forty-ninth birthday—the phone rang. We were still in fire season, so I picked it up.

I was needed at a fire about thirty-five miles south, out in the bog country near Sax. A train with hot brakes had ignited multiple fires along a remote stretch of rail. I'd tangled with a railroad bog fire in that same area three years before. After slogging through scorched sphagnum moss for several hours, dragging hundreds of feet of one-inch hose, we were told to quit for the night and go home. We climbed into the open box of a "high-liner," a truck outfitted with a set of retractable train wheels, allowing it to both ply the highways and ride the rails. An evening temperature inversion capped the smoke, blending it with a rising bog mist, and the high-liner's headlights drilled into a ghostly, shifting brume. The gleaming strands of the rails, buffed by reflecting dew, seemed to disappear into a tunnel. Behind, in the soft cherry glow of the taillights, black daggers of spruce thrust out of the enveloping smog, and the tendrils of cloud smoldered—as if a weirdly silent fire pursued us in the night.

I faced forward again and was startled. In the play of beams and shadows, a dark circle appeared—more cavelike than ever—and in the center was a brilliant point of light. My first thought was an oncoming train, but in a moment I realized it was Jupiter. The rails converged just below the planet, and I briefly felt as if we lifted, our high-liner aimed for the sky and the volcanic blazes of Io. The tunnel of smoke and mist was a corridor from the bog into the depths of the solar system.

I swelled with euphoria, sensed a spike of happiness like a shaft of sunlight through overcast. I was buoyant and immortal. I knew the sensation was generated and magnified by chemistry, by natural secretions associated with strenuous labor and physiological excitement—the usual, high-octane fireground fuel additives. I almost always feel good on a fire, but when I saw Jupiter I was blissful. The planet, glimpsed unexpectedly in fresh perspective, like an apparition, triggered an acceleration of joy. I suspect a similar reaction would've been fused by a wolf or cougar darting across the tracks or by a goshawk swooping out of the smoke, parading the resplendent grace of the wild, driving a point into the beating core of the hunter. For hunters we still are, questing feverishly for the prize of revelation, for some assurance about our role in the universe. And working in the wildlands of the nation is advantageous to the quest. Jung wrote,

> The danger that faces us today is that the whole of reality will be replaced by words [that is, information]. This accounts for the terrible lack of instinct in modern man, particularly the city dweller. He lacks all contact with life and the breath of nature.

And what is more the vitalizing breath of nature than fire—negotiator of every ecosystem?

In that sense I worship a fire god, a deific natural force of destruction and regeneration that gilds my life with purpose and led me long ago into an *ecclesia* of hunters and warriors who share the duty, pain, and joy of the fireground. We're a cadre of killers; a priesthood of healers. We attack fires and snuff them; we ignite fires and help them nurture the renewal of forest and meadow. We are, for good or ill, mediators between pervasive fire and invasive human.

And it's often humans, in the form of politics, rather than perilous but neutral fire, that confront us with the bitterest fights. Indeed, at the end of May, forty-eight hours before our DNR helitack crew members were to assemble at the Minnesota Interagency Fire Center in Grand Rapids, I lost 30 percent of them. It was politics driven by history.

The general public entertains the perception that the hardworking, geared-up wildland firefighters they see on television newscasts are full-time professionals. A few are, but most wildland firefighters fall into three categories. The first group is made up of full-time government employees (federal, state, local) who perform fire work when the need arises but whose "real" job is in timber, wildlife, recreation, hydrology, and so forth. In the second group are seasonal government employees hired on for three to six months specifically for fire duty. In the off-season they may take another job or survive on unemployment compensation. The third, and largest, group consists of fireground freelancers, referred to as "casuals" or "emergency firefighters" (EFF). They are neither official government employees nor contractors. They are denizens (or perhaps inmates) of a legal limbo. The Department of Natural Resources calls these people "smokechasers," and though they are the core of wildland fire operations—the veteran shock troops—they are also second-class citizens, living artifacts from the earliest days of organized American wildfire suppression.

In 1886, the U.S. Cavalry was assigned to prevent and extinguish wildfires in Yellowstone National Park, setting a tone of relatively low pay and expendability. When the U.S. Forest Service and state forestry agencies were formed, they often relied on temporary hires, convicts, and even conscripts to work the firelines. During the New Deal, many Civilian Conservation Corps units also fought fires. In tough economic times it was common for rural residents to go "job hunting," lighting fires in hopes (relatively assured) of being hired by the government to fight the blazes. As a result, firefighting wages were kept low to discourage arson for profit.

So although smokechasers are assigned employee numbers and taxes are withheld from their modest paychecks, the Department of Natural Resources emphasizes they are not employees, and they possess few of the rights and privileges that most American workers take for granted. There is no guaranteed term of employment, no health benefits, no sick leave, no vacation time, no seniority consideration, no grievance procedure, no career path. A smokechaser might work long hours for several consecutive days during a hot fire season, then be instantly laid off when the third raindrop splatters in the dust. There is no opportunity to negotiate, to set some conditions and boundaries.

In a 1925 statute, the state of Minnesota created a class of people who work or don't work at the whim of the government or the weather and yet are expected to respond immediately when called— either to a particular fire or to the seasonal fanfare in the spring— and to rise from long, lean winter struggles like mushrooms from dung, expected to briefly thrive in manure.

I began as a smokechaser and chafed under the yoke of the system for years, enduring the low pay, inequity, and disrespect only because I was passionate about fire. I watched dozens of good firefighters regretfully quit the profession because they couldn't afford homes, families, or even a reliable vehicle. In those days we had to work 106 hours in a two-week pay period before earning overtime, and the final straw for me was the day Richard and I accidentally saw a memo instructing our supervisor to prevent us from making over-time. If we were approaching the 106-hour threshold, we should be given a day off. We were working long hours because there was much work to be done. To cut us off not because we weren't needed, but simply to cut us off, was a kick in the ass. I finally resolved to kick back.

I called a meeting of smokechasers. In early November 1997, eight of us sat in a circle at the fire hall in Side Lake and formed the Minnesota Wildland Firefighters' Committee. I shipped out a press release, and when reporters began calling DNR honchos in St. Paul for information, the honchos began calling me. We set up a gathering for December 18, and sixty disgruntled smokechasers from across northern Minnesota squeezed into the French town hall.

It was a hard-bitten crowd, rough at the edges, with an average of ten seasons on the fireline. I contemplated the faces, some grim, some bemused, many of them weathered. From the Rockies to the Appalachians, from the Canadian Shield to the Okeefenokee, these people had battled not only fire, but also bureaucracy. I was proud to be in their number, but I guessed at the impression they'd make with the three DNR administrators—two from St. Paul—who came to listen: wood ticks, backcountry folk without real jobs, and people low on the socioeconomic scale and therefore dumb. They'd think: These are people we can bully and ignore—been doing it for years. I hoped I was wrong.

The administrators admitted that smokechasers were the back-bone of the DNR fire program, but after listening to a litany of grievances and suggestions—some delivered with visible emotion—the bureaucrats claimed they could do nothing. As much as they appreciated us (verbally patting our little heads), their hands were tethered by statute. They could offer us a small pay raise, but for anything more we should go to the legislature.

It was a polite brush-off, and my guess seemed confirmed; but if so, their impression was wrong. A month later we had a bill—written by wood ticks—introduced in both houses of the Minnesota Legislature, and though we didn't prevail, the DNR suddenly discovered their hands were not as tightly bound as advertised.

Wages increased; overtime was sanctioned after 40 hours per week rather than after 106 hours in two weeks; a hiring form (a protocontract) was drafted and implemented. Subsequent to our second offensive in the legislature the next year, the DNR created forty-five new fire positions, with full employee status. It was a start.

I was hired in one of the new positions and guaranteed three months' work with standard benefits. Good for me. But the rest of my proposed helitack crew for summer 2000 were all (but one) still smokechasers. They'd been told if they accepted the three-month assignment, they'd be treated like bona fide employees, in that they'd be paid for meals, mileage, and travel time, since they'd all be working far from home. It was the fair deal I'd have as an official employee.

Just forty-eight hours before we were to report, Sheldon Mack phoned me with the bad news. One of the St. Paul administrators who'd been at that first meeting in December 1997 decided that my crew members should be temporarily transferred to Grand Marais rather than be merely stationed there. That meant they'd actually be working at "home" and were therefore ineligible to be paid expenses. It was a low and devastating blow. As crew leader, I volunteered to call each member and explain the new order. It was a significant change in the complexion of the summer. I told them there would be no hard feelings if they changed their minds and no professional repercussions. Three of them quit.

I decided to conclude it was not an omen.

ALPHA-HOTEL-
ROMEO

There's an old trick used by firefighting instructors. Write a list under Column A on the blackboard: water, rock, concrete, steel, asbestos, brick. Then under Column B: gasoline, wood, paper, charcoal, kerosene, cow chips.

"Now," you say, suppressing a benign smirk, "which of these lists is composed of materials that will burn?"

Many students sense a trap, but few know the correct answer: neither. None of the listed substances actually burns. No solids or liquids do, just gases. It's possible to douse a small fire with diesel fuel.

Only when the materials in Column B are heated to the point of outgassing will they ignite. Since gasoline, for example, vaporizes easily under normal atmospheric conditions, it readily and violently burns; hence our difficulty with the flaming furniture van. Wood is tougher to light.

Most children quickly learn the hazards of extreme heat—the pain of touching a hot frying pan, the potentially destructive character of a kitchen match. But the nature of fire itself is largely ignored, assumed as a given. We think we know fire. It's heat and light, a utility. Despite occasional unruly disasters, we've largely tamed it, especially in the paved and sprinklered enclaves of our metropolitan sanctuaries, with a fire hydrant sprouting at every intersection.

Fire, however, transcends infrastructure. Our lives, our history, and our environment are shaped and directed by flames. We live on a fire planet. The fire triangle requires three ingredients to produce and sustain burning: fuel, oxygen, and heat. Thus we, and the rest of the living world, are carbon based, that is, combustible. Our atmosphere is oxygen rich, promoting the combustion reaction. Each day, lightning strikes the earth about 100 times per second—heat ignition.

It's easier to appreciate the impact of wildland fires when you purposely light them and view the results. When you note, for example, that the five acres of broadcast (as opposed to piled) logging slash you burned the summer before last is now thick with jack pine seedlings; or the 1400 acres of grassy bog you've burned every other year for the past decade now supports enhanced populations of sharp-tailed grouse, sandhill cranes, and yellow rails; or you enjoy the rich and diverse native prairie that must periodically burn to survive intact. Wildland fire is a tool of decomposition and recycling. It transforms the matter/energy that organisms create from solar radiation, releasing locked-up chemical potential. Geologic processes that provide chemicals (nutrients) are too slow for the demands of the biosphere. "The necessity for decomposition on a grand scale is such that if fire did not exist, nature would have to invent it" (Stephen Pyne, *Fire in America*). Especially in the temperate zones of the planet, where biological growth outpaces "normal" decomposition, fire is a critical component of ecological balance. Fire-dependent ecosystems are the norm.

And that included the Boundary Waters Canoe Area Wilderness with its Blowdown fuel. We all knew it was not a question of if, but when fires would occur in that region—perhaps newsworthy ones. The exhaustive research of the late Miron Heinselman, a U.S. Forest Service researcher, showed that, historically, every acre of high ground in the Boundary Waters Wilderness was swept by fire at least once every 122 years—boggy areas were on a longer cycle—and that since white settlement, with the introduction of aggressive fire suppression, that figure could be extrapolated to once every 2000 years. The northern forest wanted to burn, but we wouldn't let it. With the Blowdown there probably wasn't much choice. The fuels specialist at the Minnesota Interagency Fire Center told us that before the wind event, 10 to 20 percent of the snow-free days in the Superior National Forest had potential for large fire growth. After the storm, it was estimated that 40 to 50 percent of those days should be considered at moderate to high fire danger.

We were warned that such fuel concentrations favor the birth of a plume-dominated, fuels-driven fire as opposed to a wind-driven blaze. The tremendous heat generated by dense fuel induces a powerful convection column, not unlike the buildup associated with a thunderstorm. Embers and firebrands are sucked upward and soar long distances, igniting spot fires a mile or more away. As the plume develops, all the perimeter flame and smoke are drawn inward, creating a relatively tolerable initial environment for firefighters, tempting them to directly engage the fire at close quarters. But when the column reaches cooler levels of the atmosphere, thousands or tens of thousands of feet up, downdrafts or even microbursts suddenly materialize—like a thunderhead phenomena—and the fire violently blows out in all directions. Imagine the approach of a summer thunderstorm, as sudden blasts of wind rouse treetops into whiplash. Then picture that wind aflame. A plume-dominated fire is as much a weather event as a fire event. Sometimes the entire column of such an intense fire can collapse, with deadly results. At the Dude Creek fire in Arizona in 1990, six firefighters were killed in such an incident.

This was all part of the backdrop when our crew assembled at the Minnesota Interagency Fire Center in Grand Rapids, Minnesota, on the morning of June 1, 2000. Before the helicopter contractors arrived—the pilot, mechanic, and fuel truck driver—Sheldon Mack met with the helitack crew. All were aware that three members had dropped out only the day before, and some were still chafing at the eleventh-hour shenanigans regarding living and travel expenses.

Sheldon drew a loaf of bread on the blackboard, representing wages and expense account reimbursements.

"Two days ago," he said, "you had the whole loaf. Now . . ." He erased about a third of it. He was acutely aware this had been a rabbit punch to the morale of the smokechasers. "But let's see what we can do."

He passed out a sheet of paper with a handwritten column of figures, denoting estimated wages, meals, mileage, lodging, and travel time. The wages were unaffected, and he pointed out that since we and the helicopter would be listed as "available for dispatch" for a minimum of nine hours per day, every day, we owned built-in overtime all summer. In addition, I'd long ago suggested and secured for the crew one hour of paid physical training each shift. Our lodging—leased or rented—was paid for by the state. Sheldon turned to the blackboard and added a thick slice to the loaf.

He reminded us we were a statewide resource, that we would undoubtedly travel, not only for fires, but for project work like heavy-lift jobs. As soon as the smokechasers were more than thirty-five miles from Grand Marais, all expenses would kick in. With a flourish, he added another slice to the loaf.

Whenever we were in the field, government meals—usually in the form of MREs (meals, ready-to-eat), military combat rations—would be in our packs. Free lunch. Another slice. In a few minutes Sheldon's revisionist arithmetic had restored the loaf to 80 percent of whole. It was creative, effective damage control.

The contractors arrived and introductions were made.

Doug Wilson, age forty-three, was my lead helitack crew member. He'd been with me on an initial attack helicopter gig in southwest Montana the summer before, and I invested high confidence in his experience and good sense. Though still mired in smokechaser status, he was being groomed as a helicopter manager and would be my second-in-command. In the off-season he was a logger. I also appreciated the fact that he was an Emergency Medical Technician (EMT). When I'd first been tapped to lead this mission back in February, I said I'd accept on one condition: "Give me Doug Wilson and Ray Leppala."

Ray, age forty-seven, was another key crew member, a long-time, hard-core firefighter who'd also been part of our 1999 team in Montana. He also worked as a carpenter. We'd first met at a training session a decade before and had shared several firegrounds since. In May 1998 we were staffing a helicopter for the U.S. Forest Service in the Upper Peninsula of Michigan when we were dispatched to a gnarly blaze near Seney. The call surprised us because it originated with the Michigan Department of Natural Resources, an organization that usually eschewed helicopters in favor of bulldozers. We spotted the smoke from fifty miles out and, when we swung overhead several minutes later, saw an extremely hot, fifty-plus-acre fire in jack pines. It wasn't crowning, but single trees and groups of trees were torching out in snapping orange fountains of sparks. It was remote, and the dozers and engines of the Michigan DNR were an hour or more away. We had little hope of controlling the fire ourselves, but we landed, hooked up the bucket, then forded a small stream to attack a flank of the blaze. There was a deep beaver pond near the middle of the black—perfect for a bucket dip site—and in the next hour our pilot dropped 106 loads on the fire, over 11,000 gallons. On the ground, our "squirt guns" quickly ran dry, but we cut balsam fir boughs and swatted the fire out along the perimeter. To our amazement, we knocked down all open flames and damped a relatively large fire with one small helicopter and three firefighters. The first Michigan DNR people were just arriving on scene as we were stowing the bucket in the rear of the ship, and one approached me and said, "Well, you guys really saved our butts on this one. 'Course, we won't tell anybody."

Dave Stern, age thirty-nine, began working helitack in 1996 but had logged a ton of excellent experience since then. I recommended him for hire by the Nez Perce National Forest in Idaho, where I'd been a helitack crew leader 1991–93, and Dave worked two seasons in the northern Rockies. If not for the Assignment, he may have returned to the Nez Perce.

I had put forth the names of three women, but only one could accept. Christina Dickson, age thirty, was also being groomed as a helicopter manager and, if she made it, would be the first such woman in the history of the Minnesota DNR. I'd met her at a mock incident drill two years before and was impressed by her knowledge and attitude.

Dallas McCloud, age twenty-seven, had also been part of the

southwest Montana adventure. When the selection of the present crew was made, there were only eight members, and Dallas wasn't one of them. He didn't allow it to stand. He vigorously lobbied Sheldon and his assistants, arguing for his inclusion with such passion that he was mustered into the crew. Now that three had quit, we needed him more than ever.

Roy Dahl, age thirty-nine, was in his sixth year of fire and second of helitack. We'd first worked together on a Boundary Waters Wilderness fire off the Gunflint Trail in 1995 and shared a wicked tour in Ontario in 1996. Roy was present the morning one of our crew members went berserk. The fire was in wild, roadless country, and for sixteen days we'd been *spiked out* (camped in isolation), supplied by helicopters and enduring our own hazardous cooking. The work and the terrain were mean, and one of our crew—I'll call him Sam—suffered a minor knee injury. The Canadians flew him out to a doctor, and he returned the next day on crutches. We assigned him to tend camp. Near the end of our tour we were transferred to a spot near the lakeside hamlet of Graham, Ontario, and made our first contact with local civilians. They were friendly and gracious, and one evening after work I noted that Sam had procured a bottle of brandy. Next morning at "reveille," we all promptly—more or less—arose, except Sam. He was twisted up in his collapsed tent, his boots and a crutch comically poking out one end. We chuckled and blamed the contraband booze. I grabbed the heel of his left boot, shook it, and said, "Hey, Sam. Time to get up." I expected to hear a groan or a groggy expletive. Instead, the tent thrashed violently, and Sam lurched upright, yelling curses. He brandished a crutch, held high and threatening like a broadsword, and swung it at me. "I'm going to kill you bastards!" he screamed. "I'm going to kill you and eat you just like Jeffrey Dahmer!" This was startling news, and our neighbors, a fire crew from British Columbia, tried to stare without staring. Perhaps this was American humor? We surrounded Sam and subdued him without injury, discovering that he'd run short of his medication and consumed the fifth of brandy. Fortunately it was our last day out. Roy and I often spoke of the incident, and it emphasized to me the value of screening crew members.

Derek Robinson, age thirty-nine, a Canadian from British Columbia, was the pilot. We would later discover he'd been a member of the Canadian Olympic swimming team, among other talents and achievements, but that first morning all I wanted to know was: Is this a nice guy? Can we get along all summer? Because in practical terms, we'd share command. As pilot, Derek had final say about the operation and disposition of the aircraft itself, but as government representative, I had control of the helitack crew, our helibase at Grand Marais, and the general aspect of the missions. To sum up the relationship of the pilot and the helicopter manager: the pilot runs the aircraft, the manager runs the mission, but we have mutual veto power. For example, we arrive at a fire and I suggest a specific spot to land. If Derek deems it unsafe, we don't land. Or vice versa if Derek proposes a landing zone that scares the hell out of me. The shared authority forges a kind of marriage relationship, and we'd be stuck with each other for at least three months. So as I shook Derek's hand, all my antennae were extended. He seemed open, cheerful, and eager to start on the right foot. I was relieved, but time and action would tell the tale.

Jim Halfman, age thirty, was the helicopter mechanic, or "engineer," as the Canadians preferred. He was young but experienced, and we found we had acquaintances in common in the fire and aviation realm of the American West.

Larry Martin, age fifty-six, was the old-timer of the crew. He drove the 2800-gallon, Jet-A helicopter fuel truck. A native of Idaho, he was a hunting guide and retired paving contractor. He'd never been a firefighter, but we'd soon discover he had a penchant for practical jokes, a skill universally admired in the ranks of the fire service.

That afternoon we attended an in-depth briefing about aerial ignition. Our helicopter was carded to drop fire from the sky, and it was assumed that *burning out* and *backfiring*—fighting fire with fire—would be useful tactics in helping to control a Blowdown fire. If the initial blaze was hot enough, we might be forced to back off into more congenial territory—say a narrow isthmus between lakes—and start another fire, using open water, bogs, ledgerock, or less flammable tracts of forest as control lines. The purpose might be to create a black zone in front of a wildfire or to influence its direction of spread by drawing a plume toward the new fire by way of an alternate convection column. These are common goals on prescribed fires.

The advantage of aerial ignition is that a helicopter can lay down fire very efficiently, even over inaccessible terrain, and often these firing techniques must be implemented rapidly and decisively. We'd use a machine called a Premo Mark-III that mounts in the rear of the ship. An operator feeds plastic spheres into a hopper. They look like Ping-Pong balls, and each contains three grams of potassium permanganate powder. The balls are routed past a set of four needles that inject about one cubic centimeter of ethylene gly-col (common antifreeze) into each sphere. They tumble through a chute and out of the helicopter. The two chemicals combine in an exothermic reaction and in about twenty seconds burst into flame on the ground. A burn boss or ignition specialist rides in the left front seat of the ship, directing the operation. It's a modern, high-tech means of doing what North Americans have been avidly practicing for millennia.

In northeast Wisconsin in the fall of 1871, it wasn't only the farmers who were wielding the torch. Hundreds of men were also building a rail line that autumn, an extension of the Chicago and Northwestern, bound ultimately for the new iron mines of Michigan's Upper Peninsula. They used the same tools—ax and fire—to hasten progress on clearing the right-of-way. The campfires of hunters and Indians, left unextinguished in the morning, also contributed to a widespread network of small, uncontrolled fires that alternately smoldered and freely burned. These blazes were largely ignored by the populace. Such fires were workaday background, especially in the fall, not unlike the more recent suburban and small-town practice of raking and burning leaves.

In fact, when European settlers arrived in North America, many adopted fire practices that Native Americans had employed for centuries. Tribes ignited and broadcast fire to herd and/or trap wild game, in some cases forcing deer onto narrow peninsulas, transforming the confined area into a shooting gallery. Or they burned off tree moss that deer favored as food, thus encouraging them to move into more open country where they were easier to hunt. Fires were set to smoke bears or raccoons out of dens. Indians used purposeful fire to harvest or nurture wild crops such as tarweed and various berries or to surround and roast insects such as grasshoppers. Burns could increase forage for wild and domestic animals; thus while driving deer or bison with fire, they were also rejuvenating the creatures' food supply as the fire released nutrients into the soil. They created firebreaks around villages, a popular and effective tactic to this day; a careful burnout or *backfire* (a deliberate counter fire set to deny fuel to another blaze) might buffer a single house or a subdivision being threatened by a wildfire. They employed fire as a tool of war, to remove the cover of tall grass or brush to preclude an ambush, or to destroy an enemy settlement. Long-distance communication, to announce a gathering or warn of an adversary's encroachment, was accomplished with large fires, though not with blankets and puffs of smoke signals, a Hollywood invention. Fire was a means to clear trails for easier passage and to fell large trees with burning bore holes or by killing standing timber with a hot, localized blaze.

Native Americans did so much burning that white pioneers in New England reported wide tracts of almost parklike forest, the understory kept open by frequent, periodic Indian fires. Due to subsequent fire exclusion and suppression, especially in the past century (and also to the decline of New England agriculture), that region of the United States is more thickly and generally wooded than it was three hundred years ago. The overall American trend since then has been to sharply curtail Indian-style fire use, chiefly by removing Native Americans from the land.

Yet in 1871, the fires still burned. Writer and historian Vernon L. Parrington dubbed this flaming era "The Great Barbecue," and Peshtigo and its citizens were fuel. After the narrow escape of September 24, some residents abandoned their complacency. The normal autumn smoke now seemed more ominous. A few people dug shallow holes and trenches and buried family treasures and heirlooms. Officials of the William H. Ogden woodenware factory, known locally as the Company, ordered a general cleanup of slabs, sawdust, and any other combustibles in the neighborhood of the factory and increased the number of hogsheads of water deployed around the town.

Father Peter Pernin deemed these "wise precautions certainly, which could have been of great service in any ordinary case of fire, but which were utterly unavailing in the awful conflagration that burst upon us."

An "ordinary case of fire" was not what we expected from the Blowdown. I'd spent two weeks cutting through it the summer before, clearing trails and portages, and I explained to Derek and the others what I'd seen.

With a six-person team, we'd hiked an hour to our first swath of blowdown. Some trees had toppled here and there, and a previous crew had bucked them. Then we rounded a bend and the trail was gone. I stopped short and lay down my saw. I faced a massive cedar root wad, twelve feet across. When the old tree toppled, it lifted the trail with it. The rampart of tangled roots clutched football-sized chunks of granite that hadn't seen sunlight for centuries, perhaps even millennia. Beyond, the forest was smashed flat. Eighty percent of the trees, including old-growth white pines, were uprooted, broken off, or simply shattered.

Then I spotted a piece of notepaper stuck in the middle of the root wad. I unfolded it and read: "Welcome to Hell. Voyageurs Nat. Park Crew."

We clambered astride the cedar trunk and surveyed the territory. It looked like photos of the Tunguska Event, when a comet or meteorite leveled 600 square miles of forest in Siberia in 1908. I fired up my saw and, using wedges to keep from pinching the bar, cut off the thirty-inch cedar. The stump and root wad sprang back, and a three-foot section of the path thudded into place like a trapdoor slamming shut. The granite returned to darkness.

With our crew leader slowly scouting ahead to locate the buried trail and flag it with orange ribbon, the rest of us waded into the mass of limbs and trunks. Some of the twisted wreckage towered over our heads, and we literally tunneled through the snarl with three chain saws. It was wicked, hazardous labor. Nearly every fallen trunk was hung up or spring-loaded or stacked, or all three. Trees bent under tension can explode when sawed, whipping up, down, in, or out with the force of a catapult. Nearly every cut had to be planned. One ill-considered move could shove death in your face.

Cutting through a crisscross of large, heavy-limbed trees is like picking a path through a minefield.

I grew fatigued near the end of the day and made a careless cut. Even as I watched the chain tear through the trunk, I realized my error. The vectors were pushing back and not down. I stumbled backward, and the butt end of a twelve-inch aspen, thrusting like a monster piston, shuddered to a quivering halt one inch from my chest. I swore and sat down for a break.

After three and a half hours we cleared a mere 330 feet of trail. We'd progressed at the excruciating pace of 1.6 feet per minute. As I sipped warm water from a sun-softened plastic canteen, I mused on the epic proportions of fuel—mounds of bug-killed balsam fir blended with cedar and resinous pine. My scalp prickled to imagine being on foot in that terrain if all was tinder dry. Welcome to hell, indeed.

But like the high-liner ride through the smoking bog, the intense travail of breaching the Blowdown offered its own gift of sanctifying grace. By our eighth day of cutting we'd established a relentless momentum, driven on by the work and the simple joy of covering ground.

When we returned to our camp on Alder Lake, we'd paddled twelve or thirteen miles that day and cleared fourteen campsites and 200 rods of portage. The weather had delivered both burning sun and cold rain. We'd fought deer flies and a bracing head wind. We were wasted. We were also content, high on the struggle and charmed by the witchery of a north woods high-summer dusk.

As we traversed two miles of open water toward camp, we watched a burgeoning thunderhead—an anvil-shaped cloud sculpted by hot, unstable air—in the southwest, its base black against the tree line, its billowing summit splashed with low-angle sunlight. The rock palisades on Alder rose 250 feet above the lake—nearly vertical—and in a few minutes we glided into their deep shadow. The water was glassy, the forest deep and dark, but overhead the sky was tattered and bright with orange and magenta streaks of cirrus.

We beached our canoes and built a fire and, as the clouds faded to bluish gray, cooked a quick meal. I nestled between the gnarled roots of an old cedar growing from riven bedrock at the water's edge. A rising full moon broke through a band of cloud on the eastern horizon, flooding the lake with fresh light and illuminating the slowly advancing thunderhead. The pleated cumulus was a vivid black and white, gleaming off and on with embedded lightning, like a divine neon display. I heard a faint rumbling in the distance.

To the west, a jagged rim of palisade was silhouetted by the last glow of sunset. The backlit tree line was sharply etched against the sky, and a single, wind-twisted white pine ranged high above the canopy. With scales of distance blurred by moonlight and shadows, the old pine seemed like a carefully sculpted bonsai, as if manicured and placed just so. And why not? It was perfect.

As the vanguard of the thunderstorm rolled in, and the night air exhaled the aroma of imminent rain, I was as happy as I've ever been. Carl Jung wrote, "There are things in the psyche which I do not produce, but which produce themselves and have their own life." Such is the nature of euphoria. It happens. For me, the blissful climax of the evening was the image of the single, wind-sculpted white pine, and that image has shaded into an abbreviation, a bookmark for the entire blowdown-cutting episode. If I close my eyes and imagine it, conjure up that silhouette as vividly as possible, I can find my way back to Alder Lake in July 1999—even now, on a snowy December day sixteen months later, and probably also sixteen years hence. It's a creative thought. "Man, I," said Jung, "in an invisible act of creation puts the stamp of perfection on the world by giving it objective reality." Then that reality cycles back into the ephemeral labyrinth of our minds, constructing in fantastical detail what memory defines as our life. It is best, I believe, if that memory preserves many episodes of seasoning in wild country.

Whenever I wish to return to June 2000, the image I raise is of C-FAHR ("see far")—Charlie-Foxtrot-Alpha-Hotel-Romeo, our Bell 212 HP helicopter. A 212 is the offspring of the familiar Vietnam-era "Huey" but bigger, stronger, and equipped with two engines instead of one. The main rotor has two blades, with a total diameter of forty-eight feet. The ship is fifty-eight feet long, with an average cruising speed of 115 miles per hour. Alpha-Hotel-Romeo (AHR) for short, was configured to carry nine passengers in back if need be plus the two front seats—one for the pilot, one for me. The main body of the fuselage was white with two horizontal stripes— one red, one gray—running just beneath the windows. The tail boom was red. She was mounted on high skid gear that made it easy for us to scoot beneath to manipulate the belly hook while avoiding the radio antennae and mirrors. It was a gorgeous helicopter, clean and well maintained. I filled out a pre-use inspection form, noting one minor dent in a rear door.

Derek gave the helitack crew a detailed briefing from stem to stern, pointing out, for example, the ELT (emergency locator transmitter), a device designed to register the impact of a crash, or "hard landing," as some in the trade prefer, and instantly begin broadcasting an audio tone at 121.5 MHz, two to four times per second, which can be homed in on by searchers. We'd all worked around 212s before, so this briefing was a general review as well as an acquaintance with the particular features of AHR.

Derek's presentation was professional but lighthearted and self-deprecating. "We really won't need the ELT," he quipped. "I'll be screaming."

He announced that his motto for the summer, which he hoped we'd all adopt, was "mock or be mocked." I laughed and agreed. The rarefied realm of fire helicopter pilots is too often characterized by arrogance and ego, and Derek was either bored with that attitude or had never shared it. Testing his commitment to mocking, I said, "You know, Derek, you don't seem to be as much of an asshole as a lot of pilots I've known."

His lips pressed into a thin, straight line, and I thought, "Oops, went too far." But then he mimed an awkward stumble over the left skid, cupped his hand to my ear, and in a stage whisper said, "Don't tell my boss, but I'm not really a pilot!"

On June 2, we flew to the Hill City airport, a grass strip about twelve miles south of Grand Rapids, to perform proficiency drills. Doug Wilson and I designed a bucket-deployment evolution that would be our standard operating procedure whenever we landed to set up for an initial attack.

Normally, we'd have three or four crew members in back, strapped into the fabric bench seats. The goal was to exit in a fluid motion, with each person assigned a specific task depending upon their seating position. When the skids were firmly on the ground, and Derek said, "Okay," the crew removed their flight helmets, buckled them securely to the aft-facing seat in front of them, and donned their wildfire hard hats. Then all slid out the right side of the ship to pull the 150-pound bucket out of a compartment behind the rear seat. I exited the left side and opened the door to another compartment where our packs, hand tools, and chain saw were stored in flight. We could have the ship ready to lift, bucket attached and tested, in three to four minutes—without running or otherwise hurrying the process. Methodical moves were the key. No scurrying.

My complication was that the controls in front of me—cyclic, collective, and pedals—were all live. I had to squirm my size-twelve boots and six-foot-three frame over and around the collective without bumping it. I practiced a kind of awkward two-step and found it best to simply grasp my left knee in two hands and lift it over the collective stick. By the end of the season I had a system down. A generous neutral observer might've noted that I didn't quite appear to be a bear attempting to mate with a Bell product.

At Hill City we watched Derek execute both *trail drops*, maintaining forward airspeed when he opened the bucket to lay water along a line, and *hover drops*, simply dumping the entire load on one spot. Then we packed a cargo net with gear and performed several hover hookups. First with 100 feet of *longline* (steel wire-wound cable with an electrical cord attached), then belly hookups. Longline is used to deliver cargo when the ship can't land or approach close to the ground, for example, in unbroken forest or on a steep mountainside. A belly hookup, with the load on a short, ten-foot cable, requires a crew member to be standing next to the load with a swivel hook in his or her hand. The pilot eases the helicopter down over the outstretched arm of the helitacker, who, when he or she can reach the belly hook, snaps the swivel into the hook and exits. It's critical to brace yourself, feet apart and firmly planted, or the galelike rotorwash from a 212 will blow you over. After an hour or so of such practice it was obvious Derek was a smooth pilot. I was also satisfied with the crew.

On the morning of June 3, 2000, we departed for our post at Grand Marais. Besides the ship itself, we had six vehicles: the fuel truck; the mechanic's chase car; our DNR helicopter support truck, which carried nets, rigging gear, fire tools, and so forth, everything we needed to establish and sustain long-term operations in the field; and three private vehicles belonging to crew members. We chuckled over the logistics. It was like a carnival, or a rock band entourage hitting the road.

When the last of the parade pulled out, Derek, Dave, and I buckled into AHR and lifted off the Grand Rapids airport. It was about 145 air miles to Grand Marais, around 1.3 hours flight time. Though the helicopter was equipped with a Global Positioning System (GPS) unit, one of my tasks remained basic, seat-of-the-pants navigation. I kept my finger on a map spread across my knees, tracing our progress across the Mesabi Iron Range and into the Superior National Forest. My goal was to always know where we were, not only for my mandatory fifteen-minute flight-following check-ins to the Minnesota Interagency Fire Center or Superior Dispatch, but also in case the GPS went "bravo-uniform," that is, "belly-up." It happened to me on the way to a fire in Idaho in 1996; an old-fashioned map and compass saved us trouble, time, and, not least, embarrassment.

So as lakes, rivers, and backcountry roads slipped by below, I ticked them off out loud, giving Derek a geographical orientation. Ten miles out of Grand Marais airport, I raised the Grand Marais DNR–Forestry station on their local frequency.

"Grand Marais, this is helicopter Alpha-Hotel-Romeo. We're showing five minutes out. The circus is in town."

It was a lighthearted comment, but we were on the threshold of our season, our mission, and I didn't feel as relaxed as I may've sounded or wished to project. I suppose I felt as Father Pernin did the day before the Great Peshtigo Fire.

On Saturday, October 7, 1871, Father Peter Pernin attempted a journey of his own to an outlying parish. He was an energetic, middle-aged priest with a high forehead, dark, closely cropped hair, and a prominent Gallic nose. In a land of pioneers and immigrants, he fit the mold, having arrived in the United States from France less than a decade before. He first served at Clifton, Illinois, from 1865 to 1869 and transferred to northeast Wisconsin only the year before. His local parishes were in the establishment phase, and the church at Peshtigo was a work in progress. The altar and pews had been temporarily removed so that a plastering contractor could begin the interior finishing work the following Monday. Pernin therefore canceled the Sunday mass at Peshtigo and notified the congregation at Cedar River, Michigan, a small town on the shore of Green Bay about thirty miles northeast, that he would report there via ferry boat for a Sunday service.

Pernin traveled on horseback to Marinette, a town near the mouth of the Menominee River, and waited on the wharf for the *Dunlap*, a steamboat that regularly shuttled along the coast of Green Bay. Several hours passed, and for the first time that year, the boat missed its scheduled stop. Two days before, the *Green Bay Advocate* reported that because of heavy smoke, navigation on Lake Michigan, particularly near shore on Green Bay, had become difficult. Compasses were required in daylight, and foghorns blew continuously. On October 7 the air was cool, and Father Pernin noted there was "no breath of wind." It's possible a temperature inversion was in place, capping the pall of smoke close to the surface. In any case, the master of the *Dunlap* deemed it unsafe to approach the Menominee wharf with such poor visibility and passed it by. I was reminded of the 1987 fires in California and the Pacific Northwest, when a dense stratum of smoke reduced the noonday sun to a pale orange orb, and just breathing outdoors was said to be the equivalent of smoking four packs of cigarettes a day.

Pernin returned to Peshtigo and fabricated an altar in his house, using the tabernacle he'd moved from the church, and the next morning offered a Sunday mass. Every other week his custom was to preach and chant vespers at the church in Marinette, and early Sunday afternoon he prepared to go. However, several of his parishioners objected, urging him to remain at Peshtigo. Pernin wrote, "There seemed to be a vague fear of some impending though unknown evil haunting the minds of many. . . ." He too felt a certain nebulous dread, though outwardly declaring the fear was groundless. He persisted in his intention to conduct vespers at Marinette until he realized the congregation there, assuming him to be at Cedar River, wouldn't assemble anyway.

I appreciated Pernin's "vague fear," though in a slightly different context. The Assignment scared me. I mentally rehearsed scenarios—both intentionally and unintentionally—and wondered: Who in the hell do I think I am? What overweening arrogance to believe that I'd successfully meet the looming challenges! I felt like a fraud. I recalled past incidents and metaphorically trembled; I conjured potential incidents and quaked. I reminded myself of the definition of operational wisdom—the balance between confidence and doubt. Was I doubting too much? But the crux of the firefighter's struggle, especially in the heat of urgent action, is to avoid overconfidence. It can mutate into careless arrogance. Too much doubt locks into paralysis. And so I teetered, never quite convinced of my worthiness. And herein cuts my double-edged faith as a firefighter. On one hand, after twenty years of experience and over 700 hours of formal training, I can rely on my competence under many fireground situations. I can believe in ability. But, given the host of variables influencing fire emergencies, I could easily be confronted by an event beyond my mental and/or physical skills. I might drill, train, and experience for forty years and still not know it all, still not be good enough. So I must also rely on instinct and luck—have simple faith that when ambushed by the unexpected, I'll somehow do the right thing. The chief comfort is the sure knowledge that such internal debate vaporizes in the midst of action. As Jung wrote, "Often the hands know how to solve a riddle with which the intellect has wrestled in vain." Father Pernin would be witness to this truth.

In retrospect, he saw the hand of Providence and destiny. On the afternoon of October 8 he found himself home at Peshtigo, "Where according to all previous calculations, projects, and arrangements, I should not have been. . . . God willed that I should be at the post of danger."

There have been times when I felt the same way.

In my second-grade classroom I sat behind a girl who lived next door to my uncle Frank. He was a member of our hometown fire department, which then was a full-time organization. One day this girl turned in her seat and asked me if I was going to be a "fireman" when I grew up, like my uncle. The idea hadn't occurred to me.

"Oh, no," I replied, "I'm going to be a baseball player."

That fantasy was eclipsed by the notion of becoming an artist or illustrator (for which I had little talent), then a writer, and, finally, in my high school years, an astronomer. But these vocations, though attractive to me, were also a smoke screen—something to tell prying relatives and school counselors. What I really wanted to be was discernible from an impressive stack of military recruitment brochures that I kept in my bedroom. As early as the sixth grade, in 1962, I regularly raided the information racks at the post office, eagerly snatching the latest pamphlets issued by the armed forces of the United States. With naive juvenescent fervor, I read them over and over, planning my career as a sailor, soldier, or airman. I couldn't decide which would be best—wanted to be all three. I eventually settled on either the navy submarine service or the marine corps. In 1964 and '65, as American involvement in the Vietnam

War waxed full scale, I assumed I would participate if it lasted long enough. Sometimes I think I just wanted to wear a helmet, like my father's hard hat.

But another strain of desire was also heating up: I needed to know and understand the will of God. Not only from natural human curiosity about ultimate origins and fate, but also from fear. Until I was five years old, I slept with a lamp on in my bedroom to ward off the Boogey Man. That childish dread was replaced by the reality of the Bomb. When Soviet premier Nikita Khrushchev visited the United States in 1959, I knelt and prayed that he would extend his visit, reasoning that as long as their leader was here, the Russians wouldn't attack, and I was grateful for the respite from worry. Three years later, during the Cuban missile crisis, I was sure our world was about to end in atomic holocaust.

Then, in 1967, even as I fantasized about the military while fearing nuclear war, I first heard a preacher named Garner Ted Armstrong on the radio. I was mesmerized. Every evening at 6:30 P.M., on WEBC, a rock station out of Duluth, Minnesota, his smooth, authoritative voice detailed one of the many woes of the planet—crime, race riots, pollution, hunger, bloodshed in the Middle East, carnage in Southeast Asia, tyranny in Eastern Europe and Red China, and of course the horrifying prospect of global nuclear conflagration. That winter I listened with the lights off in my room, gazing out the north-facing window at Cassiopeia and the Big Dipper. His tone was friendly but dire, and at the end of each seamlessly eloquent half hour, he'd state with assurance that he knew solutions, that there was a way out. He never mentioned God, just offered an address in Pasadena, California, where you could write for free literature. He never asked for a dime. It was a brilliant pitch, even sincere so far as it went. He sounded like a particularly wise and concerned newscaster—like Walter Cronkite.

I sent for dozens of booklets and tracts, hiding them from my scrupulously Catholic mother, and they soon outstacked my recruiting brochures. Then, on July 3, 1969, while studying one of Armstrong's treatises about biblical prophecy, I was overcome by a deluge of emotion. I slid from my desk chair to my knees and, grasping a dog-eared Bible in two hands, fervently whispered, "I accept Jesus Christ as my personal savior!" After wavering for almost two years, I rejected eighteen years of Roman Catholicism, which at that moment I considered counterfeit, and resolved to attend Garner Ted Armstrong's Ambassador College in Big Sandy, Texas.

A by-product of this conversion was a vehement spurning of human warfare and military involvement. As a new member of the Worldwide Church of God, I was automatically a conscientious objector. If I was drafted, my God-directed duty was to refuse induction and go cheerfully to federal prison. About that time, a local businessman whose son was one of my friends offered to lobby our Congressman if I applied to the U.S. Air Force Academy. I turned him down. I threw away my recruiting brochures along with dozens of science fiction novels the church deemed sinful and demonic.

I matriculated at Ambassador College in August 1970 and wrote in my journal, "I'm just another lost and lazy, disillusioned clod who came stumbling out of the muck and mire of the world into something so awesome and beautiful that his semi-perverted mind can't even fully grasp it." Self-abasement was crucial to the program, but I also noted with pleasure that our instructors referred to Ambassador College as "the West Point of God's work," and we were considered "soldiers of God." It seemed I'd just needed to enlist in the right army. I was a ministerial candidate. My training would qualify me as an "officer" in the church.

I stayed four years and collected my unaccredited B.A. degree in

Judeo-Christian theology, but by then I no longer believed many of the doctrines and was scandalized by the thought of a twenty-three-year-old, inexperienced whelp such as I posing in a pulpit and telling people twice and three times my age how they should live. Even Jesus was age thirty before he started that. In 1974 I left Big Sandy, Texas, and the Worldwide Church of God—discharged, as it were, from the army of Christ. More on that later.

It's easy and fashionable to speak of epiphanies. Our modern usage—an insight or revelation, often sparked by a chance occurrence—was instigated by James Joyce. But nominally, Epiphany (from the Greek, "appearance; manifestation") is a Christian festival celebrated on January 6 in honor of the magi's visit to the infant Jesus and his unveiling to the world. So my 1969 conversion was a genuine personal epiphany—my exposure to Jesus Christ in vivid, heartrending action, and not from the bland pages of the *Baltimore Catechism*. My mind was changed. I felt I'd become enlightened. I "snapped"—in the sense that I underwent a sudden personality change that distanced me from family, friends, and what had been my normal routine. Since my mind had changed, so did my life.

Almost twenty years passed before I had a similar experience of such magnitude. It was in Oregon in September 1987 as I packed a chain saw up that mountainside, leading nineteen firefighters and suddenly realizing I was inadvertently acting out a fourteen-year-old fantasy in startling detail. When I stopped in my tracks in wonderment, one of the thoughts that flashed through my mind was: *this is what I was born to do.* I was enamored of everything around me—the aroma of smoke, the heft of the saw, the sensation of fatigue spiced with fear, the sound of helicopters, the sight of flame, and dozens of other images and impressions. But most of all I loved the nineteen firefighters hiking behind me. Not necessarily as individuals but as an idea, as a living system of comradeship, sharing trials and small triumphs—a "happy band of brothers" (and sisters). A congregation. And yes, to a certain extent, an army. I felt as if I'd arrived full circle to my goal of a military career.

The simple, clean power of being in that line of uniformed firefighters (with our helmets) is not to be underestimated. At Ambassador College, for example, our physical habits and practices were highly regulated. There was an approved way to do almost everything—from dressing and grooming to eating and working. The list of do's and don'ts was explicit and exhaustive. Bodies can be more easily disciplined than minds, and if one relentlessly directs the former, you may gain control of the latter. Generals have known this for millennia. In his book *The Pursuit of Power*, historian William H. McNeill highlighted the efficacy of military drill in creating cohesive congregations:

> For when a group of men move their arm and leg muscles in unison for prolonged periods of time, a primitive and very powerful social bond wells up among them. . . . Consider how amazing it was for men to form themselves into opposing ranks a few score yards apart and fire muskets at one another, keeping up while comrades were falling dead and wounded all around. Instinct and reason alike make such behavior unaccountable. Yet European armies of the 18th century did it as a matter of course.

Firefighters are not conditioned to that degree, nor should they be, but we are subject to the same general principle: the potency of the trained and integrated unit; the happiness of belonging to "the flock"—whether as sheep or shepherd.

In July 1969 I surrendered my will to Jesus Christ, though in reality I gave it to a specific religious organization that began to provide my thoughts for me. In September 1987 I also surrendered my will to a certain extent. A part of my thinking and activity was controlled by the fire service and community of firefighters. It was less intrusive and restrictive and made no appeal to a deity, but it was just as powerful in molding conduct and desire. In place of the crucifixion were our personal opportunities to die on the fireground.

FOUR

DREAM FIRE

Before the Blowdown, the territory protected by the Grand Marais Department of Natural Resources Division of Forestry was considered a wildland fire backwater—the "asbestos forest," as some firefighters quipped. Chiefly because of a lack of fine fuels, like grass, and a low human population density, there simply weren't many wildfires. Generally, more people equals more fires, especially in locales where *one-hour fuels* abound—one hour referring to the approximate time lag between the last rain and when a fuel is dry enough to burn. Officially, a one-hour fuel has a diameter up to one-quarter inch and is found in abundance in grasslands, savannas, and grass-shrub combinations. The Grand Marais region is mostly forest. At the opposite end of the scale are logs and heavy limbs, classified as *1000-hour fuels*. When the 1000-hour fuels are dry, you may certainly expect action.

In Minnesota, roughly 95 percent of wildfires are human caused, either accidentally or otherwise. By contrast, in a sparsely populated state like Wyoming, most wildfires are ignited by lightning. Minnesota and the Upper Midwest in general have significantly more lightning strikes than the Rocky Mountain states, but the storms are usually accompanied by heavier rainfall, and many incipient fires are doused at birth. The Blowdown provided tons of one-hour fuels in the form of conifer needles and small branches. (At Peshtigo, the Blowdown was mimicked by vast tracts of logging slash and the cuttings of farmers and railroad laborers, who were also supplying ignitions.)

So the stakes were higher in Minnesota than they'd been since the deadly fires of 1918, the last big outbreak of the pioneering and logging era. Since I was a fire instructor as well as a crew leader, it was my job to emphasize the ratcheting up of jeopardy.

One of my classroom specialties is firefighter safety and survival—how to avoid trouble on the fireground but, failing that, how to get out of it. At root, it's about managing stress. Since the Storm King Mountain tragedy in Colorado in July 1994, where fourteen colleagues died in a burnover, all wildland firefighters must take an annual refresher course in fireground safety. Thus I'm attuned to finding fresh material for these refreshers—interesting and important knowledge to spice the mandatory review of standard operating guidelines.

So when I discovered a book entitled *The M.A.P.: Mental Aspects of Performance for Firefighters*, I was intrigued. One of my classroom sermonettes emphasizes that we consume most of our precious training time focusing on techniques and technology, and we offer little guidance about how fallible humans should handle decision making under pressure; situational awareness in confusing, dangerous environments; and the acute stress of facing injury, loss, and death. We demonstrate the use of tools and tactics, but what about the psychology of "combat"? What about mind and emotions?

Clever gadgets are useless if human hands and minds are paralyzed by fear or bullied by doubt.

The M.A.P. said, "Our goal is to help firefighters increase their chances for success while decreasing the effects of stress." Stress can make you sick. Hell, stress can kill you. Fortunately, there are effective ways to manage it, but people must be convinced of their innate powers of mind. The key words in the book's preface were *confidence*, *control*, and *concentration*. The manual outlined several mental drills, and among the "sensory enhancement exercises" was a "suggestibility test." It was designed to show how potently mind affects body—highlighting their unity—and I adapted it for my classes.

From *The M.A.P.* I learned the bucket exercise, and I employed it with relish.

I told my students, "Let's see how powerful you are." Some fidgeting and worried glances.

"Take a deep breath and slowly exhale. . . . Okay, another one." Some smiles.

"Now close your eyes." And I'd sweep the room until they all did.

"Stretch your arms out in front, level with your shoulders." I'd catch a few more grins, occasionally an impatient frown.

"Okay. You are holding a bucket in each hand. The one in your right hand is made of birch bark. It's empty and very light; you can barely feel it. The bucket in your left hand is cast iron. It's heavy—extremely heavy—and I'm placing rocks in it, round chunks of granite, and now it's full, heaped with dense, heavy rocks."

More smiles appeared around the classroom, people struggling to hold their arms level. As I forcefully repeated the suggestions, I watched left arms twitch and dip, fighting to support the imaginary bucket.

After a minute or two I'd clap my hands and say, "All right!

We're done." I was amused to see that in every class there were many who required a second clap to return.

"That is mind over body, people; mental driving physical. You have far more control over how you react and perform than you probably think." It was a path to approach Standard Fire Order #10: *Stay alert, keep calm, think clearly, act decisively.*

A month later I had a frightening opportunity to practice what I preached. During a helicopter manager refresher session, we learned about *water ditching*, what to do if our ship crashed into a lake or river. We were offered a hands-on exercise. Most helicopters are top-heavy and will roll over and sink before the crew has a chance to exit. Surviving the ordeal—assuming the impact doesn't kill you—demands presence of mind. If you panic, you'll probably die—horribly.

The exercise is simple and, for most folks, terrifying. Students squeeze into a mock-up of a two-place helicopter cockpit, complete with seats, restraint harnesses, and an avionics plug. Once they're strapped in, the "fuselage" is dumped into a swimming pool. It sinks instantly, settling on the bottom upside down.

I long harbored a fear of water. At age eleven a lifeguard pulled me off the bottom of a lake. I was unconscious. He saved my life. Technically, I'd drowned, and for several years I so lucidly recalled the panic of slipping beneath the waves—the pattern of the cumulus clouds overhead etched into memory—that my life was shadowed by dread. Since I grew up in Minnesota, "Land of 10,000 Lakes," water was often difficult to avoid. "Chicken!" burned my ears. By refusing to divorce myself from water, and by vigorously improving my swimming skills, I caused the fear to gradually abate. But the prospect of being shoved into a pool while restrained and enclosed in a "cockpit" hotly rekindled a familiar terror. Was it more than I could handle?

We began the exercise in a classroom. Our instructor was a Coast Guard veteran with rescue experience, and I was soothed a little when his first move was a mental drill. He had each of us announce our name and say, with conviction, "I am a survivor!"

Sounds hokey, doesn't it? Too pat, too easy; almost Polly-annaish. But I knew better. I sensed some skepticism in the room and credited it to ignorance. Under stress, attitude is paramount, and attitudes aren't accidental; they're generated by the individual. We program our responses. Fear is a natural reaction, but we can easily nurture it into a demon.

Student by student, the simple mantra rippled around the room. "I am a survivor! . . . I am a survivor! . . . I am a survivor . . . !" (You have a heavy bucket in your left hand.) Until Harvey, a U.S. Forest Service firefighter, startled us with, "Well, I don't know . . . this scares me. I don't know if I can do it."

I was stunned by his candor. Would it work for him or against him?

"We'll help you get through it," replied the instructor.

We resumed the roll call, and the final trainee, a woman from Missouri, mumbled. Her "I am a survivor" was barely audible, her eyes downcast. It sounded like an embarrassed confession, as if she'd just been confronted with some petty misdemeanor. Would it make a difference in her performance?

An hour later we were poolside. The "cockpit" was poised on the edge. It was a tight framework of PVC pipe that the instructor unfelicitously dubbed "the cage." We all entered the pool and proved we could hold our breath underwater for at least fifteen seconds. Then the instructor called for two volunteers to go first.

Since 1981 the fire service has generously provided me several educational opportunities to joust with fright—penetrating the depths of a burning house, crawling through a small pipe with a limited supply of breathing air, breaking through lake ice in a rescue suit—and if nothing else, I've learned this: go first. Always go first. Especially if you're frightened. Because (1) the longer you wait, the shakier your knees become, and (2) if you watch someone else screw up or freak out, you'll gain nothing but magnified dread. Trust me. Go first.

I snapped my hand into the air and was instantly joined by Pat, a U.S. Forest Service seaplane pilot. We donned flight helmets, scrunched into the narrow seats, and fastened our harnesses at the waist. Once secured, we plugged our helmet jacks into the "console."

I was acutely afraid, but as soon as we'd left the classroom, I'd begun my concentration drill. Over and over I'd recited the seven steps we'd been taught:

First, remove any loose items such as eyeglasses. Second, unplug your flight helmet to avoid snagging the cord and being hung up. Third, unlatch the helicopter door. Fourth, establish a reference point by fixing a death grip on something inside the ship—the door handle is a good one—and don't let go no matter what. Fifth, as the aircraft sinks, count slowly to five; this allows all movement to cease (spinning rotor blades, for example), reducing the risk of exiting into greater danger, and allowing the storm of bubbles to clear. It also has a calming effect—if you're counting, you're in control. (I'd been taught the same technique many years before when making a parachute jump.) Sixth, use your free hand—not your reference point grip—to undo the harness. Seventh, transfer your reference point, moving deliberately hand over hand, to exit the cabin.

Once out, follow bubbles to the surface. We were told that during the rolling and sinking of a helicopter, disorientation is a given, and some survivors of crashes had tried to swim downward and died after safely escaping the ship. The instructor told us that after the class we'd never look at an aircraft the same way again—even an airliner.

"Ready?" he asked.

Pat and I said yes in unison.

The instructor looked me in the eye. "Okay, give me the seven steps!"

I chanted them, miming the actions. Pat did the same.

"Good. Establish your reference point, and prepare to count."

I grasped the door frame with my right hand, placed my left hand over the harness buckle, and drew in a deep breath. We'd already unplugged our helmets, ready for the "crash."

The instructor flashed a thumbs-up to three of our colleagues standing behind the cage, and they tipped us into the pool.

The water slapped our faces and I closed my eyes. There was a rolling sensation, then I felt the cage bump the bottom. The harness clutched my shoulders. I started counting, "One thousand one, one thousand two . . . ," and opened my eyes. A froth of bubbles was rushing toward my knees and feet. I immediately understood that unless I'd grabbed a reference point, I'd be shockingly confused. I could imagine the panic. There was a jolt of anxiety with that realization, but the counting short-circuited the fear. ". . . One-thousand-three, one-thousand-four . . ."

By the time I reached five, I was relatively calm. I unbuckled the belt with my left hand, fumbling a little. I was dimly aware of Pat squirming beside me. I grabbed the lower edge of the door frame and wiggled out of the cage. Pat and I broke the surface at the same moment.

The class applauded, probably out of nervous relief that we first two weren't dead or vomiting. As we clambered back onto the deck, the pool crew hoisted the cage out of the water, and we reentered, strapped in, plugged in, and did it over—plunging in backward. By the third "crash," in sideways, it was almost fun.

It was a literal baptism, a burial and resurrection, and I was joyful at having mastered this latest terror. I remembered the time a fundamentalist Christian minister had ducked me into a cattle trough in his basement, held my head under for a moment, then intoned, "You have risen to new life in Jesus Christ!" Born again. And I felt new—then, and certainly after the cage. I understood that this relatively benign submersion into a heated pool did not guarantee my survival in a real water-ditching, any more than the cattle trough dip had assured a Christlike demeanor. But it reinforced the efficacy of mind work, of symbolic practice, of emotional confidence. Jung wrote, "We should not pretend to understand the world only by the intellect; we apprehend it just as much by feeling."

Relaxed, I could study the rest of the trainees. Just before Harvey's turn I assured him that as long as he held a reference point and remembered to count, it was a piece of cake. Others encouraged him as well. He still seemed doubtful, and a few minutes later as the cage tilted over, his eyes were wide, his face pinched and pale.

He did fine. Had the brazen honesty helped? Or rather had the extra assurances and support he'd garnered through the open admission of fear carried him through? I believe the latter. Simply admitting fear doesn't banish its effects. You need a tool to mold and manipulate it. For him it was the support of the "community."

The woman from Missouri waited until the end. Her face was also ashen. No one had experienced major difficulty—a tribute, I think, to our instructor—but she was so palpably afraid it was distressing to watch. My pulse rate climbed. Anxiety is contagious. It's why I preach to rookies that firefighters must cultivate as much cool as they can—not only for themselves but also for the sake of their comrades.

As the cage was tipping toward the water, she ripped open the harness and literally dove out the doorway before the cage was even fully submerged. In a real crash such action could well be fatal. She refused a second try. At least on that day, she was not a survivor. She did not have a reference point. Perhaps, I thought, she hadn't been scared enough. I knew what it felt like to drown. My own dread of the exercise had swelled two weeks before, and that's when my preparation began.

From colleagues who'd been through it a few years before, I learned the basics of the water-ditching drill and twice a day mentally practiced it. Withdrawing to a quiet place, I drew a few centering breaths, then imagined myself calmly and successfully exiting a submerged aircraft. Over and over I was a survivor, establishing a pattern of victory in my head—victory over terror and panic. It was a kind of prayer. Later, in the classroom, when it was my turn to state, "I am a survivor!," I knew that at least then and there, it was true.

The manual we were issued summed it up: "Your mind is your best survival tool. . . . Positive control over your mental and emotional state are key factors to survival." And also to leadership.

It's not all in your head, but most of it is.

That's why it was critical to keep our crew exercising, mentally as well as physically. I was thinking about that at dawn on July 1 as I drove to Grand Marais after two days off at home. I was apprehensive because a new pilot was on duty. Derek had twelve days off and was back in British Columbia. He'd assured me that his replacement, Mike McKenzie, was an excellent flyer and a good guy. I hoped so, because Derek and Mike would tag-team for the rest of the summer—twelve days on and twelve off.

I was at the helibase when Mike arrived on shift, and we shook hands and made small talk, metaphorically circling and sniffing like wary rottweilers. I figured the best way for us to get acquainted, and to furnish Mike some familiarity with the turf and our operation, was to conduct a "wet run" initial attack drill. We'd load up as if dispatched, fly ten or fifteen miles, and find a helispot near a lake. Then, timing the evolution, we'd land, hook up the bucket, and Mike could do proficiency water drops while the crew deployed as if on a fire. It was not only useful but also a congenial way to pass the morning.

When AHR was warmed up, we waited briefly for a small private plane to clear the airport on takeoff, then lifted at about 10:30 A.M., bound northeast for Greenwood Lake. We were airborne no more than two or three minutes when we heard a radio transmission that changed everything. A male voice said, "There's a fire north of Tofte, and the smoke is building."

Mike shot me a glance. "Did you hear that?"

"Yes, I did."

Understand that Mike and I were monitoring four radios in the front seat—two FM and two AM. The latter were primarily for air-to-air communication with other aircraft or airport control towers. The two FMs were mostly an air-to-ground link with the Department of Natural Resources or the U.S. Forest Service, whether on a fire or doing project work, and for contact with our dispatchers. As a rule, the FM radios were "mine," and the AM or "victor" radios were used chiefly by the pilots. Each of us had a console beside us that allowed quick switching among the four units, and either or both of us could transmit on any of the radios at any time if need be.

I assumed that the smoke report had issued from FM-2, the radio currently dialed into Superior National Forest Dispatch, since all the ground north of Tofte—a small town on the Lake Superior shore—was under Forest Service fire protection. Unless you happened to be looking directly at the radios when a transmission came through, there was no way to tell which had "spoken" except from the context of the message.

I punched a button that switched my helmet microphone to Superior Dispatch.

"Dispatch, this is helicopter Alpha-Hotel-Romeo. We have a report of a fire north of Tofte. Do you wish us to respond?"

There was a longer silence than I expected, then, "Affirmative."

I suggested Mike turn 180 degrees and head southwest. I pointed out the general location of the fire on my map, then had an idea. In our GPS unit's memory we'd stored the coordinates for the Britton Peak gravel pit, a site the Forest Service maintained as a regular helispot. I had no exact fix on where the fire might be in relation to the site, but the GPS coordinates gave Mike a specific course to follow, and it was north of Tofte. He plugged it in. Ray was staffing our support truck that day, so I hailed him on the DNR frequency in FM-1, requesting that he and the fuel truck—the "road toads," as we dubbed them—head for Britton Peak.

We heard Superior Dispatch page a Forest Service engine crew and inquire about the fire. During the brief exchange it became clear that our call to dispatch was the first word the Forest Service had about the incident. Strange. So who had we heard on the radio? The engine crew called us and asked where the fire was.

"I was hoping," I replied, "that you could tell me."

"Negative. We're waiting on you."

I cocked an eyebrow at Mike and we shrugged. Wires were crossed somewhere.

A few minutes later Mike said, "There it is." He had an eagle eye for smoke.

A small white column was puffing out of the trees about two miles north of Oberg Mountain. It was almost dead ahead. My guess about using Britton Peak coordinates had been a smashing stroke of luck. Mike, flying this territory for the first time in his life, thought I was a genius. Taking advantage of good fortune, I said, "I figured it might be in this area." Yeah, right.

In a minute we were circling the fire. It appeared to be a single-tree lightning strike in a broad tract of unbroken forest, primarily hardwoods. It was not in the Blowdown, the wind was light, and there'd been recent rains, so it was unlikely to be a big deal. Mike tapped the buttons of the GPS and a *lat-long* (latitude and longitude) popped up on the screen. I radioed dispatch with the coordinates and gave them a size-up. I asked again if they wished us to respond. Yes.

"Okay, we'll look for a helispot."

But all we saw in the immediate area was a solid canopy of maple and birch. According to the map the nearest road was a mile or more away. Mike swung southeast toward Oberg Mountain, and we spied a modest opening—an old cutover—just above a brown, sluggish creek called, grandiosely, Onion River.

"That should work," Mike said, and we dropped past a picket line of tall firs and settled among clusters of stumps and deadfalls. The crew was pumped, and we quickly hooked up the bucket. As Mike took off for Oberg Lake to pick his first load of water, I turned to the crew and grinned. "So, how do you guys like this little drill I arranged?" After two weeks of wet weather and helibase duties, this first fire of our summer season was a potent elixir.

I tried to radio Superior Dispatch on my King handheld but couldn't trip a repeater from that spot. I asked Mike to relay the message that we were on the ground and to hover high over the fire. The smoke was invisible from the helispot, and we'd have to key off the ship for a bearing. I pulled out my compass and sighted in on AHR to establish an azimuth.

"Okay, Mike, got it. Just drop on the fire until we arrive."

Before I'd exited the helicopter, I learned from the GPS that we had a 0.76-mile hike to the fire. Not far as the raven flies, but between us and the blaze lay a boreal jungle.

We hefted our packs and tools, and I held my compass at arm's length until I centered the needle at 290 degrees. I looked up and selected a large balsam fir snag as our first landmark. It was only fifty yards away, but there wouldn't be a longer vista than that in this thicket. We slipped into the woods and pushed our way through alders to the Onion River. It was unimposing from the air but too wide to jump, and we wasted no time and energy hunting up a ford or a natural log bridge. We waded into cold, thigh-deep water and an oozing mud affectionately known as "loon shit."

On the other bank was a jumble of downed and jackstrawed firs forming a kind of breastwork, and we hacked at branches with pulaskis or broke them with our boots. At one point it was easier to drop to all fours and shove through at rabbit level. Beyond that rampart the going was merely rugged—a winding course through an aging hardwood boscage on a footing of slippery, moss-shrouded rocks. Shafts of sunlight penetrated the canopy as if from the high clerestory of a Gothic cathedral, and on a more leisurely morning it would've been an ideal setting for a slow, meditative stroll or a peaceful rest against the trunk of an old maple. Instead, I focused on the loud circuit of AHR from Oberg Lake to the fire, matching the noise of the helicopter to my compass shots. Nothing we did in the forest would be easier than getting lost.

By then the radio traffic was buzzing. A Forest Service two-person crew was packing in from the nearest road, and a Beaver single-engine seaplane was inbound from Ely. I relayed messages through Mike, amused that he didn't yet know my last name, referring to me on the air as "Lester." I enunciated "Leschak" more carefully, but such unfamiliarity is common on the fireground. We are often thrust into the intimate company of strangers amid hazard and trial, and we rely on a hopeful faith that they know what the hell they're doing. Few other occupations require taking such chances, and veteran wildland firefighters understand they must trust themselves first, must possess confidence in their own knowledge and abilities, before they can offer a measured, sometimes forced, trust in others.

When I was a ministerial candidate in the closed, authoritative regime of Ambassador College, I was taught to obey the elders of the church without question. I did so for years, to my spiritual and intellectual detriment, until I gradually realized that what kept me pressed under the thumbs of the faculty and the clerics was not so much a devotion to the organization and its dogma as a basic distrust of my own experience and perception as a free human being. The church capitalized on that insecurity by reminding me of my sins and shortcomings and by aggrandizing the power of the hierarchy. That's probably an effective method for nurturing an intolerant fundamentalist sect, but it's no way to run a fire crew. "Lester" had faith in just-met McKenzie because I knew enough about helicopters and helitack to recognize that at least in the scope of that day's battle, Mike was unlikely to do anything stupid. Perhaps not a rousing vote of confidence, but on the hard ground above the Onion it would suffice. We were committed.

I'd estimated a twenty-five-minute slog through the woods, but exercising caution to stay on course and zigzagging around deadfalls stretched it closer to forty. Finally Roy called out, "I smell smoke!" and in moment we all did. Another minute, and we saw a gray pall, like mist in the trees.

It was indeed a single-tree fire. An ancient, lightning-struck white pine was burning fiercely deep inside, in a cavity from the base to about eye level. Mike's drops had soaked the forest floor, and no fire had spread, but the hot, kilnlike interior was untouchable from the air. I radioed Mike and requested he hold off until we could open the flames to the sky.

That presented a political problem. The tree must fall, but it was at least thirty-six inches in diameter. My *red card* (national firefighters' credential) specified I was a Faller Class B and, by federal definition, qualified to drop any tree up to twenty-four inches in diameter. According to the rules, we needed a Faller Class C (unrestricted) on scene, or we couldn't touch the burning pine. It was a standard the Forest Service enforced, and correctly so; felling large trees is one of the most dangerous pastimes on the planet. Technically, it was irrelevant that I'd successfully cut even larger trees—up to forty-eight inches—and wasn't cowed by this one.

On the other hand, since I was a state employee working in Minnesota, I didn't have to hew to the rule, and since the felling to be done was within my range of skill, it made no sense to increase the cost of the fire by keeping an expensive helicopter and crew waiting for a Faller Class C to hike in. It also seemed prudent to finish the job so our ship and crew could be ready for another initial attack, not tied up guarding a simmering tree.

So after a careful study of the lean and the crown spread, plus a consultation with Doug, our experienced logger, I felled the pine without incident. I passed off the saw to John, a Forest Service employee who happened to be with us that day on a training assignment, and he began bucking the first twenty feet of the trunk into three-foot lengths. The Beaver seaplane from Ely had arrived a few minutes before, and the pilot wondered over the radio what he was doing at a fire where a medium helicopter was dropping and people were on the ground. The Forest Service crew requested his assistance to guide them in. I called Mike to say we were ready to resume the water drops. The stump, gouged out by rot and fire, was burning like a huge brazier. But from the air it was a difficult target—a small bulls-eye in a small opening in the forest canopy. On the first pass Mike was able to key off the smoke to find the opening, but his drop was a partial miss.

"Lester, this is Alpha-Hotel-Romeo. You'll have to talk me in."

"Ten-four, Mike."

As he fetched his next load, we rolled the bucked lengths of trunk next to the stump, and John ripped them in two, exposing the charred, piping hot interiors. When Mike returned, he approached slowly into the wind, fifty feet above the treetops. I stood near the stump and focused on the dangling bucket.

"Keep coming, Mike . . . left about ten feet . . . keep coming . . . now!"

I had just enough time to skip into the trees as 320 gallons of water cascaded down. I had him make four more sorties, and the area was cold and soppy. Mike flew to Britton Peak to tie in with Ray and Larry and our support trucks and to fuel up. He'd wait on the ground until we hiked back to the original helispot in the cutover above the Onion. We felt the remains of the tree for heat, and chopped out the final embers with our pulaskis. As a precaution, we scratched a shallow line around the stump.

By then it was past noon, and, settling into luxurious ferns and moss, we lunched on MREs—meals, ready-to-eat—the unfairly maligned military combat rations. I savored the chicken à la king.

For the past hour I'd been in radio contact with the Forest Service firefighters hiking in. The first transmissions had been weak and broken, but the most recent was loud and crisp. They were close. I yelled, and we heard an answering shout. The leader was a smokejumper from Missoula, Montana, detailed to Grand Marais to help with the Blowdown fire preparations. He was packing a chain saw, and I discovered he was rated as a Faller Class C. I noticed his long look at the big stump and volunteered that yes, though I was only a Faller Class B, I dropped the tree anyway. He said nothing. We discussed the original smoke report, but its source was still a mystery. What little remained of the incident was now officially his, so after our combat lunch I dialed the back azimuth of

110 degrees (290 minus 180) into my compass and we set off for the Onion River. It had been a "dream fire"—a swift, stimulating event that we handled ourselves from start to finish, just difficult enough to be interesting but not so trying that we weren't ready for the next one.

As we drew close, I called Ray at Britton Peak and directed him to launch AHR. Mike landed at the helispot, and we loaded our gear and flew to Grand Marais. I phoned the DNR dispatcher, and she related the story of the mystery smoke report. The fire was called into the airport manager by a private pilot. We'd therefore heard the transmission on "victor," one of the AM radios, and not over the Superior National Forest frequency. It was the pilot of the small plane that took off just before we did. The airport manager had phoned the DNR, and the Forest Service wasn't in the loop until I called them.

It was definitely an atypical circumstance, and red with irony. Especially over the past year, the U.S. Forest Service had taken pains to define and enhance all aspects of its fire response, including fire detection and dispatch protocols. Solid plans were in place. Then, on one of the first incidents of the summer, it all reverted to riddle and confusion.

Nevertheless, the fire was out, and it was a valuable drill for us, plus a superlative shakedown cruise for Mike. Most important, it had engendered a basis for mutual trust between our new pilot and the helitack crew—a priceless commodity that doesn't always birth easily. A year before, in southwest Montana, we'd experienced a harder road to trust.

We'd helitacked a fire below Shaw Mountain, near Wisdom, Montana, and were just wrapping it up when we were dispatched to a new fire about seventy-five air miles away. Our support truck and fuel truck would be forced to take a much longer, more circuitous route to the scene. As the helicopter, a French-made, single-engine A-Star, was being topped with fuel, Doug and I studied a map. There were two ways to travel by road, and route "A" looked shorter. But Doug, who'd had occasion to drive both over the past few days, was sure that route "B," though longer, was faster, since it featured significantly more blacktop and straight stretches, and fewer mountain switchbacks. Our priority was time rather than distance, so I said, "Do what you think is best." I instructed him to meet us near Dell, at a small private airstrip. He drove off, followed by the ship's fuel truck.

Our pilot was Harold, a savvy veteran of both Vietnam combat and the fireground. We'd worked together in seasons past, and I considered him a magnificent flyer, one of the best in the nation. But he had a temper and was famous for hotly expressing it when he thought wise practice was being violated. As he fired up the A-Star, I strapped into the left front seat, and Dallas and Ray climbed into the back.

After we pulled up and cleared the first ridge, Harold asked me which way the trucks were going. I told him Doug intended to take route "B."

"What! That's too long!" He was instantly hot, concerned that since it was already late in the day, his fuel truck wouldn't arrive in time to do us any good. We'd burn about half our Jet-A en route, and we'd need to refuel near the fire to be of prolonged use and perhaps not even have enough fuel to return to base before dark.

I assured him that Doug had driven the roads, he knew what he was doing, and I had complete confidence in his judgment. Irascible Harold wasn't convinced. In a pique of anger, he keyed the FM radio and barked at Doug.

"Which way are you going!"

Doug replied route "B" because it was faster.

"No it's not!" Harold snapped. "See you after dark!"

I was pissed. He'd questioned my judgment and Doug's, lost his temper in flight, and jumped on "my" radio to chastise one of my crew. I was tempted to point out that he'd never driven either road, so what the hell did he know, but I bit my tongue. En route to a fire was not the venue to hash out an issue of trust. But I fervently hoped that Doug and the fuel truck arrived in time.

We landed near the fire, and after the bucket was hooked up Harold flew to a small mountain lake for water. I turned to Ray and Dallas and said, "If there's any justice in the world, those damn trucks will be at Dell when we get there."

After cooling the fire with several bucket drops, Harold landed to retrieve us. The incident commander wanted us to fly to Dell and begin shuttling people and supplies to a helispot near the fire. We dropped off Ray at the spot and continued east toward Dell, about fifteen miles away. If our trucks weren't there, we'd be dead in the water, with not enough fuel to sustain the operation. And worse, Harold could tell us he told us so.

"Those guys better be there," he said, and by the tone of his voice I heard he was still skeptical.

As we crested the final ridge before Dell and Interstate 15, I anxiously scanned the airfield and the highway. At first, nothing. Then I spotted our trucks just turning off a service road for the airstrip.

"There they are!" I exclaimed, and pointed.

Harold grunted. I swiveled in my seat and glanced over my left shoulder to exchange a wide, shit-eating grin with Dallas.

Harold flared in to land, and our skids touched the tarmac at the precise moment that Doug's wheels rolled to a stop. Swear to god. I couldn't resist comment. In as innocent of a gee-whiz tone I could muster, I said, "Man! What timing." Harold said nothing.

A few days later we were dispatched on another initial attack, and again we huddled around the map to determine a route for the road toads. Sensitive to Harold's concerns, I tried to brief him on our decision before we took off.

"Yeah, yeah," he interrupted, "that's fine, let's go." There was no interrogation of the road toads. They were *skookum*, and that made his life easier. He'd decided to accept it and trust.

After Onion River, I felt Mike was there already. He should always be alert, of course, but it was plain this was no gaggle of greenhorns.

With scattered showers predicted for the Grand Marais area, we assumed that our fire work was finished for a while, and we returned to the helibase remodeling project we'd undertaken. But in late afternoon, Betsy, a DNR dispatcher, called with an initial attack mission. A three-unit condominium on the Lake Superior shore near Lutsen was fully involved with flame, and a trio of local fire departments was losing ground. One of the fire chiefs, who was also a Forest Service firefighter, requested AHR. He feared they were on the verge of losing two additional condos. While not unheard of, it's unusual for a helicopter to be dispatched to a structure fire. I sensed desperation.

We scrambled to the ship, and I was struck by the contrast between this assignment and the last—from a remote, pack-in forest fire involving lightning and loon shit to a blazing, high-rent condominium on Highway 61. "Expect the unexpected" is a shopworn fireground platitude.

We spooled up and headed southwest over Deviltrack Lake, on a course nearly identical to the Onion River heading. The western horizon was painted an ominous blue-black—an approaching storm front. The vanguards of the storm were immediately in front of us. Several scattered thunder cells, each perhaps a mile across, were drifting toward Lake Superior. They were compact globes of seething cloud and downdrafts, flared at the base by sheets of rain. It was soon apparent that one of the cells was directly between us and Lutsen. Mike banked west, diverting inland to circle behind it.

Meanwhile, I was on the radio, trying to raise the Cook County Sheriff's Department. That office was our contact for the mission, and as Mike curved around the rear of the cell, I tried a half-dozen transmissions. We needed to talk to someone on the ground. It would be dangerous for us to show up and initiate an air show without ground coordination, especially with fire department personnel unaccustomed to helicopters. There's nothing more maddening than dead silence on the radio when it's vitally important that you talk to someone. You catch yourself speaking louder and pushing harder on the microphone key, as if to project a more potent signal. There's no way to know why you're not receiving a response. Hardware problems? Signal weakness? No one listening? Wrong channel? We discovered later that because of a programming or transcription error, we had an incorrect frequency in our radio, and I was broadcasting impotently into the ether.

Frustrated, I switched to Fire Mutual Aid, a statewide tactical frequency dedicated to interdepartmental use by fire departments.

"This is helicopter Alpha-Hotel-Romeo to the incident commander at the Lutsen fire, on mutual aid. Do you copy?"

On the second try the fire chief who requested us answered, and I sighed with relief. But I heard a nervous edge to his voice when he requested our ETA (estimated time of arrival).

We rounded the cell over Caribou Lake, and even before we cleared the final ridge above the North Shore of Lake Superior, we spotted a tall column of coal-black smoke. In a moment we saw flames and understood why the chief sounded anxious. The large, two-story townhouse was a writhing clot of fire, and the neighboring, identical structure was only several feet away. Despite access to the largest freshwater lake in the world, the fire departments obviously couldn't pump sufficient water fast enough to establish control. They were concentrating their efforts on protecting the intact condo by drenching its exposed wall and roof. The first building was a loser. As we circled in low, scouting for a landing zone, I could see that savage radiant heat had already scorched the unburned structure. There was a light onshore breeze from Superior, but if—or rather, when—the wind shifted as a result of the approaching storm, and it was from any direction but southeast, the next townhouse, and perhaps even a third, would certainly burn. It was the equivalent of an urban fire that starts in one apartment and takes out an entire block. The primary danger was to the firefighters: under pressure to save high-value real estate, and clearly losing the battle, they'd probably push themselves, taking abnormal risks to prevent that row of townhouses from collapsing like flaming dominoes. In order to help we'd have to land.

We saw an open area less than a hundred yards from the fire, but given the firefighters and rigs, condo tenants and staff, and gawkers, it was too busy. A nearby power line, though avoidable, was one more reason to reject the site.

"I don't like it," said Mike.

The fire chief understood. He suggested we fly back up the ridge to the parking lot at the Oberg Mountain trailhead and set up there. In a minute Mike was landing—and wincing, as our rotor-wash blasted a couple of parked cars with sand. I shrugged.

"Can't help it, Mike. This is an emergency." I was just glad the lot wasn't full.

We piled out and hooked up the bucket, mildly amused that we were just over a mile from where we'd worked the Onion River fire only hours before. Mike flew off to the condos, and the fire chief sent a truck to deliver us to the scene.

Since the structure was only yards from the Lake, Mike was able to drop thirty-eight buckets (about 12,000 gallons) on the fire in twelve to fifteen minutes. When I arrived, it was apparent the key service he provided was to collapse the burning condo with the force of the drops, instantly reducing the flame lengths and thus the hazard to the adjacent building. The quick and massive airborne dousing allowed the fire departments to gain control of the blaze with their hoselines.

I inspected the scene with the fire chief, and we agreed that Mike had undoubtedly saved the next condo. Heat impingement had not only scorched the siding but also cracked windows. Thus preheated, it would've caught fire in a few minutes, rapidly ballooning into flames and driving firefighters from the dangerous defensive positions they'd taken inside the building. The third townhouse would've become the new front line.

"That place is worth a half-million dollars," said the chief.

I was delighted to hear it. Our summer was paid for. In May I'd scribbled some back-of-the-envelope arithmetic, estimating our operation would cost at least $450,000 and probably more. The helicopter alone was worth a minimum of $3610 per day, whether it turned a rotor or not. Of course, no one actually cut us a check for the "save," but it was a public relations bonanza. (Next day the property manager told me the value of the townhouse was $525,000, and he was effusively grateful.) On the report I filled out daily for the Minnesota Interagency Fire Center was a line for the dollar value of saved buildings. This was not only for the edification of the media and the public, but also for the legislature, the governor, and other arbiters of state treasury expenditures. Wildland fire aviation resources can be difficult to fund because they're not needed every day, may be "profitable" for only a few months out of the year, and can be breathtakingly expensive. And, yes, though the

Lutsen condominium was worth more than three months of our helicopter operation, it was merely a paper relationship without tangible relevance to the bean counters, entering the ledgers in invisible ink. You can never prove your helicopter or air tanker is worth the price tag, and we find ourselves great champions of circumstantial evidence.

For example, in early summer 1998, Florida was ravaged by an amazing tidal wave of catastrophic wildfires. Tens of thousands of people were evacuated from their homes, and costs were tallied in the hundreds of millions of dollars. Texas, which was also tinder dry, realized it could easily share Florida's troubles and decided instead to spend money up front. When I was dispatched there in July, the joke was that if there was a spot big enough to land a helicopter, then by god, there was one sitting on it. The goal was to preposition an effective initial attack force to keep the inevitable fires small and relatively inexpensive. From May 1 through August 23, Texas had 8,445 wildfires that blackened 365,675 acres, but the state lost only two homes. They'd spent $36,260,000 to achieve that remarkable record. Was it worth it? Did Texas avoid a Florida scenario and save hundreds of millions? Affirmative—there's no doubt in my mind. But I can't prove it. Nobody can. Thus the eternal battle over wildland fire funding drags on yearly in every nook of the nation.

The fire chief released AHR from the incident, and we all returned to the Oberg parking lot. Larry had just finished refueling the ship when our fire department chauffeur dropped us off. I'd been watching the clouds on the drive up the ridge, and the storm front was closing in. The sky was the color of wet cement, and the rattle of a rising wind was accented by an occasional distant rumble. As I approached the helicopter, Mike wordlessly pointed upward, and I said, "Yeah, it's definitely time to boogie." We were about twenty-four miles from the helibase, less than a fifteen-minute flight.

We lifted off and turned northeast for Grand Marais, into the wind. Our last glimpse of the Lutsen condo showed a white, steamy column of smoke blowing directly over the two unburned structures.

"Look at that, Mike," said Doug. "If not for you, that wind shift would've taken out the next shack, maybe both of them."

"Yeah," Mike grunted. "That was fun, eh?"

We already knew he was no blabbermouth. But I could see he was happy. His face, if not his voice, was brightened by a warrior glow, the radiant expression of a challenged winner, the satisfied demeanor that softens the visage and hardens the eyes.

Four miles from Oberg we flew over the Poplar River. On our way in an hour before, it was transparent, almost crystalline in the afternoon sunshine. Now it was full and frothing, the color of creamed coffee. Miles inland, a downpour was glutting the creeks and bogs, washing sediment down to Lake Superior. Over my left shoulder to the northwest, the sky was dark, dense, and spitting lightning. We were racing the storm. Our ship was a tiny speck in an ocean of choppy air. I wasn't afraid of the weather per se, but I was superstitiously nervous about our insolence, and by the bedrock hubris of flying itself. On calm summer days with fleecy blue skies, when even chickadees are eagles, it seems benign and almost natural for humans to fly. But when the atmosphere is rough and sunless I begin to think about aircraft parts—bearings, bushings, linkages, shafts—and how complex and relatively fragile is our tiny, featherless speck. It's irrational to consider the sky angry at our presence, but it is useful to remind myself that it's *not* natural to be racing a storm 2000 feet above the ground. Rather, it is an astonishing privilege.

We were supported not only by the laws of physics, but also by the dedicated effort of the team. Jim, the mechanic, spoke of "air worthiness" as a technical concept. I thought of it in moral terms. We were worthy to fly only if we continued to strive for perfection. My playful superstition said we'd make it back to Grand Marais because that afternoon, at least, we deserved it. But I knew that all we truly deserved was the opportunity to fly and fight fires. How it all turned out in the end might have little to do with our personal success or failure. The sky—or a control linkage—was free to punish us no matter what.

Fifteen minutes from Oberg we flew over the Cascade River, and it was still running clear. Heavy rain had not yet churned its inland headwaters, and I knew we were winning the sprint. We arrived at Grand Marais several minutes ahead of lightning and gusty winds, exultant over a two-fire day.

At sunset, after the storm had passed, I drove into Grand Marais and strolled out to Artist Point, a forested spit of ledgerock jutting out into Lake Superior. In the wake of action I was in a contemplative mode. I thought: this forest, this lake, and certainly this Precambrian bedrock will remain when I am gone. That sense of a continuity transcending my short life textures the mind. It packs substance into the images and sensations processed by the brain. The world is real. I no longer believe in a personal, manipulative god, and I don't worship trees either. But I can hear wind in the swaying needles of a white pine, can smell the sweet smoke of burning, can admire an aged, furrowed trunk—or can make it fall down. I believe in life. It exists outside me and is not a dream. I believe in action. We start "doing time" at birth, and memory is our holy ghost. To love, we need only act for good. To learn, we need only explore with an open mind. To laugh, we need only love and learn. And what infuses it all with zest is the certain prospect of death.

I cherish working fire because there's no escaping the gritty verity of action and life. Fire is brash and in your face. It demands attention. It punishes apathy and ignorance. It kills. It's real. Fire will still burn when my mind has vaporized.

But I'm also a romantic. I have an afterlife fantasy: when I die, I haunt the northern forests, not as a human spirit, but as a sentient wildfire. Rebirthed by lightning, I explode into flaming action—a fire wraith born to test the firefighters who come after. For a while, even some of those I've taught and led. I will battle and prove them. I'll be their dream fire.

From early June and into July, we were doused by frequent showers and several times relegated to "one-hour callback." It meant we were free to leave the base and do anything we wished— laundry was popular—as long as we hung near a phone or carried a radio and could be fully mobilized and in the air within sixty minutes. On one rainy day, I conducted a test. After we'd been dispersed for a couple hours, I made two phone calls and one radio broadcast, and the entire crew was at the helibase and good to go in twenty-nine minutes. As Doug teased, "That's because we don't have a life."

During the soggy periods I owned a few more free hours and continued studying the Great Peshtigo Fire and the experiences of Father Peter Pernin. I focused on the weather that helped generate the event. Wildland fire, of course, is a slave to weather, and not only to extremes such as prolonged drought but also to nuances. For example, I've been on prescribed burns whose success or failure turned on a 10 to 12 percent range of relative humidity (RH). Given the fuels, topography, air temperature, wind velocity and direction, the past week's weather, and our particular management goals, an ideal RH might be 42 percent. We begin burning. If, say, a thin overcast moves in and the RH rises to 47 to 48 percent, we're wasting *drip torch fuel* (a mixture of gasoline and diesel); the fire won't consume what we want or perhaps will even sputter out. On the other hand, say the temperature rises and the RH drops to 36 to 37 percent, we begin to scare the hell out of ourselves and cease lighting before the abruptly rambunctious fire compromises our control lines, or our safety.

The nut is that fire, like its sibling weather, can be notoriously unpredictable. Two years before, I'd helped with a prescribed burn that strikingly demonstrated that oft-repeated lesson. The morning dawned moist and overcast, and as my partner and I drove to the site—a wet expanse of primarily lowland brush—we figured the burn boss was either desperate or demented or both. During the preignition briefing we were spattered by a light, intermittent drizzle, and I saw a firefighter roll his eyes as the boss said, "Well, let's get this one done before we lose our window of opportunity." Say what? The "window" needed wipers, and I didn't see a fifty-five-gallon drum of drip torch fuel. This damp brush wasn't going to sustain fire. But the boss, by god, was sure it would. I thought, What the hell, money's the same.

So with the RH at 82 percent and beads of condensation on the drip torches, we lit the first strip, then gaped in astonishment as a vigorous backing fire exploded from grass and leatherleaf, pushed beneath a fifteen-foot balsam fir, and immediately torched it out. Moments later a twenty-foot birch snag was flaming, top to bottom. Someone yelled, "Good thing it's too wet or we'd be chasing this thing already!" No kidding. I was suddenly grateful for the drizzle. Later, as we admired a near-perfect *backing fire* (flames proceeding against the wind) munching briskly through head-high green willow, I slapped the boss on the shoulder. "You're my hero, man." Yes, according to the prescription and the plan, the RH had been far too high, but the boss knew his site and his fuels and we skeptics had been confounded. (I did note, however, that the boss did not say "I told you so"; he was nearly as surprised as we, and it became clear that one of our suspicions was correct: he was desperate. It's not easy these days to assemble a professional crew, and he wanted to go for it while he had the people to pull it off.) Unpredictability, of course, is one of the charms, and dangers, of fire.

On the afternoon of October 8, uncertainty and the weather plagued Father Peter Pernin. He vacillated between an apprehension of impending doom and a conscious denial of his foreboding. He felt in a torpor, almost paralyzed, and recorded, "The afternoon passed in complete inactivity." Except for his internal debate.

He was influenced by the heavy pall of smoke, accompanied by a strange silence suggesting the eve of a storm. The stillness seemed to transcend what might be expected on a calm autumn day bereft of the normal clamor of summer birds and insects. It was too quiet; it unnerved him.

Yet the streets of Peshtigo were alive with young people out for Sunday recreation, singing and laughing, indifferent to the menace he sensed. And, he reasoned, since the scary evening of September 24, citizens had taken even more precautions against fire. Fewer combustibles were exposed, more hogsheads of water were ready. On its face, the town appeared safer. Sentinels had been posted.

An elderly Canadian immigrant noted for his dedication to the parish showed up that afternoon and asked Father Pernin for permission to dig a well close to the partially completed church. Though it was the sabbath, the man argued he had no time during the week, and the plasterers would no doubt be grateful for the water next morning. Pernin was persuaded, and the man turned to his digging with religious zeal. A few hours later he informed the priest the well was sufficiently deep, providing an abundant supply of water.

With obvious satisfaction he said, "Father, not for a large sum of money would I give that well. Now if a fire breaks out again it will be easy to save our church."

Pernin fed him supper, then walked over to see his neighbor, Mrs. Dress, an elderly widow whose children were still at home. As the priest and the widow strolled across her fields, they noticed a breath of wind had begun to stir the dead air. An intermittent breeze appeared, "as if to try its strength and then as quickly subsiding." At one point, a stronger gust arose, and an old tree trunk at the edge of the field burst into flame. They stamped out the fire, but to Pernin's eye there'd been no "tokens of cinder or spark, just as if the wind had been a breath of fire. . . ." No doubt the dead tree was sheltering latent heat from the last blaze, smoldering deep in its punky core. Continued dry weather kept the heat slowly feeding away, waiting for wind to supply more oxygen.

Mrs. Dress urged her children to pull water and make other preparations, but they laughed her off. Pernin returned home, more troubled than ever, but "the wind fell again, and nature resumed her moody and mysterious silence." He was restless but also enervated. There was work to be done, but he couldn't concentrate.

Then, at about 8:30 P.M., he glanced out a window to the southwest. In a deepening dusk darkened by smoke, he saw an immense red glow. He stepped outside for a better view and heard it: a distant, continuous roar.

Three hours earlier, at 5:35 P.M., a massive low pressure system was centered over southwest Nebraska, with a barometer reading of 29.00 inches of mercury. Near the center of the low it was 52 degrees Fahrenheit and overcast, with a northeast wind at 19 miles per hour. On the "backside" of the low, at Salt Lake City, Utah, it was 35 degrees and clear with a northeast wind at 12 miles per hour. In contrast, it was 83 degrees at Milwaukee, Wisconsin, that afternoon, under clear skies with a 32 mile-per-hour wind from the southwest. The barometer read 29.80.

A dramatic cold front was surging into the Midwest, riding a temperature gradient that spanned fifty degrees. The low cell was a giant vortex of air, rotating counterclockwise and slouching west to east. Atmospheric air rushes from higher pressure to lower pressure, like water flowing downhill. The steeper the slope, the faster water will fall, and likewise, the "steeper" the pressure gradient—caused by temperature differences—the stronger the wind being drawn around the center of a low cell.

At 5:35 P.M. the temperature and pressure gradient was steepest on the northeast arc of the low. In northwestern Minnesota near Roseau, the temperature was in the 40s. About a hundred miles southeast in Bemidji, it was in the mid-60s. In St. Paul it was in the low 80s, as was all of Wisconsin. The passage of such a burly cold front is accompanied by high and shifting winds, and a modern fire behavior manual sums up the concern: "Firelines are most often lost, large acreage burned, and property and lives lost when strong winds fan a fire out of control."

Wind force-feeds oxygen to a fire at the same time it's helping to dry fuels. It bends flames into the grass, brush, or trees, thus preheating them before the fire. Wind increases the rate of spread by transporting heat and firebrands to fresh fuels ahead of the flaming front, and of course the direction the fire runs is most often determined by the bearing of the wind.

Firefighters are taught to beware of cold fronts because they can pass with startling rapidity. At 3:00 P.M. you may have a southwest wind at 15 to 20 miles per hour, and by 3:30 P.M. it could be blowing northwest at 20 to 25 miles per hour because of the rotation of the low cell. So imagine you're working a fire pushed by that southwest wind. It's running northeast, narrow and long, say a mile long. Once the cold front arrives and the wind shifts ninety degrees, your mile-long right flank is no longer a flank but rather a blistering headfire a mile wide. If firefighters are on that side, they're in trouble. What was once a relatively benign perimeter is now charging. The passage of a cold front was a significant factor in the tragedy at Storm King Mountain in Colorado in 1994, where fourteen firefighters died.

So a vast cyclonic storm was bearing down on the Peshtigo region, poised to hammer a hot, dry, smoldering forest with strong and shifting winds. Father Pernin and Mrs. Dress had felt the first gusts as they walked her fields in the late afternoon and saw a snag rekindle from the latent heat of a fire almost two weeks old.

Such heat and open flames were scattered across northeast Wisconsin—multiple but discrete fires responding to their immediate fuels and local weather. But the continued drought and the cyclonic storm conspired to merge disparate hot spots into a single spectacular blaze: "In heavy fuels and under favorable conditions, the coalescence, which begins with the upper convective columns, occurs rapidly. The resulting holocaust is a synergistic phenomenon of extreme burning known as mass fire" (Stephen Pyne, *Fire in America*). A stationary mass fire—like Dresden, Germany, in flames after a World War II incendiary bombing—is called a *firestorm*. It's a plume-dominated inferno sucking oxygen from all directions. A mass fire that covers ground is a *conflagration*. These terms have often been employed poetically to simply denote a large fire, but it seems that both types of mass fire played a role in the Peshtigo disaster. When Father Pernin heard the distant roar at 8:30 P.M., a conflagration was in progress, the fire front a kind of rolling explosion.

In 1889, Robert Bell of the Canadian Geological Survey described a similar fire:

An irresistible front of flame is soon developed, and it sweeps forward, devouring the forest before it like the dry grass in a running prairie fire. . . . The irregular line of fire

has a height of a hundred feet or more above the trees. . . .
Great sheets of flame appear to disconnect themselves from
the firey torrent and leap upward and explode. . . .

Fires in this category have been estimated to release energy on
a par with an atomic bomb every five to fifteen minutes.

Such a blaze can spread with frightening speed. In 1971, the
"Little Sioux" fire in the Boundary Waters Canoe Area Wilderness
ripped across seven miles of woods in about six hours, a 9000-acre
run in relatively gentle topography—without the extraordinary fuel
loads of Peshtigo or the Blowdown. In his 1999 book, *Fire on the
Mountain*, about the Storm King incident, author John Maclean
described what happened when the cold front hit the fire:

An enormous wave of flame arose from the western
drainage and began to sweep the ridgetop, driving firefighters before it. It swelled to a height of 50, 100, and then 150
feet. . . . The flame wave began to break over the ridgetop,
transforming the people into surfers riding the curl of a
scarlet-orange wave of fire.

As cold June rain pattered on my roof, I was struck by Father
Pernin's apprehension of fire as opposed to mine. I longed for
another "dream fire." He was about to descend into a nightmare.

FIVE

"MADAM, SEEK
THE RIVER"

As early as February I'd been concerned with preparation, trying to foresee what tests we might face. Some—a single-tree fire, for example—were expected, almost routine; but fashioning or even imagining specific provisions for every eventuality is impossible because they are unknown. In fire and other emergency operations, you must not merely tolerate uncertainty, you must savor it. Or you won't last long. The most efficient preparation is a general mental, physical, and professional readiness nurtured over years of training and experience. You live to live. Preparing is itself an activity, and action is preparation. You can design it only in part; the rest just happens. Nietzsche wrote, "That which does not kill you makes you stronger."

Father Pernin, as we'll see, made decisive, even amazing, preparations on the eve of the great fire, then executed a coherent plan of action under circumstances that massacred most of his neighbors. I believe he prepared for that night all his life, with nary a thought about fire, unless it was Lucifer's brimstone. His long-range strategy did not encompass the agonies of a Wisconsin forest fire that would consume his town. Probably his goal was to create a life record worthy of heaven and the beatific vision. If he was a good priest, his life was dominated by service and sacrifice, with a tempering of ego and personal desires. Such a code would've seasoned him for the ordeal of October 8 and days following. He was not a firefighter, but he was a survivor. I doubt he audibly, or even mentally, intoned, "I am a survivor," but he had a mission that in his mind equaled if not transcended his own life.

That was the way I felt at Ambassador College. I was dedicating my life to God. It was a strict authoritarian regime that venerated its leadership. From Herbert W. Armstrong, founder of the sect and self-described apostle, to the greenest local minister—all were to be accorded the utmost respect and obedience. All were anointed deputies of the risen Christ. I was told (and believed) it was a privilege from God to be associated with such sanctified men. I was flush with hope and idealism. I'd enlisted in the vanguard of the returning Savior, who would banish evil and suffering from the world. I was ready to obey and conform. It was good for me, and I was good for humanity. Toeing the line would make us happy, and when you're supposed to be happy, and unhappiness is the result of sin, then you act happy even if you're not. Can smiles be pernicious? There was always a certain fakery to it all but also a genuine comfort in fully accepting and being fully accepted. Into an army.

In hindsight, I'm tempted to view many of those aggrandized men as small and venal, but I resist. They were seduced by a potent mix of doctrine and power (as was I), and while I eventually deemed them wrong, most were sincerely wrong. They were frozen at an emotional and intellectual level that fogged their judgment and worldview. W. A. Overstreet wrote, "A person remains immature, whatever their age, as long as he thinks of himself as an exception to the human race." And how could we be more arrogantly exceptional than as the few humans handpicked by God? To believe that was to host a virus that could ultimately twine itself through your mind and choke compassion and reason.

In a third-year Bible class misnamed Theological Research, my friend Bill asked a penetrating though innocent question, tactfully (I thought) disputing the conclusion we were intended to reach as the result of a homework assignment concerning the canonization of the Bible. I saw the instructor and minister, Mr. Chapman, stiffen and bristle, like a German shepherd confronted by an intruder. He had no answer to Bill's challenge, and he lashed out, hurling accusations of arrogance and insubordination. Bill protested that he wasn't questioning the instructor's authority, but Chapman ridiculed him, demanding to know if Bill even trusted the Bible.

I was astounded and dismayed. The *Ambassador College Bulletin* stated, "Students are vigorously encouraged to use their own minds to think, to question, to check up on doctrines, concepts, and philosophies, to search for proof before accepting any." The conceit was that we were being trained in the liberal arts.

Instead of earning praise for his insight, Bill was humiliated in front of his classmates. Despite feeling violated by the instructor's verbal assault, he was wracked with guilt and that evening presented himself at Chapman's residence to apologize. He hoped the minister would reciprocate, but Chapman received the undeserved apology without grace, indicating that Bill's obeisance was merely his due.

Bill was angry. He'd paid a high price to attend "God's college." When he'd announced the intention to his parents, they'd dispatched him to a psychiatrist. Chapman's attitude disturbed him deeply, so he arranged an official appointment with the instructor and asked me to go along. Our intention was to achieve a reconciliation and to make some points about the inconsistencies in the classroom material.

On a Friday evening three weeks later, Chapman warmly welcomed us into his office. We spent two hours discussing the nature of his class and the notion of individual thought in a religious context. It seemed to go well, and Bill and I congratulated ourselves when we left. It appeared we'd made some progress, and Chapman had been receptive.

But next morning—probably according to a plan that was about three weeks old—Chapman delivered the sermon at the sabbath service. For an hour and a half the minister ranted against academic theological scholarship and those who questioned or doubted the doctrines of the Worldwide Church of God. Though he didn't mention our names, it was clearly a personal attack on Bill and me, and several students in the audience glanced my way in alarm. Chapman referred to points we'd raised in his office only several hours before, viciously demeaning what he'd pretended to receive with equanimity. He ridiculed any and all who critically examined what he heralded as the Truth, spiraling up to a shouted crescendo: "It's not your place to question what your teachers tell you!"

I was stunned. Hurt. Enraged. My impulse was to leap up in the midst of his tirade and spew one of my own. But that would've simply demonstrated that I was indeed a rebellious sinner. I bit my tongue and held my seat. Later I wrote, "I won't sink to his level. I still believe in Ambassador College. Chapman is just a bad apple."

A few months earlier, a minister named Howard Clark had transferred to the Big Sandy campus from the headquarters in Pasadena, California. We'd not seen an authority figure like him. Most of the faculty took their meals in a special dining room, but

Clark regularly mingled with the students, pushing a plastic tray along the rails shoulder to shoulder with "the flock." His booming voice, often bracketed with laughter, echoed through the cavernous hall—rendered all the more striking by the aluminum cane he used to support his limping frame. As a marine in the Korean War, he'd been horribly wounded in combat. His mangled body had been found by the graves-registration unit, and it was believed he would die. Instead he emerged from a military hospital as a quadriplegic. He was awarded a 100 percent disability and ensconced in a wheelchair. But God "called him into the Work," as we liked to say of ourselves, and subsequent to being anointed with oil by a minister of the Worldwide Church of God, he rose from his wheelchair and walked. He became a minister and teacher and something of a legend as a preacher. At one sabbath service he flailed at a side of beef with a homemade cat-o'-nine-tails, graphically portraying the sufferings of Jesus at the hands of the Romans.

There were whispers about him. He was, some said, a renegade, banished from Pasadena to the hinterland of East Texas because he made the church hierarchy uncomfortable. I later decided they feared his personal power to gather disciples around him. And how do you deal with someone who shed paralysis, who was apparently healed by God? He was magnetic, not only because of his remarkable history, but also because he challenged people to think. His mind and his tongue were razor sharp.

In the English class he taught, he once railed at the collective timidity and mediocrity of a student body afraid to stretch beyond the ambient dogma. Brandishing a sheaf of our lukewarm papers he bellowed, "There's not even a successful failure in this bunch!"

After hours he occasionally convened what he called the Waffle Shop, a free-flowing bull session over which he presided, "waffling" from one topic to the next—from current events to church doctrine—prodding us with barbs of wit and wisdom. One evening, during a discussion about translating theology into everyday living, he stated, "If Jesus Christ was a student here today, we'd kick him out." We'd strayed too far from the original precepts to stomach the original teacher. We were all taken aback, but I saw a staid upper-classman (on the inside track for the ministry) blanche. Next day, word filtered down from the dean of students' office that the Waffle Shop was closed. Such independence of thought and expression was not conducive to solidarity in the ranks. Soon after, we heard that the chancellor of the Big Sandy campus had remarked in the faculty dining room, "We must get rid of all the doubters."

It was two months later that Bill asked his question in Chapman's class. As he and I prepared for our fateful Friday meeting with the instructor, Clark called me into his office. He was concerned that Bill and I intended a belligerent, verbal assault. (As if we dared.) I assured him our plan was to proceed calmly, rationally, and respectfully.

"Be careful," he said.

The day after Chapman's livid attack sermon (a technique that was taught in homiletics class), I returned to Clark's office. I sat down across from the veteran of the Yalu River, aware that his body was still peppered with shrapnel, that he had a steel plate in his head and only one good lung. Aware also, that he'd once been paralyzed and that he was one of the smartest, most articulate men I'd ever met. He'd heard Chapman's sermon.

He grinned at me, studied my face for a moment, and said, "Well, what are you going to do? Run off screaming into the night, or laugh about it?"

We laughed.

He read me a quote from Walter Kaufman's book *The Faith of a Heretic:* "The aim of a liberal arts education is not to turn out ideal dinner guests who can talk with assurance about practically everything, but people who will not be taken in by men who speak about all things with an air of finality. The goal is not to train future authorities, but men who are not cowed by those who claim to be authorities."

I would not have understood that passage a year before. Howard Clark—warrior, teacher, cleric—taught me to say no. There is drama in that, and it would serve me well on the fireground. I understood Clark tapped a reservoir of self-confidence that allowed him not only to lead people through adversity but to laugh at the challenge. I also understood that pain was the source of his confidence. He was a Christ figure—"saving" us through his suffering. It was a path that Father Peter Pernin would literally take on the night of October 8, 1871.

In retrospect, it seems clear that I tried to mimic Howard Clark's pain. At Ambassador College I became obsessed with long-distance running. It was a genuine escape from the waxing perception of intellectual and emotional tyranny. I ran four marathon races and, while training for the twenty-six-mile ordeals, tallied fifty to seventy-five miles per week, pounding along the red clay back roads north of the campus. My buddies and I likened our eight-, ten-, and twelve-mile workouts to the pot, LSD, and cocaine that our cohorts "out in the world" were using to blaze their trails through adolescence. We chose pain, release, and the mind-goosing endorphin highs that often materialized on the backstretch.

One autumn afternoon I cut through the pine woods on a joyful whim and leaped over a coiled copperhead rattlesnake in the middle of the path. Rushing back onto the road, I yelled to my partners, "I can fly! I can fly!" Their goofy grins displayed the same conviction.

The incessant running was a revelation, no less powerful than the exposition of scripture. Back in high school, at the hands of a particularly driving and driven assistant football coach, I'd experienced a glimmering of the truth that pain is a means of transcendence—not the pain of a laceration or fractured bone but the controlled agony of pushing your mind-body to the far rim of endurance. In East Texas, we tortured ourselves in order to run farther, faster—and to forget about sin. We racked up 3000, 4000 miles (or more) each year, in hot sun and cold drizzle, in parched dust and leg-splattering mud. We ran when we felt good and ran when we were sick. Vomit in the grass was not unheard of. During one marathon I lost twelve pounds in three hours, and when I finished, my pulse rate pegged past 100 for over an hour. I lashed myself in training and in races until my thighs were spongy and my mind—floating somewhere above my heated head in self-defense—begged for a halt. I guiltily compared running a marathon to the sufferings of Christ, who turned willingly to hard trial. I mortified the flesh. And in the process of self-submission and discipline I found a strain of happiness. It was good to hurt. It became natural to steer for the hard road. In sweat and mud I discovered a sublime cleanliness. Gasping lungs and shin splints were righteous, our running coach a prophet.

Years later, on a fireline in Idaho, filthy and exhausted in three-day-old underwear and four-day-old socks, wondering if I could marshal the energy to pick up my chain saw and hike the mile back to spike camp, I conjured up the red roads of East Texas. Or rather, a certain smell electrified my memory. I never did identify it, but the fleeting odor of something—perhaps a tree or forest forb—delivered me to the twelve-mile course we used to run at seven minutes to the mile. I heaved to my feet, shouldered my pack and chain saw, and startled my weary colleagues by shouting, "I can fly!" And despite my black face and crusted shirt, I felt that energizing wash of purity. The dreaded upslope march became an unaccountably pleasant hike. I had confidence in the pain. I knew that in the fireline marathon I had to push just a little bit longer. It was possible, it was necessary, and Clark would be proud of me. You cannot lead unless you know how to hurt. And yes, the marathon running, like the marathon reading, had been an escape from perceived religious oppression. But I needed no escape from the honest, forthright fireground. It's what I'd been escaping to all along.

There's a patina of romance to fighting fires, and yes, I was drawn by that, but for the long haul you must relish the blue-collar core of sweat, blisters, and steel, and recognize the verve in hard labor. Eric Hoffer, laborer and philosopher, wrote,

> My 25 years as a longshoreman were a fruitful interval in my life. I learned to write and published several books. My becoming a writer did not impress anyone in the union. Every longshoreman believes that there is nothing he could not do if he took the trouble.

My fellow firefighters are likewise unimpressed by my books, and that's fine. I earn more regard for applying razor edges to saw chain or building efficient loads for cargo nets. And we had the opportunity in 2000 to work that solid, bread-and-butter angle of our profession.

On the morning of July 26 we flew to the Orr airport, about 115 miles west of Grand Marais. The cloud deck was low and gunmetal gray, rain streaking the windscreen, but we had just enough ceiling—about 1200 feet—to comfortably ferry to Orr.

Our mission was to sling a decommissioned fire tower off a remote ridge in Voyageurs National Park. A crew of contractors had disassembled the angle iron and cupola, and total weight was estimated at 9000 pounds. Rigging it to fly would be an interesting challenge.

To me, fire towers are one of the few man-made structures that don't blight a forest. Though certainly symbolic of overly aggressive suppression policies past and present, they also support an aura of romantic isolation. Especially when first erected, most fire towers were the only obvious human colonization in vast realms of forest, seeming to emphasize the hegemony of the trees. For many of the towers the only access was a long, no-nonsense hike. At one time the Minnesota Department of Natural Resources alone maintained 132 of them. Most are gone. The bulk of routine wildfire detection is now accomplished with aircraft, a program that began as early as 1919, when the U.S. Forest Service and the young Army Air Service teamed up to initiate fire patrols in California and Oregon. Until the biplanes were equipped with radios, observers dropped messages in cans or by small parachutes. The advantage of planes is obvious, but they aren't cheap, and the national fire tower infrastructure remained viable well into the second half of the twentieth century, with some still in use today. Not, however, the one above Shoepac Lake in Voyageurs, though I was gratified to learn it would be reerected at a museum.

We camped that night on the west shore of Pelican Lake, generously sharing our tents with a fresh mosquito hatch. Next morning dawned warm and mostly clear, and though thunderstorms were forecast for late in the day, we hoped to finish the job by then.

We flew twenty-five miles north to an established Voyageurs National Park helispot and shut down for a planning session with the U.S. Park Service firefighters who'd help us with the project. Part of our premission helitack job was to make sure all those who worked in or around the ship were given a safety briefing, even if they were veteran firefighters. We joked that we were a lot like airline flight attendants, though not as debonair, and forbidden—regrettably—to sell miniature bottles of gin. After ten years of pointing out seat belts and emergency exits to bored old-timers, I actually feel empathy for flight attendants and always fake attention while they demonstrate buckling.

We're trained to assume nothing regarding the helicopter and its environs, and we try to remember we're providing information that could save someone's life. When I was in Ontario in 1996, I received a memorable safety briefing. My squad of Americans was assigned to initial attack, and a Canadian firefighter offered us a detailed rundown on a Bell 204 Huey—all the standard items, plus the responsibilities of the "saw dude." In the thickly forested lake country of northwest Ontario, they sometimes had difficulty locating a helispot near the fire. If there was nothing reasonable, the pilot would hover low over shallow water, and the firefighter sitting left side rear—the "saw dude"—would slide open the door, drop a chain saw wrapped in plastic, then climb out onto the skid and jump in after it. Retrieving the saw, he or she waded (or swam) to shore and cut an opening for a helispot.

"Of course," said the Canadian, "we practice that, eh, and we won't expect you guys to do it."

Two hours later we were dispatched to a fire, and I happened to sit left side rear. Just before he closed the door, the Canadian plopped a waterproofed Husqvarna at my feet and cheerily proclaimed, "I guess you're the saw dude!"

Fortunately, we found a good helispot, because I figured there was at least a 50 percent chance I would jump—not out of bravery, but because it was expected and assumed. Firefighters must sometimes resolve the conflict between doing what they're told and doing what is prudent. I'd face such a challenge in the weeks ahead.

When our safety briefing for the Voyageurs job was complete, Mike flew us over the eastern end of Lake Kabetogama to a grassy meadow below the tower, and we hiked about three-quarters of a mile to the crest of rocky ridge. It was classic north woods high country—exposed slabs of Canadian shield granite carpeted by multicolored lichens, with small but old jack pines rooted in shallow soil or in rock fissures.

At first glance the old tower site looked like a junkyard, but the contractors had organized the piles. When we'd discussed the project weeks before, I suggested the dismantlers pack in a small banding machine so they could tightly bind lengths of angle iron with metal straps, as is done with heavy shipping crates. We closely inspected the loads and they seemed secure. There were nine in all, including the conical roof of the cupola. Our assignment was to design rigging arrangements that would allow the loads to fly safely and efficiently below the ship. It was critical to avoid creating any airfoils that might generate lift in flight and endanger the helicopter.

I'd recently read an account of a mishap during the Vietnam War. The main rotor blade of a Huey damaged in combat was fixed on a line beneath another ship. The plan was to fly it a few miles and dump it in the sea. Shortly after takeoff, the blade—an excellent airfoil after all—lifted into the helicopter and chopped off the tail boom. The ship augured straight into the ground and burst into flame. All aboard were killed, including three mechanics along for a joy ride. It was an extreme example, but the cupola roof definitely had lift potential.

The long bundles of angle iron were fairly straightforward, and our goal was to prevent pronounced oscillation in flight that would increase drag and make them difficult to fly. We'd hauled in a couple dozen heavy-duty strap chokers. We wrapped one on each end of the first bundle, looping them into themselves—one winding clockwise and the other counterclockwise, so when tension was applied the vectors canceled out and the load wouldn't roll. The free loops of the chokers were locked into a clevis and the clevis inserted into a swivel hook. The swivel allowed the load to spin if it needed to, so the longline wasn't dangerously twisted up in flight.

With the bundles rigged, we called for AHR. Mike hovered overhead and slowly descended until the remote hook was on the ground next to the first load. While I monitored the radio, Doug strode in and slapped the swivel into the hook. I called the elevations to Mike as he lifted. The angle iron was spinning slowly but otherwise appeared stable and secure.

As Mike made return trips for the rest of the bundles, we discussed the cupola roof. With items that "want to fly," the basic tactic is to break up the airfoil. For instance, if you're hauling sheets of plywood, you rig them from the four corners to a single point so they'll fly flat, then affix a blocky object on top—a case of nails, for example—to disrupt the airflow that induces lift. The cupola roof was round, smooth, concave, about six feet in diameter—essentially a jumbo Frisbee, virtually guaranteed to soar. It had a small circular hatch, and we removed the cover. That would allow some air to rush through the side and roughen the flow. Christina, our first female helicopter manager prospect, and the Park Service firefighters dragged up some heavy pine limbs, and we used baling wire to lash them atop the roof, further upsetting the aerodynamics and adding some stabilizing weight. We then placed it in a cargo net and cinched it closed.

I warned Mike he was picking up a load that might have a mind of its own, and after it cleared the trees and AHR established forward airspeed, the roof did lift fifteen or twenty feet.

"What do you think, Mike?"

"It'll be fine if I go slow."

And the last of the Shoepac Lake fire tower exited the park.

It was grunt work—the labor of stevedores—but hazardous, and played out on the threshold of the fireground. Muscling an old fire tower out of the woods doesn't sparkle like the outward romance of battling fire, but I learned how to savor the more prosaic aspects of the fireground while working on a logging crew. At the time I was merely grateful to survive logging, but now I understand it was an academy.

In the summer of 1973, between my junior and senior years at Ambassador College, I took a logging job in the Oregon Cascades. It seemed an adventurous thing to do. I was possessed by a youthful restlessness, a hot yearning that blew away caution and calculation. I called it the Foreign Legion Syndrome. It was a seminal summer, like the reading binge of 1963 that fed the yearning. I had a good job on campus that paid $1.60 an hour, but R. J. Hehn of Glide, Oregon, was paying $4.50 per hour for brush stackers, and in '73 that was big money. Mr. Hehn was a respected member of the Worldwide Church of God (that's how I discovered the job), but out in the woods he was the "Hook," as the logging bosses were called, and while mercy is a Christian virtue, there was little offered on the steep mountainsides of the Umpqua River country. There was no labor union, and the only required safety practices were those mandated by a compromise between common sense and high production. For the first time in my life I worked a job where it was simply assumed that a certain number of us would be killed. Years later I read an article about lumbering in the Pacific Northwest that termed our attitude "proud fatalism." The carnage reached a level that's unacceptable in most First World professions. Two percent of the fallers died each year.

On the afternoon of my seventh day stacking Douglas-fir limbs, I looked up to see the Hook striding though the woods. There were four or five of us on the brush crew, but I was the first one he saw. He pointed at me and crooked a finger.

"C'mon," he said, "you're my new chaser." It seems his regular chaser had just quit and walked off.

"But," I protested, "I don't know how to do it."

"I'll show you."

A "high-side chaser" runs from one duty to the next—from cutting limbs to log branding, from greasing machines to hooking up truck trailers. But my premier mission was on the landing, releasing chokers (steel cable slings) from around the logs after they were skidded up the slope by the yarder.

The yarder was a tracked crane with a towering boom. From a pulley at the apex of the boom, we strung up to three-quarters of a mile of large-diameter wire-wound steel cable down the mountain through the trees. Another large pulley was bolted high up on the most massive fir we could find, then the cable was pulled through it and back up to the yarder. A hoist carriage the size of a Volkswagen Beetle was driven along this steel "clothesline." Four chokers dangled from this hoist to the forest floor and were looped by hand around the bucked logs. These "sticks" were thirty-five feet long and two to six feet in diameter—big-league timber, old-growth.

The yarder and hoist "walked" these logs up the hill and dropped them on the landing. My job was to unhook the chokers, then smack the ends of the logs with a branding ax, leaving a deep impression, the Hook's mark to be tallied at the mill. You could train a chimp to do it, but there were variables that added a treacherous playfulness to the operation. The unstable pile sometimes grew to fifteen or twenty feet high, like a stack of three-ton rollers. But the scariest aspect was the brutal dance of our machines. While the yarder reeled in the logs, they were simultaneously loaded onto trucks. The loader—also on tracks—swung a huge set of toothed jaws, like the pincers of a monstrous crab. The Hook manipulated the loader with methodical swiftness, swiveling the machine from the log deck to a waiting tractor-trailer truck. It was a violent scene as logs were slung through the air, jaws gnashing into bark, cables whining under the strain (and sometimes snapping, whipping like charged power lines)—all of it conducted in the relentless roar of smoking diesel engines. And I was stationed smack in the middle.

My training lasted only a few minutes, but it was obvious that timing was the key. Estimating how long it would require to release the chokers compared to how soon the jaws would return for another bite, I had to quickly decide if it was reasonably safe to scale the log pile or wait until the next pass. The wild card was that the Hook couldn't see me until he'd already committed the jaws to the pile, and I'd been grimly informed that I bore "responsibility for your own ass."

One hot afternoon the log pile was unusually high, burgeoning beyond the point of efficient handling. To hurry the process along, the Hook became selective about what he loaded on the trucks. Smaller logs he simply cast aside, rapidly spinning back for higher grade timber. I lacked the experience to reliably guess which were keepers and which were despised "pecker poles," and thus my customary sense of timing was upset. At one point he snagged what I assumed was a keeper for the truck, and decided I had a minute to scramble up the pile and brand several logs.

I was swinging away when an alarm jangled in my head. The cue was a certain grinding of gears. The loader was swiveling back to the pile. The log had been a pecker pole. I jerked my head up and saw the clenched steel jaws, bark smeared on the teeth, aimed right for my face. I dropped the ax and jumped ten feet to the ground, running upslope to the yarder. The jaws slammed into the log on which I'd been standing, bounced off, and swung up the hill after me. I didn't see any of that. What I saw was the yarder operator. His eyes were wide, his hands frozen on the controls. He was watching the jaws close in on me from behind, certain he would witness me crushed. At that moment the Hook finally spotted me and, reacting quickly, opened the jaws. They sailed by, bracketing my head. All I saw was a shadow on the ground, like the silhouette of a swooping raptor. I felt a rush of air.

I slumped against a track of the yarder, winded. I figured the Hook was going to be mad at me for my mistake. I feared for my job. The yarder operator climbed down from his cab, ashen faced, hands trembling as he tried to light a cigarette. The Hook hopped out of the loader and strode toward us, and I braced for his anger. I was shocked when he bellowed with laughter and slapped me on the back.

"Well!" he chortled. "That'll put the fear of God into you!"

Of God? No. But it did instill a fear of ever having a soft, safe, secure job. As the yarder operator finally succeeded in lighting his cigarette, and the Hook walked back to the loader, still chuckling, I looked around for my branding ax. I liked it that logging was risky. I liked it that I'd had a narrow escape—the kind of cinematic episode I'd read of so often a decade before. And I liked it that the Hook had laughed it all off. But most of all I liked it that the following winter he wrote a letter inviting me to return. Despite my tenderfoot beginnings I'd been accepted as a member of the crew. I was briefly tempted to brave the chokers again. The lure of working with people who almost routinely die on the job is strangely seductive. Years later, when I matriculated on a fire crew, I understood I'd returned to the sturdy and strenuous realm of the Hook.

After the fire tower job, I left for two days off at home, with the usual mixed feelings. I certainly relished time with Pam and the pleasing ambience of our self-built log house, but I also hated to be out of the helitack loop; I might miss something. Fortunately, when I arrived home and was quickly and congenially distracted by all the inherent pleasures and obligations, my firefighter's restlessness abated, and there was typically no way for me to monitor what I might be missing. However, Orr was only forty miles north of our house, and since the ship would remain there flying recons until I returned, it was within radio range.

I didn't think about that until July 29, when I walked into our fire hall at Side Lake to catch up on a few of my chief's duties. The scanner was on, and as soon as I opened the door I heard, ". . . this is Alpha-Hotel-Romeo."

I hurried over and turned up the volume, but it was near the end of the exchange and all I gleaned was that they'd been dispatched for something, then canceled, and were returning to the Orr airport. I assumed there'd been a small fire somewhere and ground forces had gained control before the helicopter arrived. I resisted the temptation to scan with my handheld radio for the rest of the day. A husband's hard-won wisdom dictated that I pay full attention to the home front, especially since I was spending most of the summer away.

That was also a wise decision for my peace of mind, because if I'd tuned in I would've heard AHR dispatched again that afternoon and been tormented by what I was missing: a plane crash.

A doctor from Kentucky took off in his seaplane from the Ely airport, neglecting to retract the wheels attached to his floats. A short time later he landed on a wide, slow-moving stretch of the Kawashiwi River, just inside the Boundary Waters Canoe Area Wilderness, an illegal act. That, however, was trivial, for the instant his extended wheels struck the surface, the plane flipped over onto its back and sunk to the level of the floats. The doctor was able to exit and swim to shore, suffering only minor injuries. His aircraft, however, was leaking gasoline into the river.

When AHR arrived overhead, all that was showing were the upturned floats and the obviously offending wheels. Mike landed nearby, and the crew hooked up the longline. Dallas, who'd lobbied his way onto our crew, and a Forest Service pilot swam out to the wreck and wrapped a strap choker around the tail section. Mike dangled the remote hook within their reach, and they linked it to the choker. He then hoisted the aircraft out of the river and set it upright on its floats. He couldn't fly away with it, but at least it stopped leaking fuel, and a photo of the operation turned up in a local newspaper. I was sorry to have missed it, but it wasn't the only plane crash we'd deal with that season.

Though northeastern Minnesota was beginning to dry after a soggy June, the fire news was in the Western states. Huge blazes in the Rockies were making CNN and National Public Radio, and we had computer access to the daily national Incident Situation Report from the National Interagency Fire Center in Boise, Idaho. Large numbers of helicopters, air tankers, engines, and crews were being deployed. Many of our Minnesota DNR colleagues had already been shipped west, but Sheldon had cautioned us on June 1: "Don't even think about an outstate dispatch." We, and our funding, were dedicated to guarding the Blowdown. The local citizenry had been promised we wouldn't desert them, even though a serious local fire seemed unlikely anytime soon.

But on July 16, while flying a DNR forester on a survey of cater-pillar damage to aspen stands, we stumbled upon a smoke near Devilfish Lake. It was another single-tree lightning strike that had been sleeping for several days. A freshening wind kicked it to active life, and there was open flame at the base of the snag. It was on DNR ground, and Grand Marais told us to extinguish it. We found a tight but doable helispot within 200 yards and made short work of the fire with seven bucket drops and some chain saw work. It was an hour's labor and we barely got dirty, but it was a promising sign. Perhaps a summer fire season in the Superior country was on the horizon, and we'd fully earn our keep.

I was surprised, therefore, by a phone call from Minnesota Interagency Fire Center three days later. We were shoveling and raking, preparing to form up and pour a twenty-foot-square concrete slab for a helipad. But Sheldon offered an alternative. He mentioned that the fires in the West were already straining national wildland resources, especially helicopters and helitack crews, and that though AHR wasn't going anywhere, I could release two of my crew members for Western duty if they wanted to go. I should phone back with the names, and he'd get the logistics rolling.

I gathered the troops and made the announcement, figuring those fire animals would leap at the opportunity and we'd have to draw cards or flip coins to determine who went. I did see eyes light up, but a short discussion formed a consensus that we stayed together as a crew. If Montana or Idaho desired us, they'd have all or none. I was pleasantly surprised.

When I phoned Sheldon with no names, he sounded a little disappointed, and I suspected he'd seen himself—not unreasonably—as bearing gifts. "Going West" holds special allure for wildland firefighters. Never mind that Minnesota, Wisconsin, and Michigan suffered some of the biggest, deadliest fires in North American history. The West is where the legends live.

During that watershed fire season of 1910, in the midst of the Big Blowup, forest ranger Edward Pulaski was anointed a folk hero. He was descended from Casimir Pulaski, the Polish nobleman who first served as General George Washington's aide-de-camp and later formed an American cavalry unit. He died of battle wounds in 1779.

On August 20, 1910, Edward was working a fire in north Idaho, between the St. Joe and Coeur d'Alene Rivers, not far from the town of Wallace. A strong southwest gale whipped the blaze into a frenzy, and Pulaski collected forty-five of his firefighters who were in danger of being overrun. His goal was to reach the relative safety of Wallace, where a burnout operation was being initiated to save the town.

But Pulaski and his men soon found themselves surrounded by fire—perhaps the burn from Wallace or spot fires ignited ahead of the main blaze they were fleeing or both. The heat was intense, the forest darkened by smoke, and the inexperienced crew was on the verge of panic. Pulaski shouted over the roar that he knew of mining tunnels nearby where they could survive the burnover. As he led them to the War Eagle mine, one man was killed by a falling tree.

Inside the shaft, he urged them to the rear, where water was seeping from the rocks. They wet their clothing, using some to cover their noses and mouths. It seemed intuitively wise, but modern firefighters are trained to protect their airways with a dry bandanna or mask. Moist air compromises the lungs' capacity to tolerate heat. If water is available, the best thing to do in an entrapment is to drink it, staving off dehydration. It's critical to keep sweating. You are physiologically more likely to panic when dehydrated because, as the fire shelter manual points out, "If sweating stops and your body is pushed to the limit, you will experience unbearable pain before collapse."

Pulaski's men were near the limits. The cramped tunnel was dark and choked with smoke and gas. Men cried and prayed, and when one panicked and attempted to escape the shaft, Pulaski pulled his pistol and vowed to shoot him or anyone else who tried to run. As evil as it was in the tunnel, outside was certain death. I wonder, morbidly, if the outcome at Mann Gulch may have been different if Wag Dodge had brandished a revolver.

Pulaski stationed himself at the mine entrance with wet horse blankets, stubbornly resolved to prevent the shaft timbers from burning or charring, allowing the tunnel mouth to cave in. Given no option, the crew huddled at the back, where they all passed out, overcome by heat and fumes—most likely carbon monoxide. There's at least one case of a modern firefighter dying of CO poisoning inside a fire shelter. Pulaski also lost consciousness while guarding the portal.

Hours later, one of the men came to, stumbled out of the mine, and made it to Wallace at about 3:00 A.M. next morning. A rescue mission was launched immediately. Back in the tunnel, five men were dead, but all the rest revived and at around 5:00 A.M. approached the entrance of the mine, where they discovered Pulaski slumped over.

"Come outside, boys," one crew member reportedly said. "The boss is dead."

"Like hell he is," replied the dauntless Edward.

They struggled outside into the black and met the rescue party on the way to Wallace. Pulaski spent two months in a hospital, temporarily blind and bedeviled with respiratory problems. But he was quickly a celebrity, later hailed as an exemplar of what President Teddy Roosevelt championed as "the strenuous life"—a path to national greatness. He also bequeathed his name to the firefighting tool he invented—the venerable *pulaski*—that's still in widespread use today.

The blowup at Peshtigo was a forerunner of 1910, without a legion of firefighters. Father Peter Pernin was not a forest ranger, but on the evening of October 8, when he spotted the hellish glow and heard the muffled roar, he surged into action as decisive as Edward Pulaski. His torpor and mental stalemate evaporated instantly, transformed into an almost joyful energy. "From listless and undecided as I had previously been, I suddenly became active and determined. This change of mind was a great relief." The balance between confidence and doubt had shifted. The fire he'd feared was bearing down, and his hands knew what to do.

His first move was to release his horse from the stable, turning it free into the yard. Then, wielding pick and shovel, he began digging a grave-sized hole in the loose soil of his garden. He worked furiously, his breathing labored in thickening smoke. The "menacing crimson" glow waxed brighter each minute, and the roar was louder and constant, like "locomotives approaching a railroad station, or the rumbling of thunder." Powered by a blend of fear and determination, he excavated a pit six or seven feet deep and six feet wide.

As he toiled, his neighbors, the Tylers, were hosting a party in a room of their house facing his garden. They weren't members of his congregation, and Pernin heard stifled laughter, assuming some of the younger guests were making fun of him and his frenetic mining operation. About a half hour after he started digging, the gathering broke up and Mrs. Tyler walked out to his garden. Pernin dryly noted, "The actions of the priest always make a certain impression, even on Protestants."

"Father," she asked, "do you think there is any danger?"

"I do not know," he replied, "but I have unpleasant presentiments, and feel myself impelled to prepare for trouble." This is a curious understatement from a man who was digging like a badger.

"But if a fire breaks out, Father, what do we do?"

"Madam, seek the river at once."

She took his advice. A few minutes later her entire family left the house and headed east toward the Peshtigo.

There was a tavern across the street that had catered all day to many of the two hundred laborers that arrived by boat that morning, bound for work on the railroad construction. Pernin suspected—no doubt correctly—that these young men "had passed the holy time of mass drinking and carousing there." As he dug his hole he noted several drunken men lingering on the porch of the saloon and in the surrounding yard. They appeared oblivious to the smoke and other cues that inspired the priest to action, and the establishment still resounded with the raucous noise of revelry.

The wind rose, and by the time his pit was finished, the air was howling. He lugged books, vestments, and church ornaments out to the garden and laid them in the bottom of the hole. The roaring was louder than ever and he worked faster, backfilling his excavation and covering all its contents with at least a foot of sand. While he shoveled, his maid rushed up to the house to rescue her caged canary. When she emerged, the wind ripped it from her hand. Terrified, she screamed at Pernin, urging him to flee.

But the priest had one more mission. He hurried to the room where he'd set up the church's tabernacle and, fumbling with a key, tried to open it. He meant to save the Blessed Sacrament—the consecrated Host, or Eucharist—and carry it with him. The key slipped from his grasp and fell to the floor. He wasted no time searching for it and simply grabbed the tabernacle—essentially a box with a small door—dashed outside, and placed it in his wagon. He planned to drag the buggy to the river, hoping to enlist help along the way.

Calling for his dog, he returned to the house to find the chalice and encountered a weird phenomenon. As he scampered through the house he saw "a cloud of sparks that blazed up here and there, with a sharp detonating sound like that of a powder exploding, and flew from room to room." He speculated the air was suffused with a "special gas" being ignited by the hot wind. Reading this gave me pause. In October 1987, in southwest Oregon, I saw a mountainside of thick manzanita brush explode into fire. As monstrous flames lashed upslope, heated gas violently blazed in midair in front of the headfire, as if impatient and enraged and fighting to be born. You'll recall that only gases freely burn, and under such extreme conditions it was as if the fire couldn't keep pace with its own volatile fuel. Nothing in the immediate path of that conflagration could live for an instant. The fuels ahead of the fire were being intensely preheated then ignited by embers.

So Pernin's speculation was at least partially correct, and the interior of his house must've been beastly hot. The fire was close, and it's possible the building and its furnishings were outgassing, approaching the point of spontaneous combustion that modern structural firefighters call *flashover*. It's conceivable that the temperature at the ceiling measured in the hundreds of degrees. Small wonder he dropped the key or that his maid ran off in a panic. The entire Peshtigo region was being heated like a casserole in an oven, approaching the microclimate of hell.

Pernin discovered his dog hiding beneath the bed, but it ignored his pleading and refused to budge. The priest seems to have become preternaturally calm. He noticed his oil lamps sedately burning on the kitchen table and imagined their glow would soon be overwhelmed by "the vivid light of a terrible conflagration." He felt almost lighthearted, keenly self-aware. Even in the moment he thought it strange that faced with such obvious peril he should possess a sharp presence of mind. Later he described it as "childish"— in the sense of innocence, wonder, and a kind of playfulness—and considered it "peculiar."

But it wasn't as peculiar as he thought. Novelist and semanticist Walker Percy wrote, "Why is a man apt to feel bad in a good environment, say suburban Short Hills, New Jersey, on an ordinary Wednesday afternoon? Why is the same man apt to feel good in a very bad environment, say in an old hotel on Key Largo during a hurricane?" One answer lies in the natural exhilaration people often experience when decisive action is not merely desirable but absolutely necessary. When the stakes are life and death. Firefighters know the feeling. We train in order to attain Pernin's state of mind on demand. We don't always succeed.

It's tempting to ridicule Father Pernin—as did the Tylers' guests—for troubling, in the face of such peril, to bury his books and vestments or delaying his departure for the sake of the chalice. But it was this very purpose in the face of grand risk that afforded him his "peculiar" potency. We may regard his personal and priestly possessions as trivial, but they were talismans, tools to forge a mind-set that enabled him to survive and to help others do so. As he later reflected on his "childish frame of mind," he noted, "It kept up my courage in the ordeal through which I was about to pass. . . ." What many might consider a more realistic approach would've paralyzed him with terror and doubt, as happened to many in Peshtigo. Pernin had a mission beyond personal survival, and, as often happens, that's exactly what saved him. It's why fireground leaders—crew bosses, helicopter managers, incident commanders—have an advantage over their firefighters. They're officially charged with thinking about the welfare of others. It's not that most line firefighters don't take care of their comrades; they do. But wearing the mantle of command is like being attired in the vestments of a priest. You are recognized as, and expected to be, a shepherd of the flock. Concern for others is a powerful anecdote to paralysis. Edward Pulaski is a perfect example. A friend once asked me what was my greatest fear on the fireground. I answered immediately: making a mistake. I don't want to be hurt or killed, but often as not, injury and death lurk in labyrinths of circumstance beyond my direct control. I do all I can and hope for the best. But I am fully responsible for the decisions I make, and the terror of deciding badly can dilute natural concerns of self-preservation. If a leader acts decisively to save his or her crew in the face of flames, it's not so much courage as it is wielding one fear over another. Perhaps that's what courage *is*. Beware the foolish firefighter who claims he's afraid of nothing. From where will he snatch courage?

At that point Pernin had snatched it from his fear of losing the sacred appliances of his faith, which, by extension, allowed him to serve his flock. Turning away from the lamps, he ran from the house, grasped the tongue of his buggy, and rolled it to the gate. Just as he reached out to open it, an Olympian blast of wind tore it from his grip and the gate simply disappeared, along with the fence itself.

He thought: I've waited too long.

That jolted me. I easily imagined the surge of alarm that electrified the priest's heart. I also had once waited too long.

It was in August 1992 in north central Idaho, not far from Edward Pulaski's War Eagle Mine. A dry lightning storm ignited 140 fires in an afternoon, similar to the rash of starts preceding the Big Blowup in 1910.

I was dispatched in helicopter Six-One-Echo (61E), a Bell 206 LongRanger, to a fire in the Nez Perce National Forest called "Scott Saddle." Ground forces were on scene, but the fire was at fifteen acres and growing. We saw the smoke from several miles out, and when we arrived overhead, Jim, the pilot, and I agreed that the initial attack would probably fail. The pine forest was gorged with fire, as if tentacles of flame were ripping out of the earth itself. It looked like a mass of spreading bonfires.

We found an exposed knob between the fire and the Salmon River, and Jim landed in a gusty wind. We had two firefighters in the backseat, and I retrieved their gear from the aft cargo compartment. They donned their packs and immediately headed upslope toward a perimeter of backing flames just over a hundred yards away. As I hooked up the bucket and fifty feet of longline, a DC-4 air tanker thundered along the crest of the ridge and dumped a load of retardant. The four-engined plane banked away to the west, and a red mist of slurry drifted in its wake. Off to our right, helicopter 699, a Bell 204, dropped 300 gallons on a hot spot. I could feel the heat of the fire on my cheek. My hands trembled a little as I taped the electrical connections then tested the control head of the bucket. I signaled Jim then backed away and crouched as he lifted off and angled down toward the river. On the opposite bank, in the Payette National Forest, another blaze was running up two steep drainages. We hadn't even heard about that one, and it heightened my sense of futility.

We had an Air Attack Group Supervisor (or "Air Attack") orbiting the fire in a twin-engined plane. His job was to coordinate the air resources and act as an aerial lookout for the incident commander on the ground. He directed the two helicopters to work the right flank while the DC-4 pounded a hotter section near the head.

The radio traffic was heavy, but a few minutes later I heard the observer at the Chair Point fire tower break through to Air Attack. "There's some weather moving in," she said, and reported 25-mile-per-hour winds. She was only a dozen miles west of us. When that front hit the flames, it would blow the fire completely out of control. The aircraft were having only a moderate effect as it was, and strong wind, especially if it was gusty, would make tactical flying too dangerous. It was time to cut our losses and get the hell out. The current operation was a loser.

Air Attack acknowledged Chair Point but continued to advise the incident commander. There was no mention of the helicopters. I tried to radio Air Attack but couldn't penetrate the buzz of traffic.

"C'mon!" I yelled at the sky. "It's time to go!"

The fire was winning. I could feel more heat on my face. The sky was torn by turbulence and darkened by smoke. The air was charged with menace. I was exposed and alone on a dry pinnacle that would embrace flame like a lover. I fondled the case of my fire shelter in a vain attempt at reassurance.

Long minutes passed, then I heard Air Attack release helicopter 699. Good! It was time to scamper. But then I heard him tell dispatch he was "hanging onto Six-One-Echo for a while." No! "Time to go! Time to go!" I shouted impotently at the airplane above. Even the big air tanker, with four 1500-horsepower engines, was off the fire. Our little ship had no business tempting the approaching cold front. I could now see a dark line of cloud to the west. I tried hailing Air Attack again, without success.

Then I saw 61E swing away from the river and head back toward me. Jim was done. I wasn't sure if he'd been officially released or not. No matter. It was time to run.

The wind was squirrelly as 61E hovered over the helispot. Updrafts and downdrafts tangled into a punishing boil, and Jim struggled to place the lurching bucket on the deck. As soon as his skids were on the ground I scuttled under the belly to pull the long-line then rushed to rebundle the bucket. I was busily bunching the suspension cables when I heard Jim yell.

Now what? I thought. For a moment it didn't register how remarkable it was for me to hear his voice. I was wearing a flight helmet, which is like having earplugs, and was working beneath the howling rotor disk; Jim was inside the ship. My next thought was, Jesus! Jim must be excited.

I looked up to catch his eye. He was literally bouncing in his seat, frantically waving his right arm. I sprang up and hurried to his side of the helicopter. He jabbed a finger downslope and shouted something obscene linked with the word fast.

A wave of fire was ripping up the north side of the knob. We'd waited too long. Our helispot was about to be engulfed in flames. I took it in with a glance and would be pleased to relate that I performed some hasty rate-of-spread calculations in my head. I didn't. Two minutes. The number simply appeared in my mind. We had two minutes—tops. And I didn't know if that was correct.

I ran back to the bucket, jettisoning my methodical protocol. I should've just abandoned it, but I'd been drilled in the necessity of caring for expensive, important equipment, and leaving the $7000 bucket never entered my mind. I grabbed the seventy-pound unit as it lay, cables askew, control head flopping, and half-dragged it to the rear of the ship, sloppy and dripping. I whipped open the cargo bay door and shoved it in. Then I seized the end of the fifty-foot long-line, and instead of twirling a careful, compact coil, I yanked it, bumping across the ground. I propped open the back door with an elbow and piled the line hand over hand into a heap. All the while I inwardly cringed, afraid of scratching the expensive door. Like an eighteenth-century European soldier standing firmly in line, I'd perhaps been too well trained.

I slammed the back door—cringing again—and all but vaulted into the left front seat. The instant my harness buckle clicked, Jim pulled the collective and 61E leaped off the helispot. One of the firefighters we'd dropped off told me later that "flames were licking your tail rotor!" I didn't believe that, but it *was* close.

As we flew down the Salmon River, Jim keyed the intercom.

"We're having fun now," he said.

And we soared away to safety on a whirlwind of human manufacture, the leading edge of the cold front lifting our rotor blades.

For Father Pernin, the whirlwind was a blast of fire and death. He'd waited too long.

SIX

TREMBLING IN
EVERY LIMB

Back at Grand Marais on July 31, I pulled the morning weather forecast off the fax—my first priority each day. Firefighters and fly-ers are obsessed by weather reports and satellite images, performing fresh auguries with each new dose of meteorological data. With the possible exception of farmers and fishermen, no one spends more time and energy divining the future from which way the wind is blowing. You quickly understand your life tomorrow may depend on what's happening three states away this afternoon.

In his book *Chaos*, James Gleick outlined modern theories in physics, proposing that small differences of input into a natural sys-tem can rapidly develop into huge differences of output: "In weather, for example, this translates into what is only half-jokingly known as the Butterfly Effect—the notion that a butterfly stirring the air today in Peking can transform storm systems next month in New York."

Though Peshtigo's firestorm was relatively brief, the violent holocaust was the result of many inputs, most of them benign or neutral in themselves: the cluster of small fires burning off and on for much of the season; the widespread, intensive logging operations; the lack of organized, effective fire suppression; unusual autumn weather conditions not only in Wisconsin but also in the Rockies and the high plains (and maybe in Peking); human attitudes toward fire and nature in general, not least the American notion of Manifest Destiny, which shaded into religious beliefs about God's will. Father Pernin, presumably unaware of nuances governing fire ecology and climatology, certainly ascribed the firestorm to divine purpose.

He was born in France around 1825 and probably held European views concerning fire. On the continent, the basic attitude was distrust of unregulated fire, and open burning was mainly confined to agricultural use, such as field cleansing. Through intensive land management (and greater population density), wildfires as known in the New World had been largely banished. When Spain established a forestry school in 1848, France was one of the sources it looked to as a guide for forest regulations and practices. So Pernin's nationality may've been one reason he was apparently more alarmed early on than many of his neighbors by the fires "gleaming everywhere" in the fall of 1871.

The weather report in my hand explained why the northeastern Minnesota summer had been cooler and wetter than normal:

> An extensive area of ice pack still covers southern Hudson Bay and northern James Bay. . . . It is rather unusual for our area to have a nearby snow-covered source of air masses during the first week of August. . . . The time will come when the ice fields begin thickening with the onset of early autumn.

More brazen than a Chinese butterfly, and a little discouraging; few masses are more intractable than an Arctic ice pack.

Meanwhile, the relentless siege of wildfires in the West continued to burgeon. It was a daily national news story—multiple fires exceeding 50,000 acres, homes burned, firefighting resources strained. A printout of the Incident Situation Report out of Boise had the heft of a *National Geographic*. Over 350 of our Minnesota colleagues had been dispatched. The potential of the Blowdown was taking a backseat to the reality of Montana and Idaho smoke filtering sunlight in Bismarck, North Dakota. Casualty reports arrived. A twenty-nine-year-old U.S. Park Service firefighter was killed in a helicopter crash in Nevada. An Oklahoma state firefighter was burned to death when overrun by a fire in Wyoming. Two convict fire crew members were struck and killed by lightning at an incident in the Stansbury Mountains of Utah.

Over morning coffee on August 5, Doug and I heard a National Public Radio reporter say that wildfires "have destroyed three and a half million acres nationwide." We snorted in disgust at destroyed. What did that mean? Nothing. Many of the fires were no doubt beneficial in some way, and a hard-core wildland fire partisan might've rewritten the report as "rejuvenated millions of acres nationwide," though that wouldn't have been strictly accurate either. But the sheer numbers were telling, and it was clear we should be sent west. Even our luster as a public relations asset was tarnished. Many local residents were anxious about the possibility of huge fires in the area. The previous autumn, when the Forest Service had burned piled brush in a gravel pit in the rain, they'd received agitated phone calls from spooked residents who smelled smoke. But by the first week in August, bombarded by television and newspaper images of ripping flame fronts and smoldering foundations, locals began approaching my crew members in the streets of Grand Marais and asking, "What're you guys still doing here?"

A fair question. And by midmorning of August 5, despite Canadian ice fields, the answer was: flying to a fire. The Forest Service had a fire near Lake Jeanette off the Echo Trail, about eighty-five miles west of Grand Marais, and we were requested. Ten miles west we flew into drizzle. The ceiling briefly dropped, and we were forced to cruise about 150 feet above the trees. Visibility was poor, and I considered canceling, but the cloud deck abruptly lifted several hundred feet, and I didn't make the call. Still, I had misgivings. It was a fickle, borderline sky.

We landed at Ely to top off with Jet-A. Dispatch indicated we'd be needed at the fire for probably an hour or two at most, so our trucks stayed at Grand Marais.

Just northwest of Ely the drizzle stopped, and, though overcast, the sky seemed brighter and less hostile. I made radio contact with the incident commander (IC) of the "Bushwack Fire." The running flames were down, but he wanted us to sling in supplies and make some bucket drops. After orbiting the burn—a remote, smoking patch under heavy timber—we landed a few miles away on a ledge-rock helispot near Lake Jeanette and prepared for bucket work.

Whenever we stowed the bucket, we meticulously straightened the eight suspension cables running from the rim of the bucket to the control head. We tied them in two bunches of four, along with the single trip cable and, after collapsing the bucket, carefully looped the cables on top, using a pair of bungee cords to secure cables, control head, and bucket into a compact package that we rolled into a zippered bag. The goal was crispness—ensuring a tangle-free setup at the next deployment—the opposite of what I'd done at the "Scott Saddle" fire.

So we were surprised and chagrined when we encountered jumbled cables. Three Forest Service folks were at the helispot, and the one time we had a bucket snarl, we also had an audience.

As we worked to arrange the lines, the sky perceptibly darkened. If not for the noise of the helicopter, we could've heard the approaching wind and had time to don ponchos. We saw it at the last moment, mature aspens whipping like tall grass as brawny gusts slammed the tree line like breakers on a lakeshore. The in-rushing squall was a curtain drawn across the sky. When it hit the edge of the opening, the surrounding trees vanished behind sheets of rain. I had time to turn my back to the wind, bending at the waist to shield my radio. The cold blast struck, and I staggered forward, instantly drenched to the skin and gasping.

Derek grimaced and shut down, and we climbed back into the ship, listening to the hammering din of rain on the skin of the helicopter. We were glad to be parked on bedrock; any soil would've been a quagmire. The windows fogged. The weather was not mellowing, and I regretted I hadn't canceled the mission. I was a victim of a common fire service mind-set: can do! When assigned a task, you tackle it with alacrity. And since fires are not often an everyday occurrence, a crew is ever anxious for the action and the novelty. That's why, in my rookie helitack class a decade before, our instructor had drummed a phrase into our heads: when in doubt, don't.

It was too late to "don't." Still, it was only discomfort and inconvenience at that point, and when the squall passed and the downpour slackened to intermittent drizzle, we emerged from the ship and finished squaring away the bucket. The IC reported they'd had no rain on the fire and still needed water drops. When Derek finally lifted and headed for a lake, the bucket looked strange, a little lopsided.

"Alpha-Hotel-Romeo, Leschak. The bucket doesn't seem right."

"Copy that. I can see it. Let me give it a try."

He flew to a small lake, dipped a couple loads and returned. The bucket looked even worse.

"We've got a problem," he said.

"Only one?"

He landed, and we swarmed on the bucket like an Indy 500 pit crew. We found one of the eight support spokes was snapped off at a bracket. It's not unheard of, but it was the first time I'd seen it. We jury-rigged a repair, and Derek was able to make four drops on the fire. By then it was beginning to sprinkle there too, so we decided to sling in the food and water before another cell rolled through or we got socked in completely. God was doing mop-up on the Bushwack. One of the Forest Service firefighters, rain dripping from the brim of his helmet, said, "Well, I don't think the Blowdown is going to burn this year."

No. No, it wasn't.

We hooked up a hundred feet of longline, and Derek flew two supply runs. By then the sky was scowling again, viscous with drizzle. We were soaked and shivering and anxious to fly away, but should we? One option was to leave the helicopter at the spot and have Forest Service rigs deliver us to Ely or Orr and spend the night. It was prudent and doable, but nobody liked the idea—no dry clothes, hassle and expense for the local unit, plus our simple desire to move on. In a cold-risk analysis, none of the objections seemed compelling. The other option was to fly to Ely—only about thirty miles, or fifteen to eighteen minutes away—and reassess while the ship was refueled. We were confident we could make it there safely. At that moment the sky seemed no worse than the crap we'd flown through to get there.

"Game on," said Derek.

We stowed our tools and took off for Ely.

Eight or nine miles from the helispot, over Bootleg Lake, the drizzle fattened to rain and visibility deteriorated. Soon we were a hundred feet above the trees, with murk overhead. Everything beyond the streaked and beaded windscreen shaded from milky white to deep gray. The dark pillars of spruce and pine, softened by mist, merged into a phantom forest, melting to opacity a mile off. If the saturated sky congealed much more, we'd be in trouble—forced to ground, if we could find a spot. It was like being on a foggy sea, close in to a rugged, unforgiving coastline.

Derek radioed Ely airport on victor, and they reported a 900-foot ceiling with three miles visibility, so it made sense to fly on for that safe harbor rather than turn back. We monitored the Ely traffic as a Mesaba Airlines commuter flight landed and a Lear Jet descended from the south. Five miles out, Derek established contact with the Lear pilot and coordinated approach plans. The sky lightened, and our view suddenly stretched out two or three miles. We gained altitude, and the treetops receded to a less threatening perspective. Even with that relatively cramped visibility the sky seemed expansive, almost luxurious. We passed south of the town of Ely and landed near the fuel tanks at the airport. So far so good, but should we bully on to Grand Marais?

"We'll check the weather computer and make some phone calls," said Derek.

As the rotors cycled to a stop, I glanced left and stared. About fifty yards off the edge of the taxiway, just inside the young woods bordering the airport, a tall aspen snag dominated the rest of the trees. It was old and crooked, seeming ready to topple. On the single remaining limb perched a large raven. It was a stark, riveting scene— would've made an arresting black-and-white photograph or a haunting watercolor. I've long been fascinated by ravens. They're keenly intelligent, uncommonly graceful in flight, and, given their total, almost radiant, blackness, are always seen in a kind of silhouette.

Even if you're close, it seems you never really get a good look. The black is like a hole in your vision, the raven an enigma. Not surprisingly, many cultures considered them harbingers of ill fortune. Just as a kettle of ravens will trail a wolf pack in expectation of carrion, so they've been known to shadow human war parties and armies with the same fond hope. Several years ago I playfully adopted ravens as my personal totem, and though the notion was more than half in jest, I've automatically paid closer attention to the birds and looked to them for omens. It's a pleasant mind game. But the danger (or the advantage) is that part of you tends to believe it. Humans can be expert at ferreting out any and all clues to self-knowledge, whether obvious or dubious.

So when I saw the raven roosting in the aspen snag, unruffled by our loud, windy landing, it gave me pause. Harbinger? Probably not. Coincidence? Probably. But I couldn't help imagining: what if it was watching us, prepared to follow if we took off, hopeful (or certain) of discovering fresh carrion between Ely and Grand Marais? I pushed it out of mind, and we all trooped over to the terminal to check the computer.

Derek studied the radar loop images and pointed at the screen. "Looks like we've got a decent window right now."

It appeared the heaviest precipitation was behind us to the west. I phoned Larry at Grand Marais, and he said it was overcast but not raining. He could see the far ridge to the north of the airport, so while the ceiling wasn't generous, it should be high enough. Derek called the Flight Service Station at Princeton, Minnesota, down near the Twin Cities, and they reported VFR (visual flight rules) conditions at Grand Marais. They cleared us for departure from Ely.

I polled the crew. Was everyone comfortable with a flight to Grand Marais? If even one person wanted to remain overnight in

Ely, we'd scrub the mission and try again in the morning. The consensus was to fly.

As we walked across wet tarmac to the ship, I saw the raven was still perched in the aspen snag. Doubts returned. Nevertheless, I climbed in, buckled the harness, and slipped on my flight helmet. Before I plugged the jack into the radio, I swiveled toward the aspen. The raven was gone. The back of my hands tingled. For a long moment I was convinced it was a sign: something bad was going to happen; it was a black satori. The raven had given me fair warning. I twisted around in the seat and looked back at my crew. They were strapping in and joshing, eager to go home. Derek climbed in smiling, ready to fly. I glanced back to the bare aspen. We shouldn't leave Ely. But what the hell would I say to them? How to explain it? I recalled the radar loop image and fixed it in my head. We did have a good window; never mind the "omen." I plugged into the avionics and flashed Derek a thumbs-up. He started the number one turbine.

Next day, over a couple of beers, I told Doug about the raven.

"I guess you should've paid attention," he said.

We left Ely just after 4:00 P.M., and the GPS indicated we had sixty-seven miles to Grand Marais, about thirty-three minutes. As we cleared the airport, Derek tried to reach Princeton on victor with no success. I hailed Trudy at Superior Dispatch on FM-1. Derek requested she phone Princeton and inform them we'd be flight-following with her. We climbed to 900 feet AGL (above ground level), with a nice cushion of clear air above. The overcast definitely seemed thinner and we had decent visibility to the east. I relaxed and traced our progress on a map. At the fifteen-minute mark I called Trudy.

"Location is one mile north of Silver Island Lake, eastbound."

"Copy. How's the weather?"

"Okay so far."

It was a timely equivocation. A couple minutes later the ceiling began to slump. Drizzle slapped the windscreen. By then it seemed routine, and that, of course, spotlighted our mistake. We were normalizing risk: we'd been through a similar situation and emerged just fine. It's a paradoxical aspect of firefighting that often it's the veterans rather than the rookies who sink themselves into trouble. If you've tallied a lot of experience in dangerous, iffy environments without significant calamity, the mental path of least resistance is to assume it was your skill and savvy that told the tale. But it's also possible, if not probable, that you were just damned lucky. A little rain? No big deal, we'd be all right. Been there, done that.

But minute by minute the cloud condensed, and Derek eased AHR lower. I was also cognizant that the field elevation at Ely was 1453 feet and at Grand Marais 1798, a difference of almost 350 feet. Cloud and ground were gradually compressing, with us between. I wondered how far back the raven was.

As we closed to within a hundred feet of the treetops, I stared ahead, straining to catch sight of any looming ridgelines. We knew the turf well, but not well enough to anticipate every high spot. About eighteen miles out of Grand Marais we passed over Clara Lake. The water looked cold and forbidding; the tree line on the opposite shore seemed nearly eye level. When we reached it, the pines were fifty feet below.

"Not far to go, Derek, but we've got a good helispot near Clara if we need it."

He scrolled to "Clara" in the GPS and entered it.

"About a mile and a half away," he said.

We were fifteen miles out of Grand Marais—eight minutes— when we "hit the wall." Suddenly tendrils of cloud were wisping in the forest canopy. The drizzle was denser. I could resolve individual treetops, but the ground was shrouded in mist. It was suicidal to proceed.

Derek banked around and punched "Clara" back into the GPS. I radioed Trudy.

"We can't go any further, and we're heading for the helispot at Clara Lake."

She came back almost instantly with the lat-long for the spot and one other in the immediate area. We had them logged in already, but it was an adroit dispatcher's move, and soothing to know she understood our fix.

"She's good," said Derek, offering the benediction aloud as a salve for our fear. We peered out the front, tearing at the fog with our eyes. We were at treetop level. The pines seemed hostile, like the claws of a monster thrusting from the depths of a murky sea.

A dirt road slipped by underneath, close enough for me to see single stones, but it was a good sign—the helispot was in a gravel pit off a forest road. The GPS zeroed out.

"It should be here," said Derek.

We were slowly sideslipping along, whipping treetops in our rotorwash. Then the pit opened up below, and I realized I'd been holding my breath. Bad move. I took a deep one and keyed the radio.

"Superior Dispatch, Alpha-Hotel-Romeo is landing at Clara Lake helispot."

"Copy. I'll send someone to pick you up."

We ignominiously settled into the hole, eighteen miles from Grand Marais. The window we'd seen on the radar image in Ely had snapped shut. It wasn't a disaster, but it was a black mark, and there would be pointed questions from the Minnesota Interagency Fire Center. I knew the first one: why didn't you stay in Ely, why push on when the weather had been marginal all day?

As Derek killed the engines, I surveyed the gloomy, wooded rim of the pit, half-expecting to see a raven perched in a snag.

I gained a valuable experience, albeit reinforcing what I already knew, and ruefully recalled an aphorism I'd spouted in class on several occasions. During the infamous *Exxon Valdez* oil spill in 1989, an unidentified Coast Guard officer told a reporter, "Good judgment is based on experience, and experience is frequently based on bad judgment."

The underlying concept is called *decision space*. When determining a course of action in tense circumstances, the goal is to retain as much room for maneuvering as possible. How much "space" you have is based on time, options, and resources. As you run out of those three, decision space shrinks. I once had a conversation with a pilot who crashed a crop duster. "What happened?" I asked. "Well," he replied, "I ran out of airspeed, altitude, and ideas all at the same time." On the flight to Grand Marais, our decision space was literally squeezed to one option: land. Provided we didn't run out of fuel or lose even the poor visibility we had. We'd been utterly focused on going to a fire.

But what encouraged me about the incident was that, though frightened, I'd remained calm. Partly it was the infectious coolness of Derek and Trudy, but there was also a core calmness within. I'd "seen a raven" long ago and learned a comforting lesson:

It's November 2, 1972. I'm sitting on the floor of a single-engine Cessna. The right door is off, and wind whips my hair and ruffles my jeans. Thirty-five hundred feet below, the arid autumn farmland of southeastern Oklahoma looks ludicrously far away—a dreamscape of patchwork fields and woods.

Billy-Don, jumpmaster and bartender, points to a D-ring in the floor, and I fumble with a hook on the end of my static line, finally snapping it into the ring. I give it a tug. He also tugs. Secure. I fondle the handle of the ripcord on the reserve parachute riding just below my sternum. I wonder: who packed it and when? And: will I have the presence of mind to deploy it if necessary? I doubt it. I've had about four hours of training—some of it while swigging beer at Billy-Don's tavern the night before. In the midst of serving a couple of rounds—on the house—he'd suddenly turned to the bottle-bracketed mirror and pulled down a roll-up chart of a T-10 modi-fied cargo chute, and—swear to god—produced a telescoping pointer from beneath the bar. I switched to Coca-Cola.

On the floor of the Cessna 172 I'm gripped by two terrors, so scared I can barely draw a full breath. The first is that I'll actually lose control of my bladder. There's a queasy tickling in my gut and groin. I fervently pray: Please, God, don't let me wet my pants! The second fear is that I won't be able to jump, that right after I soak my briefs I'll simply seize up. I cycle between the pair of dreads as we reach the appointed altitude. It's not the height that's fearful. We're so far beyond the tiny barn roofs and filaments of barbed wire that elevation is abstract, almost meaningless—I could just as well be jumping off the moon. No, the airplane ride is fine, the sky and land are beautiful. I'm terrorized by terror itself. I came to the Hugo, Oklahoma, airport with three college buddies. It's a rite of passage, and I volunteered to go first. Could I possibly endure the shame of landing with the aircraft, my face pale and pinched, my butt in a pool of piss? I consciously and firmly decide I'd rather die. Death indeed before dishonor.

Billy-Don leans past me and looks down. He pulls back in and touches his helmet to mine.

"Put your feet out the door!"

It's the first of three commands, and I'm surprised when I instantly obey. I thrust my boots into the prop wash and fold my calves outside the fuselage. I'm ecstatic. Because I'm abruptly preternaturally calm and absolutely certain that I'll jump.

"Get out on the strut!"

I ease my left foot onto the locked wheel of the Cessna and reach out to grasp the angled wing strut with both hands. I slide out the door, and my right foot extends over nothing. I stand outside the plane. My hands are steadier than when we briefly rehearsed the maneuver on the tarmac.

"Go!"

Billy-Don slaps my left thigh, and I drop off the wheel and wing into blue silence. I forget to count to six and check the canopy. I just wait in amazed happiness for the parachute to open.

Reliving that moment, I cannot deny the jump smacked of reckless derring-do. But after I landed in a minefield of Oklahoma cow pies and quickly gathered up the folds of the billowing parachute, I reveled in a few minutes of intense joy. The "canopy ride" had been fabulous, but more important was the realization it was possible to function in an atmosphere of almost crippling dread. The key was to think beyond the moment at hand. It's a traditional religious concept. Look ahead to consequences—to reward or retribution. Exercise foresight. And take a few deep breaths.

As August 2000 wore on, the increasingly common opinion, inside the government and out, was that our helicopter and crew were a wasted resource. But we seemed trapped in northeastern Minnesota, our forced landing in a wet gravel pit symbolic. The day after, we were assigned one-hour callback, the weather so low and lousy that Derek wasn't able to retrieve AHR and fly her to Grand Marais until late afternoon. The local forest was sodden, with no indication the pattern was going to dramatically change.

Meanwhile there were eighty-two major fires burning in thirteen western states, encompassing 920,000 acres. It was being hailed as "the worst wildfire season in fifty years." Because of a shortage of wildland firefighters, the National Interagency Fire Center had dipped into the military to help staff the lines. There was an alarming dearth of helicopters. We heard that over 100 standing orders for ships were going unfilled. Fire personnel from Canada, Australia, New Zealand, and Mexico were being tapped, but a wicked test of our morale was an Associated Press story headlined "Retirees Returning to Help Fight Fires." It detailed how federal agencies were soliciting exforesters in their fifties and sixties to respond to the emergency, and while most were filling support roles, the article was illustrated by a photo of a seventy-one-year-old crew boss working a fireline in the Bitterroots. Meanwhile we hearkened to the rhythm of the falling rain, south of the Hudson Bay ice pack. Derek suggested we all take an early retirement then volunteer for duty in the West.

On August 8, my wife, Pam, a seasonal dispatcher for the Department of Natural Resources, phoned to say she was being shipped to a busy command center in Helena, Montana. Then Sheldon called with the electrifying news that we'd be sent to Dillon, Montana, as an initial attack crew. We were ecstatic. We'd worked out of Dillon the August before and knew the people and the territory. And it was burning. But an hour later the deal was dead. That afternoon we installed wheels on the skids of AHR and rolled her into a hangar ahead of thunderstorms packing hail and heavy rain.

There was a political battle being waged at the Minnesota Interagency Fire Center and at Department of Natural Resources headquarters in St. Paul, between those who wished to contribute us to the national effort and those demanding we stay to protect people and property on the periphery of the Blowdown. The reason our ship and crew were on the payroll at all was because officials had stressed the high potential of a blowdown fire and allocated money to establish a credible initial attack. If they now sent us to the Rockies, then why were we there in the first place, and what if a serious fire broke out while we were gone? On the other hand, in a national response system dependent on close cooperation between the feds, the states, and multiple agencies within each, there was resentment that Minnesota was "hoarding" a type II helicopter and crew that could be put to instant use on fires in the West.

New rumors circulated every day, and though the official word from the fire center was that we'd remain on station in Grand Marais, we sensed the leash was loosening. Sheldon was in Missoula, Montana, assisting the Forest Service, and he thought it merely a matter of time before we were shipped out.

On the morning of August 19, I walked into the helibase office and found a faxed Aircraft Resource Order. I snatched it up. Palmer, Alaska? What? Had to be a prank. It was an official form and perfectly executed, but any doubt of its illegitimacy was dispelled by the notation, "Support truck should be equipped with a snow plow." Someone familiar with the federal ordering system was jerking our chain.

That afternoon the aircraft dispatcher at the Minnesota Interagency Fire Center called and said we might expect a request from Montana in the next few days. A plan was in the works to replace us in Grand Marais with a smaller helicopter and crew. He'd have more information next day. Meanwhile, we installed new skirting around the helibase trailer and replaced some bad plumbing.

Next day arrived with no word. It poured rain, and again we endured one-hour callback.

On the morning of August 22, everything changed. As is common in the fire service, we exploded from dead stop to full bore. The aircraft dispatcher called. A resource order was expected anytime, and we should mobilize immediately and report to Grand

Rapids. Yes! It was a gloriously sunny day, finally, and we matched it with our mood. A replacement helicopter and manager were headed for Grand Marais, and Roy and Christina would remain behind as crew.

Since we'd maintained a ten-minute readiness regime all summer, preparation was uncomplicated. The road toads inspected the trucks with an eye for the long haul and steered for Grand Rapids. After I stuffed extra forms into my briefcase, the rest of us strapped into the helicopter. Mike McKenzie, who'd recently returned from twelve days off, warmed up AHR, and we flew to Rapids.

Upon arrival I reported to dispatch at the Minnesota Interagency Fire Center. I learned our resource order would probably materialize next morning; we'd motel-up in Grand Rapids for the night. The center was roiling with activity. Hundreds of Minnesotans were either still outstate on fires, returning home, or in the process of being mobilized. I found a free phone for last-minute business. With Roy and Christina gone, I wanted another crew member for the western gig. There was only one available, Jeff Niemala, and I called him. He'd go. I told him we expected a hot tour of duty, but he should be keenly aware he was joining a team in midstream that'd been together for almost three months, and he was an outsider. He should be prepared to work hard and pay some dues. It was a pro forma admonition I'd have given to any "newbie," but I had little idea how quickly and intensely his hard dues would be paid.

Quick and intense was the whirlwind of heat that slammed Father Peter Pernin at the front of his house. The storm was at hand. Though he'd been shadowed by a sense of impending doom for at least two weeks, he was surprised by the swiftness and violence of the fire he'd feared. When his fence and gate were ripped away, he staggered, fighting to keep a grip on his buggy. He steadied the tabernacle, afraid it would be sucked off the wagon and into the sky. He pulled his load out into the street, but after three or four steps was blown onto his back, still grasping the tongue of the buggy. The surface winds ahead of the low cell were only 15 to 40 miles per hour, but the spinning action from the convection column produced by the fire was ferocious. Heat-induced winds reached 60 to 80 miles per hour. Trees were uprooted and half-ton wagons flung end over end. Papers turned up 200 miles away—across Lakes Michigan and Huron into Canada. The wind pushed Pernin's wagon, dragging the priest with it to the front of the neighboring tavern. The raucous patrons who'd so recently been scattered across the yard, drinking and laughing, had retreated inside and shut the doors. Pernin wrote, "A death-like silence now reigned within it, as if reason had been restored to the inmates, or fear had suddenly penetrated to their hearts." A few minutes later the tavern was swept by fire and destroyed.

Pernin's house was west of the Peshtigo River, and under normal conditions it was a five- or six-minute walk to the bridge and dam at the center of town. But as he struggled back to his feet, each breath was a gasp. The air was choked with dust, grit, ash, embers, and smoke. It was difficult for the priest to keep his eyes open in the punishing blast, and, peering though slits, he tried to discern the edge of the road and stay on track. Several times his heaving chest filled not with air but noxious gas, and, unable to breathe, he instinctively threw himself down. It's a sick sensation on the fireground, and no human reaction seems as quick and wrenching as panicky gulping for oxygen. Fortunately there's almost always a vestige of usable air on the deck, and whenever I've made that involuntary dive—perhaps thrusting a sharp tool away from my torso—I feel a spike of fear, even when I know the smoke will likely shift or lift in minutes or seconds. But when you can't breathe, nothing else matters. You'd probably flop onto a rattlesnake if your lungs were empty.

The atmosphere at Peshtigo was also charged with sound, a discordant symphony of terror. Amid the steady thunder and howl of wind, he heard neighing horses, the crash of toppling trees and collapsing chimneys, and the dire undertone of crackling fire as houses burst into flame. It was a wooden town, one step removed from the forest. Homes and shops were merely a type of fuel arrangement, with beams and planks instead of trunks and limbs. What struck Pernin about the "deafening noises" was the utter lack of human content. "People seemed stricken dumb by terror." But the sound that would haunt him for the rest of his life was the mad ringing of his own church bell, hammered by the wind and sounding distant in the general roar.

The street was crammed with people—jostling and bumping on foot or sideswiping wagons pulled by lathered horses. The frenzied stream of humans and animals was rushing in both directions, some toward the river with Pernin, and others away in the direction of Oconto. There was no doubt in the priest's mind that his route was the better, and it didn't occur to him to turn and follow the crowd headed west. "Probably it was the same with them. We all hurried blindly on to our fate."

He was being modest. At that place and time Pernin was taking the only reasonable—if desperate—course. His decision space was reduced to one option—seek the injury zone of the river. In modern firefighting we speak of four zones in a fire entrapment. First a *safety zone*, where a firefighter can retreat, relax, perhaps eat lunch and watch the fire; a *survival zone*, where you deploy a fire shelter and weather an entrapment without ill effect; an *injury zone*, where a firefighter deploys a shelter and lives but suffers burns, smoke inhalation, or carbon monoxide poisoning; and, last, the *dead zone*, which is self-explanatory. For anyone in Peshtigo the river was the only hope. Those pushing west may've been simply fogged by panic, but, in their defense, they were also fleeing flames, for at that point the town was probably surrounded by fire. The general conflagration was likely advancing from the southwest, then switching to northwest, driven by the cold front winds. But spot fires ignited by firebrands, plus the reawakening of smoldering hot spots from previous blazes, were joining forces to create a gargantuan mass fire with Peshtigo near the epicenter. One witness said, "The heavens opened up and it rained fire."

Another factor in the panic may've been carbon monoxide poisoning from the pervasive smoke. A common by-product of burning, carbon monoxide has a 250 times greater affinity for hemoglobin than does oxygen and is thus more readily absorbed into the bloodstream. We teach firefighters that a .05 percent concentration is normal, just from background pollutants, and in doses as little at 1 to 5 percent, cognitive abilities are compromised—time interval discrimination, visual acuity—and also muscle coordination. Symptoms of poisoning such as headache and dizziness are not apparent until the 10 to 20 percent range, so we stress that when firefighters are sucking smoke, they need to be aware they might not be as quick and smart as they are in clean air. Everyone at Peshtigo had been breathing increased levels of carbon monoxide for days. Since drowsiness is also a symptom, perhaps the "torpor" described by the priest was influenced by the toxin.

Not far from the tavern, Pernin tripped and fell. Recovering to all fours, he realized he'd stumbled over a prostrate woman and a small girl. He lifted the woman's head, and it "fell back heavily as lead." They were both dead. He rose, and the wind knocked him back down. Up again, he grabbed the tongue of the buggy. At that moment his freed horse appeared at his side and leaned its head against his shoulder. The animal was "trembling in every limb," and Pernin called its name and motioned it to follow as he moved on. The horse refused to budge, and the priest pushed on. He felt the ground shaking, a phenomenon reported by firefighters inside fire shelters during the approach of strong fire fronts. Other Peshtigo survivors thought an earthquake had accompanied the "hurricane" of fire.

Pernin's street angled into Emery Avenue then cut straight for the bridge across the Peshtigo. In that district the frame buildings were tightly packed, providing continuous fuel. They flared like a fuse on a stick of dynamite, until the street was an erupting swell of flame. As Pernin approached the river he saw houses on the bank ablaze. Embers and long flames were blowing into the water, and it seemed pointless to enter the river there. Though the bridge to the east side was burning, he decided to cross and seek safer water. The span was jammed with people, wagons, and cattle—again, battling to flee in both directions. He shouldered into the fearsome chaos, still dragging the buggy and tabernacle. On the bank behind, a man staggered a few steps then fell, burning like a torch. If his clothing had ignited from radiant heat, it indicates a temperature of 375 to 600 degrees. Forest Service data shows that in a dry environment at 300 degrees, the breathing sensation becomes unpleasant within ten minutes. At 500 degrees, breathing is painful in two minutes, without exertion. During fire shelter training, students are advised to breathe through the mouth, since nasal inhalation becomes uncomfortable around 220 degrees and oral at 280. For perspective, consider that book paper ignites at 451 degrees.

At this stage of his account I was in awe of Peter Pernin. Each breath would've been rasping and painful, his eyes stinging with sweat and grit, his mind pummeled by the infectious terror of a mob. His first access to the river had been cut off by fire, and that must've been a crushing disappointment. A burning death was minutes away. It would've been so easy (and wise) to simply drop the tongue of the buggy and worry only about escape. He did not.

In the wake of the fourteen firefighter fatalities at Storm King Mountain in 1994, the U.S. Forest Service conducted a workshop focusing on firefighter behavior during crisis. It was noted that some of those who died trying to outrun the flame front might have succeeded if they'd dropped tools and packs. Why are firefighters so reluctant to jettison their gear in a run-for-your-life situation? Not surprisingly, studies demonstrated you could hustle 15 to 20 percent faster without the equipment. The conclusion was that when a firefighter drops the pack and the hand tool or chain saw, it's a tacit admission that he or she is no longer a player but a victim. The mission has deteriorated from the noble cause of beating the fire and saving natural resources (or houses or lives) to an ignoble affair of frantic personal survival. Nobody wants to be a victim. As a "Standards for Survival" instructor, I'm now directed to emphasize the abandonment of packs and tools (except fire shelters and radios) in a run-for-it arena. I would've advised Father Pernin to leave the buggy.

But it was in fact his lifeline, and the thought seems never to have entered his mind. He had a mission and believed he was doing God's work. No doubt he exposed himself to greater hazard and physical stress by acting as his own horse, but he was probably buoyed by faith that God would aid the protector of the Blessed Sacrament. He was like Jewish rabbis in Nazi-occupied Europe who risked their lives to preserve the Torah. He was, I thought, like me in 1969, when I fell to my knees beside my desk and converted—in that instant—to a fundamentalist. For after the initial euphoria, I had to *practice* my newfound faith. It was a Thursday, and I had to tell my mother I could no longer attend Sunday mass, that now I had to observe a strict Friday-sunset to Saturday-sunset sabbath. I knew there would be outrage, sadness, and tears. My mother and father were on the brink of divorce, and my "snapping" would be one more trauma in the midst of family upheaval. I agonized for twenty-four hours, practicing the speech I'd deliver. But I couldn't do it. Finally, I wrote a letter and left it on her pillow. The blowup that followed encompassed some of the most painful hours of my life, but never did it enter my mind to avoid it. God came before my feelings and those of my family, no matter how unpleasant the outcome. I was prepared to pay any price to fulfill what I deemed to be God's will. Father Pernin would've been horrified by my rejection of Catholicism, but in the act of doing so, I became more like him— passionately wedded to a faith. I understood why he didn't abandon his buggy and the tabernacle.

On the burning Peshtigo bridge, his exertions added to the momentum of surging people and beasts, and he was carried along with the tide—almost deposited in the midst of a crowd on the east bank of the river. He intended (a strong word in that context) to work his way downstream along the shore to a stretch below the dam where he knew the water was shallow and the slope gentle, but again his plan was frustrated. The Company's sawmill adjacent to the dam, and its boarding house just across the street, were both ablaze with flames leaping between them, obliterating the passage with sheets of fire. Intense heat forced him back above the dam toward the factory and warehouse, which had been successfully defended on September 24. The ferocity of the fire was peaking. A phenomenon that Pernin didn't witness was reported by other survivors. One described "a large black object, resembling a balloon" spinning in midair over the treetops. When it struck a house, the "balloon" exploded with a loud boom and the structure was instantly engulfed in flames. It was probably a cell of superheated gas ignited by embers or radiant heat or a partially observed *horizontal vortex*. Under extreme burning conditions, counterrotating vortices—or tornadoes—of flame and/or hot gases can form at the edges of a large headfire, then collapse and roll along the ground, violently consuming fuel. They're often associated with the flatter terrain of the Lake States. For instance, in 1980, a Michigan prescribed burn near Mack Lake jumped out of control and rambled over 45,000 acres. The intensity of the blaze caused vortices to appear, and they in turn ratcheted up the intensity. A firefighter was trapped and killed, and several structures were lost.

Pernin pulled the buggy past the bridge for what he deemed a safe distance, expecting the span to plunge into the river at any moment. He backed the wagon down the bank and shoved it into the river as far as he could. At that point the horrendous convection currents were generating a whirlwind effect that inhaled smoke and embers upward, and Pernin could suddenly see better than at any time since he'd fled his house. Under extreme burning conditions the vertical vortex phenomenon can quickly develop. At the Tyee fire in Washington State in 1994, such a vortex was potent enough to tear lodgepole pines out of the ground, spinning them into midair, where they erupted into flame. In the forests surrounding Peshtigo, large, mature maples were uprooted and twisted into pieces. After the fire, "a tree standing upright here or there was an exception. . . ."

With the sudden clearing of vision—tinted bright orange—Pernin saw the riverbank was lined with people "as far as the eye could see." They were eerily statuesque—stupefied—some staring wide-eyed at the sky, tongues sticking out. No one was moving. No one was in the water. Survivors told him later they thought Judgment Day had arrived and there was nothing to do but accept fate and the Wrath of God.

Ironically, that was not the conviction of the priest. Since "the violence of the storm entirely prevented anything like speech," he strode up and shoved two people into the river. One bolted out immediately, muttering, "I'm wet." Pernin dragged him back into the river, lunging out for deeper water—"immersion in water was better than immersion in fire."

Then he heard multiple splashes along the bank. His decisive action had mobilized them all, and they tumbled into the river.

But the night was only beginning.

SEVEN

A GLIMPSE OF
MEDUSA

At sunrise on August 23, I hiked the three-quarters of a mile from the Super 8 Motel to the Minnesota Interagency Fire Center. It was clear and cool, and residential lawns sparkled with dew. Robins skittered in the grass. I could've called for a ride, but this was ceremony. I desired a quiet interlude before we flew west, trailing the sun into "battle." From the moment of dispatch until the day we returned, I'd be pinched by tension almost every waking moment. There's a profound difference between operating from your home base and being "expeditionary," as the military terms it.

The chief stress is working with people you don't know in a place you've never been. We'd plunge into action, enmeshed in critical relationships with firefighters from across North America. As with Mike at Onion River, it would be imperative to rapidly learn (and memorize) names, radio frequencies, and individual levels of expertise, not to mention landmarks of the territory. Everyone in the business knows this is hard—even a bit crazy—but nobody's interested in excuses. "If you can't run with the big dogs then stay on the porch."

So, though excited to launch the expedition, I was also nervous. I focused on the soothing, small-town yards, garnished with flower beds and tricycles, relishing birdsong and the yellow warmth of sunlight on my face. As my lug-soled boots scuffed the civilized sidewalk, I consciously drew energy from swinging arms and legs, instructing myself to be calm and calculating—meditative action. There was important mind work ahead.

The fire center was already buzzing, and when I walked into the aircraft dispatcher's office he handed me the long-awaited resource order, received by fax at midnight. We were bound for Kalispell, Montana, assigned to initial attack for the Northwest Land Office of the Montana Department of Natural Resources and Conservation, and the Flathead National Forest. Six years before I'd worked for three days on a fire near Kalispell. Two images sprang to mind: steep, merciless terrain, and the wonder of Flathead Lake—blue-green depths the color of Lake Superior, hemmed in by mountain ranges.

I commandeered a telephone and dialed the number on the order—for Flathead Dispatch. The mere fact my call was answered at 6:00 A.M. mountain time indicated they were busy, probably staffing the office twenty-four hours a day.

Dispatchers are esteemed in emergency operations, and a smart, tough, experienced dispatcher is a golden blessing. They are often female, taking on the stern, matriarchal aura of "she who must be obeyed." Stationed at the center of a throbbing network of incoming information by radio, phone, fax, and computer, a good dispatcher anticipates your request before she hears it, suggests alternatives as they gel in your brain, understands your message when it's cut off. She monitors the radio and reads your mind. And if she's top-notch, her voice invariably sounds composed, perhaps even a trifle bored, no matter what craziness and chaos is afflicting the fireground. I've been conditioned to treat dispatchers with deference—to listen, report, and comply. Not only because it's efficient and courteous, but because effective communication is the key to success and survival in emergencies. You can order expensive, high-tech aircraft and engines, staffed by elite personnel, but if they aren't communicating and coordinating—facilitated by dispatchers—they may be liabilities rather than assets, figuratively and literally bumping into each other.

There's a firefighters' proverb that summarizes our relationship with dispatchers: "You may know where you are and what you're doing, and God may know where you are and what you're doing, but if your dispatcher doesn't know where you are and what you're doing, you better have a good relationship with God."

I introduced myself to the all-important dispatcher, emphasizing we were anxious to get there and do whatever they desired. I briefly explained our complement, stressing that we'd been organized and operating since June 1 and were not a typical helicopter module potpourri assembled at the last minute. I hoped my tone conveyed a blend of competence and humility. Everyone despises know-it-all outsiders, no matter how fancy their toys.

A helitack mentor once suggested to me that when approaching an alien dispatch center for the first time, you should metaphorically enter on your knees, head bowed, and softly say, "I come before you a pathetic wretch, barely a step above dog excrement. Yet with your expert guidance I'm confident I can rise to a plane that pleases you. Your wish is my command." I stopped a little short of that.

The Flathead dispatcher gave me an initial contact radio frequency and the lat-long for the work station near Little Bitterroot Lake that would be our base. I reckoned our estimated time of arrival would be before noon next day.

The Flathead National Forest and nearby Glacier National Park were involved in the 1910 complex of fires. In the park alone, 60,000 acres burned, some reputedly ignited by "job hunters," though most of the largest northern Rockies fires that year were started by lightning in remote country. Without a fire detection system—neither lookout towers nor aircraft—and poor communications, backcountry fires grew large and unruly before the Forest Service was aware of them. In early August, before the Big Blowup on the twentieth, President Howard Taft ordered the regular army to aid the 4000 men working the lines who'd been drawn out of the labor pools of western cities from Missoula to Spokane. It was a crucial juncture for the fire infrastructure of the five-year-old U.S. Forest Service. The army, with long experience in basic logistics, impressed the rangers with their organization and communications, including early employment of telephones. (They even tested the use of fireline explosives, a tool that's still being refined.) The influence of military command-and-control techniques—with modifications for wildfire operations—is apparent to this day. In fact, the wildland fire agencies of federal and state governments have so excelled at the speedy mobilization of personnel and equipment that they're migrating toward an all-risk response—to floods, hurricanes, tornadoes, and even the *Exxon Valdez* oil spill. And the backdrop remains "the moral equivalent of war." During World War II, the connection was made explicit in government propaganda. For example, the May 17, 1942, issue of the *American Weekly* featured one of the vivid advertisements of the day. A forest fire is portrayed in the shape of a ravening wolf bursting from the trees. A clean-cut young man is poised in front of the beast, swinging a double-bit ax.

The header reads: "Strike Down This Monster." A line of smaller type asserts, "Forest Fires Delay Victory"—presumably by siphoning off valuable human and mechanical resources.

The key to emergency operations is the Incident Command System (ICS), a nationally accepted tool for organizing everything from major disasters to Fourth of July parades. The gamut of needs from helicopters to timekeepers, fire engines to bandages, are supplied and managed by individuals assigned to preexisting positions in the ICS. Thus when I was sent to a helibase near Red Lodge, Montana, in 1996 as a deck coordinator, I was unfamiliar with details of the particular emergency but understood precisely what my duties were, what positions were subordinate to mine, and who was my superior. The ICS channels not only people and tools but also information. And it was time for us to plug in.

Mike arrived, and the dispatcher handed us a blank Aircraft Flight Request form to record our itinerary for the ferry to Kalispell. We bent over a map, and Mike sketched a route across Minnesota, North Dakota, and Montana—airport fuel stops about one and a half-hours apart. Every airport in the nation has a three-character identifier. For example, GPZ designates Grand Rapids, FAR is Fargo; but I noticed that as Mike filled in the stops, he wrote out the full names of the towns. It seemed an insignificant detail, and when the route was plotted, I finished the form, manifesting passengers and cargo. Mike drove to the airport to file an official flight plan with the Federal Aviation Administration (FAA) in Princeton, Minnesota.

I huddled with the rest of the crew and appointed Dallas and Jeff to be the cross-country road toads. Larry, of course, would pilot his fuel truck. They needed to leave immediately, riding U.S. Highway 2 all the way from Grand Rapids to Kalispell. As Dallas prepped the support truck he noticed one of the rear dual tires was flat. We groaned. Déjà vu. A year before, the truck was brand-new when Doug and Ray left the fire center for Dillon, Montana. The odometer read 100 miles. That evening at Billings, with 1000 miles on the meter, the transfer case disintegrated. I'd flown out ahead by airliner that morning and was in bed in a Dillon motel when I received Doug's message. The truck was belly-up, requiring major repairs, ETA unknown. I called Sheldon at home, and without missing a beat he said, "I guess I should've sent a newer truck."

As Dallas drove off to a tire shop, we told him we'd expect him no later than Thanksgiving.

I handed the completed form to the aircraft dispatcher. The information would be relayed to the Eastern Area Coordination Center in Minneapolis and to the National Interagency Fire Center in Boise. It was my responsibility as helicopter manager to phone Boise at every stop with a progress report, not only as a safety check, but also so the helicopter resource could be tracked. It wouldn't be unheard of for us to be diverted en route.

"How's that look?" I asked.

The dispatcher scanned the form, presumably noting the lack of airport identifiers, and said, "Okay, looks good. Hit the road."

At the airport, Doug, Ray, and Dave were loading our personal gear into the ship. They'd already stowed the bucket and 100 feet of longline in a rear compartment, and we'd arrive in Montana ready for basic business. Jim the engineer was also flying, in case of mechanical trouble on the long flight.

Mike had news. While filing with the FAA, he was informed that the airport at Valley City, North Dakota, was closed. That was to be our second stop, so he was forced to revise the plan, and Jamestown would now be our destination after Fargo. I radioed fire center with the change so it could be passed to Minneapolis and

.. it seemed a minor adjustment, and we were square with the FAA, so we finished the preflight checks and loading and took off.

It would be a long trek into the prevailing wind, in a sinewy aircraft built for work and not comfort, but our spirits soared with the ship. We were embarking on a quest—pursuing a burning grail—and, in the American tradition, bearing west. It was an expedient journey but also symbolic, a summons to adventure as old as the myths of humankind. If asked why we were galvanized to be going, the ready replies would've been: more hours, so more money; the plain excitement of motion and travel; the opportunity to fight fire, our favorite job; a break in routine. But the deepest impulse, usually unstated and perhaps not thought, was the prospect of adventure encompassing danger.

At the root or our excitement was our discourteously treated companion, Death. The surface reasons were all valid, but the lust and joy of the quest originates in what Joseph Campbell called "the standard path of the mythological adventure . . . separation-initiation-return." We were electrified to lift from Grand Rapids because we were acting out an ancient human passage from darkness to light, youth to maturity—the voyage of the archetypal warrior to the den of the dragon, to slay it and return triumphant—or die. And we flew!—the elemental eagle, blood brother to thunderbolts and fire, representing height, velocity, flight. The brightest human lives are dramas reenacted from scripts created ten thousand years ago. Our excitement was rooted in antiquity, surging up from the depths of the human spirit.

Though we were tied in with the Princeton Flight Service on victor, and under control of the federal agencies in Boise, I was maintaining radio contact and flight-following with the fire center as a courtesy, at least until we flew out of range. Our first stop was Fargo, and north of Park Rapids, Minnesota—flying at 4000 feet—

we saw a distinct line in the distance where the forest ended and the prairie began. On the ground it's a feathering boundary; from the air the break is sharp. We wouldn't see appreciable forest again for over 800 miles.

At that moment the fire center called, but it wasn't the dispatcher. It was one of Sheldon's bosses, and he sounded angry.

"Who filled out this Aircraft Request Form!" His voice boomed into my headphones, and it was less query than accusation.

I was caught off guard. What was this about? Though Mike and I had completed the form jointly, for the sake of radio brevity I simply replied, "I did."

"Well, it's messed up! Why didn't you use identifiers?"

Mike and I exchanged looks of incredulity. Our radio transmissions were being broadcast over most of northern Minnesota, and I could tell from the boss's tone that identifiers were not the only issue. I made a snap decision.

"Fire Center, Alpha-Hotel-Romeo. You're coming in broken. I'll phone from Fargo."

It was inappropriate to conduct such a petty inquisition over an aircraft radio. For some reason I was being chewed out, and there was no way half of Minnesota was going to be party to it. I switched off FM-1.

A few minutes later Mike contacted the Fargo control tower, and they directed us to land at a private air service terminal. A teenager on a riding lawnmower scowled as our rotorwash swirled a squall of fresh grass clippings. Our tail boom obstructed his path, and I saw him eyeing the distance between the ground and the spinning tail rotor, as if he was determined to cut regardless. I opened the door, prepared to hop out and stop him, but he shrugged and shut off the mower. It was a clear demonstration of why we needed constant vigilance around the ship. The year before in Montana, we'd flown a Forest Service technician to a ridgetop radio repeater site. We had to land on slanting terrain below the crest, which meant it was imperative to exit the ship downslope, since the main rotor disk was closer to the ground on the uphill side. I casually assumed that the technician, who'd worked around fires and helicopters for many years, was aware of that. As I got out, the pilot pointed sharply, his eyes alarmed. I turned and saw our passenger striding upslope beneath the rotors, his head approaching the level of the blades. He was supposed to wait for me to open the back door and direct his exit. He didn't. Dropping to a crouch, I hustled after him, half-expecting a burst of blood and brains. He cleared the disk with inches to spare before I reached him. I explained my concern and he shrugged, obviously irritated that I'd mentioned it. I was tempted to archly quote the cost of replacing a rotor blade dented by violent skull impact but held my tongue. I shook my head in disgusted sorrow, and he got the point.

As AHR was being refueled, I found a pay phone in the terminal and called Boise flight-following, told the pleasant woman who answered that we were in Fargo, and gave her an ETA for Jamestown. There was no problem on her end. I dragged in a deep breath and called the Fire Center air desk.

The big boss ripped into me immediately: "You can't just take a helicopter anywhere you want to go!"

At first I was nonplused, but as he ranted it dawned on me that the last-minute itinerary change had been fouled up somewhere, and he assumed I was out in the wild blue yonder making it all up as I went along. But rather than beginning with questions about what I knew and what I'd done, he presumed it was I who screwed up. What burned me was that I understood where his incendiary animosity originated. I used to be a lowly smokechaser, and I was told this guy had been opposed to smokechasers as helicopter managers.

I was automatically guilty. I mused later that this first challenge of our quest was the traditional battle against "the ogre aspect of the father," our struggle to birth from the metaphorical nursery into the wider world of the initiated warrior. I needed to stand on my own and meet the challenge to my integrity.

When he paused for a breath, I interjected that we'd notified Fire Center and the FAA of our revised route, and that I'd done precisely what I was told to do all morning, including fly away. Despite myself, I also flared.

"Look," I spat, "if you're going to chew on somebody, chew on your dispatcher!"

Another pause.

"And what about those identifiers?" he retorted.

"I'll look them up!"

Another pause, and I filled it.

"Is there anything else?"

My voice, I confess, sounded like sulfuric acid dumped into a toilet bowl. Doug was standing a few feet away listening to my side of the sparring. His expression was rapt with wonder and dread. It's a fierce joy to defy the father. I fully expected the big boss to launch another fusillade, but apparently he was now nonplused. After a short silence he simply, and uncertainly, said, "No."

I slammed down the receiver.

"Well, Doug," I sighed, "I don't know how long I'll have a job, so we better get to Montana while we can." I learned later that the big boss fired a dispatcher instead.

As we whirled the grass clippings and lifted for Jamestown, I chided myself for losing my temper but was also elated for confronting a bullying attitude. Over the course of two decades I'd prided myself for being a "good soldier" and team player (a good son), but I was also taught that a firefighter must be an independent observer and thinker, that it was often appropriate to question authority, especially if safety issues were involved. We were not expected to ape the charge of the Light Brigade. I told rookies there might be a time to "just say no" if faced with a command or request that appeared to threaten life or safety. That telephone exchange had not been such an issue, but I felt the satisfaction of refusing to be intimidated by an abusive application of power. There is a time to resist or you sacrifice dignity, and in that loss you jeopardize respect—of others and of self. You thus undermine your leadership, your maturity. If I'd meekly knuckled under to an unjust charge, what confidence could the crew have that I'd resist a misguided order on the fireground that might endanger our lives? We'd discover that such a test was only forty-eight hours away.

I made it my mission to flight-follow with an aeronautical chart, and across North Dakota, as we shadowed Interstate 94 west, it was easy to identify the small farming towns, each sprouting grain elevators—Medina, Crystal Springs, Dawson, McKenzie, and west of Bismarck—Mandan, the huge Holstein statue astride a hill above New Salem. I'd seen the bovine colossus from the highway years before, but viewing from 2000 feet overhead a cow monument that still looks monstrous is a special Dakota experience.

The weather forecast showed clear sky all the way to the Rockies, and from altitude the tawny green patchwork of intensive cultivation ticktacktoed from horizon to horizon, defying your ability to say if you were over South Dakota, Kansas, Nebraska, or southern Manitoba. That is, until we left Dickinson and passed over U.S. Highway 85, sighting the eldritch badlands of Theodore Roosevelt National Park. The most startling aspect of the terrain is that stark topography abruptly appears below the level of the plain. The rusty, wind- and water-sculpted turrets and merlons of the badlands, lavishly veined by arroyos fringed with juniper and grass, are a revelation, like a lost antediluvian world. Punctuated by the occasional oil well. I've never hiked the sinuous trails in that wild region, but it speaks to me in the language of coyotes and rattlesnakes. As we flew over, I mused that unless it was burning, I'd be unlikely to confirm that language from the ground. So many trails, so little time.

The smoke from the northern Rockies was by then evident—a thin, high pall to the west that would only thicken. Our cruising altitude was gradually dropping with the visibility. And of course the ground was rising. The elevation back at Grand Rapids was 1355 feet. At our next fuel stop—Glendive, Montana, on the banks of the Yellowstone River—it was 2456. So we were being squeezed by land and sky, just as we'd been on the wretched flight between Ely and Grand Marais a couple weeks before. We planned to steer for Lewistown and Great Falls, but the elevations out there topped 7000 feet, so Mike thought it best to divert north, out of the worst smoke and into lower terrain. We'd consult a map when we landed.

Before our turbines cycled down on the tarmac at Glendive, a middle-aged man rushed out of a hangar and approached us with a look of concern. I thought something was wrong—that he'd just run dry of Jet-A or we'd parked in a bad spot. But soon it was apparent he was merely enthused. He recognized us as a fire ship, and he had a grill in the hangar. He insisted on cooking us lunch. Since our butts were flight weary, and our last snack was a vague Bismarck memory, he was preaching to the choir. After a round of custom-grilled hamburgers, he posed us at the helicopter and snapped away with a digital camera.

"I'll have these pictures on the Web this evening," he said. "And be sure to stop here on your way back!" We promised. I phoned Boise and advised them we'd be altering our route and proceeding northwest to Glasgow.

Eastern Montana is one of the bleakest landscapes on the planet, especially under smoke-filtered sunlight—arid, rugged, and sparsely populated. I once traversed the region alone in a rattletrap station wagon and at one point failed to tune in a radio signal—AM or FM—for about forty miles. It was easy to imagine I'd missed a nuclear war and would discover only smoking ruins if I ever made Billings. The two lonely highways we crossed on the 110-mile trip to Glasgow were jolting, as significant and out of place as waterfalls or skyscrapers. We saw no vehicles.

Just south of Glasgow we skirted a jagged arm of the Fort Peck Reservoir, a massive swelling of the Missouri. The main channel reached west-southwest as far as the eye could follow, vanishing into bluish gray haze.

A short stop at Glasgow, and we took on the long, 150-mile leg to Havre, paralleling U.S. Highway 2. Our ground speed, tempered by the prevailing head wind, hovered around 100 miles per hour—relatively slow. After Havre, we intended to remain overnight at Cut Bank. Mike was permitted only eight hours flight time per day, and that would put him at around seven and a half. It was getting to be a long day. I glanced to the rear. Jim was slumped over, asleep. Of the other three I saw only one pair of open eyes, and they were glazed. Intercom chatter had faded to stillness an hour before, and Mike and I were startled when Dave suddenly called, "Ninety-four!"

"What?"

"That train down there has ninety-four cars."

I grinned and turned to Mike. "Are we there yet, Dad?"

To battle my own sleepiness, I announced the place names to Mike, whether he cared or not, noting it was possible to trace immigration patterns through the town monikers: Malta, Harlem, Zurich. I also programmed the Flathead Dispatch frequency into FM-1.

As we came up on Havre we noticed a huge white X on either end of the runway. Closed? The FAA out of Great Falls had said nothing to Mike when he filed his flight plan at Glasgow. We could see laborers and construction equipment. Low on fuel, we landed near bulk tanks at the small terminal. The place was deserted except for a stranded mail pilot. He'd loaded his airplane that morning and was ignorant of the closing until he taxied over an X. The work in progress was for new lighting and not for the airstrip itself, so it was physically possible to take off, but he'd been waiting in vain all day for special permission from the FAA.

Since the airport was closed no one was around to sell us fuel. The mail pilot provided a number to call, but there was no answer. We were dead in the water. Our own fuel truck wouldn't pass that way until sometime the next day, assuming we could contact Larry. A construction crew foreman drove up and informed us the airport would be shut down for at least two more days. He knew the manager and tried a couple of phone calls for us without success.

Mike had an idea.

"You know," he said, "we don't need to run the ship on Jet-A."

He and Jim explained that #2 diesel fuel would work fine, as long as it was employed short-term and was well filtered. In fact, we weren't even compelled by regulations to note its use in the maintenance log. The turbines weren't that fussy as long as the stuff was clean. They'd run on nail polish remover if we had enough, and Jet-A itself was just fancy kerosene. The foreman called a friend who delivered fuel, and a half hour later he arrived with his tanker. Mike confirmed the fuel was filtered, then pumped 100 gallons of #2 diesel into AHR.

"If we'd known this," said Doug, "we could've landed at a good truck stop and gotten some pie and coffee while we filled up. And probably some green stamps."

I'd conveniently forgotten that such fuel was proscribed by our Minnesota contract. It was about 122 miles to Cut Bank, on the doorstep of the northern Rockies. Not far out of Havre we passed about twenty-five miles south of East Butte, a 7000-foot promontory close to the Alberta border. It's a sentinel for the mountain ranges to the west, a bedrock rhizome with subterranean links to Glacier National Park, ninety miles away—a vague rampart on the horizon. We also saw the spoor of three or four recent fires—patches of black crisscrossed with the tire tracks of the engines that extinguished them.

At Cut Bank I made a final call to Boise for the day. We pulled our overnight packs off the ship and locked her up. Two cars showed up from town and ferried us to a motel. I called Pam in Helena, and she assured me Montana was still jumping and short of resources. She figured we'd be in the middle of initial attack immediately.

So before bed that night I dug out my *Tactical Supervisor Checklist*, a tally of reminders for crew bosses and initial attack incident commanders. I considered it a rosary or phylactery—an aid to prayer and meditation concerning the duties and vagaries of the fireground. As I read each item, I conjured up an image from the past to highlight the point, imagining it as an example for a classroom. I paused longer at item 3: "Have you been briefed about hazards in the area including fire behavior, local weather conditions, expected weather, terrain, fuel types, public activity, equipment on the line, road conditions?"

The next day would present a blizzard of information once we arrived at our duty station, and it's always more dangerous to fight fire without "home field advantage." I recalled an episode from our tough tour in northwest Ontario in 1996, an operation that almost killed me.

A fire was threatening a small lakeside community called Graham, about eighty miles north of the Minnesota border, and our twenty-person crew was dispatched to aid in its defense. But before we even smelled smoke, we were held in Thunder Bay for a day and given a thorough briefing about what to expect on the Canadian fireground—communications, local fuels and fire behavior, air operations, water supply techniques, the map grid system, and command structures. We were grateful. It enhanced our comfort level considerably, but it didn't account for human factors or ensure our safety as a "visiting team."

On the sixth day of the campaign, our crew boss was asked to provide one squad for a special mission early next morning. The Ontario Ministry of Natural Resources incident commander intended to launch an aggressive assault on a section of uncontrolled fireline that was most directly menacing Graham. Three teams—our American squad and units from British Columbia and Alberta—would be helicoptered to three separate locations in front of the fire. Each would set up a pump at a small kettle lake (a glacial "pothole" surrounded by bog), then run one to 2000 feet of hose up to the fire perimeter. At that point each team would be about a half mile apart, and we'd all begin laying hose to the west, snuffing fire as we advanced. By early afternoon we'd have a continuous hoselay in place across the fire front, then settle in to defend it with air support.

Our crew boss produced a clutch of straws, and we four squad leaders drew out of his fist. I won. Three others and I, accompanied by our assistant crew boss, were instructed to assemble at a nearby helispot just after dawn. The key to the success of such a bold attack was to start early, before the temperature rose, the relative humidity dropped, and the breeze freshened. Every afternoon so far—not surprisingly—had seen a significant increase in fire behavior.

We arose a half hour before sunrise and after a quick breakfast gathered at the helispot and watched the surrounding forest gradually suffuse with rich morning light. It was chilly—near frost—and a heavy dew sparkled in the hazel brush. The air was exquisitely still, and the first calls of the jays and red-winged blackbirds were startlingly sharp. It was precisely the conditions we needed to get a jump on the fire.

An hour passed. Once we heard a helicopter in the distance and assumed one of the Canadian teams was being airlifted into position. Perhaps we were next. Another hour passed. The dew was slowly vanishing, and we felt the first hint of a breeze. I was restless. We should've had a couple thousand feet of hose strung by then. If we delayed too long, the plan was probably doomed. Finally, sometime after 9:30, a Bell 204 Huey arrived at our spot. We'd been waiting three hours. In reality, it was already too late, but the incident commander was obviously wedded to his plan, and like so many schemes it had probably generated its own momentum. We should've suggested that the assault be canceled, but being firefighters in a foreign country, we were reluctant to back out and lose face with the Canadians. We proceeded. It was an unwise decision.

After a short flight, the Huey—with tundra pads on the skids—settled onto a bog mat next to a ten-acre lake. We off-loaded a Mark-III pump and several pack frame boxes of one-and-a-half-inch hose then crouched in wet sphagnum moss as the helicopter departed. A humming film of mosquitoes embraced us immediately.

The sun was getting hot, and as one of the squad began setting up the pump, the rest of us hefted the cardboard boxes onto our backs and briskly bushwhacked for the fire. The hose was packed and coupled so that it played out the top of the boxes as we marched, and in less than a half hour we made it to the fire's edge, about 1500 feet from the lake.

It was an irregular, fingering perimeter, mostly smoldering, with scattered pockets of low flames. I twisted a smooth bore nozzle onto the hose and worked the hot spots as the others began laying hose to the west. Our tactics were simple. As soon as I reached the limit of that first stretch, I clamped the hose, removed the nozzle, then coupled the charged hose into the next length. Someone else advanced the nozzle, then I released the clamp, charging the next 500 feet. And thus we bumped down the line, soaking it as we went. Simple, yes, but our main concern was that we were living a lucid demonstration of Watchout Situation #8: *You are constructing fireline without a safe anchor point.* In other words, at the spot we met the fire's edge and steered west, there was nothing but fuel—all the way east to where the British Columbians were doing the same thing. If we'd taken off from the shore of a lake or stream, or the side of a road or bulldozer trail, we would've had an anchor. What the incident commander and we were hoping was that British Columbia would tie in with our line and we'd link up with the Alberta team before our positions were compromised by the daily reawakening of the fire. It was risky, made more hazardous by a late start. Our minds were eased to an acceptable extent by the knowledge that a helicopter was supposed to be kept aloft over the area to act as an aerial lookout.

We made encouraging progress for an hour and a half, snaking another 2800 feet of hose through thick brush and trees. The assistant crew boss flagged a line with orange ribbon, forced to tie a streamer every thirty to thirty-five feet or we couldn't readily see the next one from the last. By the time we broke for a snack, the air was definitely hotter and drier, and wind was rustling the canopy. The flames were higher and tougher to extinguish. We'd heard no cautions or alarms from above, but we were slaving in solid fuel, so before resuming work we scouted out a potential safety zone—a five-acre wet bog just north of our hoselay.

After our break the assistant crew boss found a large spot fire—about fifty feet across—between our hose and the safety zone. As he called for our attention, a balsam fir torched out in the middle of it, then another less than a minute later. A bad sign. We clamped our line, decoupled, and placed our nozzle at the joint. Grunting and swearing, we dragged the heavy hose to the edge of the spot and began working the edges. The assistant crew boss contacted the helicopter and ordered bucket support. Then he found a second large spot fire on the opposite side of our safety zone. Meanwhile, we discovered the torching firs had scattered enough embers to create a half-dozen more nascent spots. Behind us, somewhere in the body of the main fire, we heard more conifers explode into flame. We were gradually being surrounded by fire.

The Huey arrived with a full bucket and dropped water at a third location not far away—a threat we weren't even aware of. Our line was seriously compromised.

The assistant crew boss appeared out of the smoke and said the radio traffic indicated that both British Columbia and Alberta were also having trouble, and two Canadair CL-215 air tankers were inbound. We decided to abandon our effort to kill the spot fires and reroute our hoselay to encompass them—a strategic retreat.

"Everyone knows where the safety zone is, right?"

A few minutes later we heard a siren. At first it didn't register—we were miles from the nearest road. Then we realized it was a *Bird Dog*, a small, fast, twin-engine aircraft that served as a lead plane for the CL-215s. The wail grew louder, and suddenly the Bird Dog screamed directly overhead, just above the trees. We scattered like rabbits, hustling away perpendicular to the flight path. A CL-215 was close behind on that same track—hard, fast, and low—to drop 1300 gallons (11,000 pounds) of water. The force of such a salvo can knock down trees. I was still breast-stroking through the brush when the air tanker bellowed in. A white wave of water and foam lashed into the trees and smacked the ground, followed by a mist of foam bubbles wafting and glinting in the sunlight. Clumps of foam clung to the limbs like bright snow. The second CL-215 was about two minutes behind and pounded our first spot with another load.

We hooted and cheered but waited. The two air tankers were skimming the surface of a nearby lake, refilling their hulls with water and injecting it with Class A foam. In seven to eight minutes they bombed our second spot fire, then peeled off to aid the other teams. We resumed the arduous task of rerouting our hoselay, attacking smaller spots that seemed to pop up wherever we looked. Off to the south we heard the whooshing of more torching trees.

We struggled for another half hour before the assistant crew boss gathered us for a conference. We decided to take a break in our safety zone and reassess, but when we arrived at the north end of the five-acre bog, we saw it was burning. A line of two- to three-foot flames was running across the leatherleaf and moss as if it were dry grass. If needed, we could've taken refuge in the blackened portion of the bog, but a safety zone afire seemed like an emphatic message to boogie.

The assistant crew boss contacted the incident commander and informed him we were quitting the line and heading back to our pump on the lake, and expected a helicopter pickup. We were grimly amused to hear the two Canadian teams immediately deliver the same message. As soon as we made the first move, everyone felt free to retreat. We'd been engaged in an international game of chicken, and we were the first to veer away from danger. How many firefighters, I wonder, have been slain by irrational pride?

As we gathered our packs and prepared to flee, I saw Ryan pick up the chain saw.

"Just leave that, Ryan," I said. We needed to move quickly, and heavy tools were expendable.

But he couldn't bear to lose the saw. "We've got time, I'll take it."

Recalling how I risked my life to save a helicopter bucket at Scott Saddle, who was I to criticize? "Okay, but if you start to lag behind, just drop the damn thing."

Our small band headed east, following the hoselay out. The last thing I saw of our final defensive position was an entire box of Ontario's hose flaming like a bonfire. Our team alone was forced to desert almost 5000 feet of hose. Flames were closing in from three sides. The underbrush was thick and difficult.

After about a hundred yards, the assistant crew boss and I decided it was best to angle sharply to the northeast and cut across country to our first line from the lake; if we kept on east to the corner it looked as if we might struggle straight into a flame front. We now heard a constant roar. The main fire was on the move, and it was a chilling sound. Through the dense foliage ahead we saw glints of orange in the forest canopy. The main fire was awake and ravenous.

Soon we reached the trail we'd tramped from the pump to the fire, and Ryan and I broke out of the trees at the rim of the bog. I abruptly stopped, transfixed by the stunning images. Less than 500 feet to the rear, the woods were clogged with flame—trees torching in loud blasts of two and three at a time. Our hoselay was engulfed. The heat pressed on us like a blast from the door of an oven. A dark column of roiling smoke painted the southern sky. Death was two minutes behind. But straight ahead, framed by a brace of leaning spruce, was a peaceful patch of azure sky dotted with puffs of cumulous. A helicopter was just banking into the "frame," preparing to land at our pump site. In the foreground our three colleagues humped through the muskeg in a line, hurried but deliberate.

Ryan bumped into me, still clutching the chain saw.

"What're you doing!" he demanded, a touch of alarm in his voice.

"Look at this, Ryan!" I said, sweeping an arm from the helicopter ahead to the inferno behind. "It's beautiful! This is a special moment. You'll remember this for the rest of your life."

He stared at me, the roar of fire in our ears. "You're nuts!" he said.

His eyes were wide, so I pushed on into the bog toward our delivering angel of a ship but called once more over my left shoulder, "A special moment, Ryan!"

I was serious. Such instants provide the emotional voltage necessary to charge our existence with significance. I regard that Ontario escape in the same category as enduring Chapman's attack sermon at Ambassador College. Our lives are a temporal tapestry of moments, bright or dull, and what we do, say, feel, or think at any given time is the measure and leavening of those lives. It's true the mission was doomed from the start, and we should've spoken up, but I don't regret the vivid images I'll carry in my head for life. How many times do you have the opportunity to flee for your life and in that flight feel the full force of living?

Only as we flew away did I realize how close was our brush with disaster. Our entire line was aflame, overrun by a charging headfire. We'd escaped the area of our safety zone by a whisker. I was exhilarated by a brush with death but also by our dramatic decision to abandon the line. We'd been so right.

A few days later, on another sector of the fire, my squad was performing heavy-duty mop-up. It was 97 degrees, and the air was viscous with biting black flies. We slogged through our work like zombies, stewing in our sweat. We paused for a snack, waving weakly at our faces to keep flies out of our mouths.

In a voice at once weary and sarcastic, Ryan asked me, "So is this a special moment?"

I laughed so hard he was forced into a lopsided grin.

"Well, Ryan, as a matter of fact, you just made it one."

So often on the fireground, the bad times are also good. Action—whether pleasing or distressing—is the crux of sentient life. That thought is the echo of the summer of 1963, that season of page-turning books.

I was hoping for some special moments in Montana. I was in charge of an excellent ship and crew, and before going to sleep in Cut Bank I reminded myself to avoid letting our prowess go to my head.

Next morning, Cut Bank was dingy with smoke and overcast, but Mike checked the weather computer at the airport, and the ceiling was high enough for us to follow U.S. Highway 2 and the Middle Fork of the Flathead River through the pass between Glacier and the Lewis and Clark Range. We picked up the black-top on the west end of town. Visibility was only three or four miles, and the murky sky was disappointing. I was hungry for the intense rush of clear mountain flying, breaching the revetments of the Rockies in the glitter and glare of glaciers and snowcapped peaks—floating the vista of corrugated ridges undulating in steel blue sky. Out of the gray morning I conjured up an image from the year before:

It's August 2, 1999, and we're returning to Dillon, Montana, after a hot and snappy initial attack on a fire above the Big Hole River. I'm in the left front seat of helicopter One-Three-Hotel-Fox, and Harold Skaar, an old colleague from my seasons on the Nez Perce, is piloting. I've just checked the GPS display and radioed a routine location check to Dillon Dispatch.

I notice the altimeter reads 9000 feet. Just ahead is a knife-edged, snow-dusted ridge. We'll clear it by less than a hundred feet because Harold likes to hug topography when he can—a legacy of being shot down in Vietnam. As we crest the ridge, I gasp. The far side is a sheer escarpment, plunging a thousand feet. Distant talus blends with dense fir to frame a small, blue-green alpine lake.

I glance left and crane my neck. Craggy Torrey Mountain is less than a quarter mile away, surging steeply to a snow-shrouded pinnacle 2000 feet above. The sun is low, directly aft, and the mountains are stained orange.

I turn forward, and now a perfect, sharply focused rainbow is projected before a blue-black tower of cumulus. It seems to span half the Pioneer Range, like an arch we must pass under to reach the yellow haze of the Beaverhead Valley fifteen miles ahead.

Then jagged lightning bolts from the cloud, as if to say, "Yes, children, beautiful but deadly." We're in the realm of vindictive mountain gods.

Harold, who's been struck by lightning in the air, nudges the cyclic stick and banks a few degrees south—a tacit admission that we frail humans are no match for such raw grandeur.

One of my crew in the backseat keys the intercom and whispers, "Wow . . . "

On the way out of Cut Bank, I cherished that memory, realizing my longing for such vistas was a kind of lust. Near Blackfoot and Browning, the foothills rose up like a staircase, the threshold of the Rockies. Then the mountains themselves loomed out of clouds, and we were funneled into the pass, below the crests, with heavy timber riding the flanks of the drainages. Southwest of East Glacier we topped Marias Pass—appreciating the anagram of Grand *Marais*—at 5280 feet, and it was literally downhill from there. When we passed beneath Lonesome Mountain, just able to make out the fire tower at the summit, I tried Flathead Dispatch on FM-1. They replied immediately, and we were tied in to our new home. A reassuring female voice—she who must be obeyed—asserted they were glad to have us.

After fueling at Glacier Park International Airport, we flew twenty-four miles southwest to Boorman Station, a state facility on the north end of Little Bitterroot Lake. The designated helispot was a half-acre opening corralled by a split-rail fence in a young lodgepole pine plantation. As Mike flared in, AHR kicked up a blinding cloud of dust. We'd have to do something about that.

We introduced ourselves to the local firefighters and found we were part of an initial attack task force that included the fire engine and two bulldozers at the station. I was given a list of radio frequencies and a copy of the *incident action plan*, a written record of who was assigned to do what and where, then phoned Flathead Dispatch in Kalispell to discuss local response protocols and flight-following procedures. The inversion was lifting, so I requested and received permission for us to make a short familiarization flight to identify prominent landmarks and test communications. While Mike programmed the ship radios, I did the same with my handheld, then hooked up a cloning cable and transferred the new channels to all the crew radios. I ordered a water tender for dust abatement at the helispot. We pored over maps of the Flathead-Glacier area, and an hour after arriving we rose in a tornado of dust to scout the region west of Kalispell, noting prominent peaks, major roads, lakes, and rivers. My head was throbbing with fresh information, and though I reported to dispatch that we were fire-ready, I secretly hoped we wouldn't have one until the next day. I needed more time to get cozy with the turf and the system. We also needed our support and fuel trucks on scene to be fully operational.

The road toads showed up by late afternoon, only six hours behind us. U.S. Highway 2 had been kind. We briefed them, programmed the truck radios, and outfitted both vehicles with local maps. By sundown I was confident we were prepared—meaning we were ready to take a credible swing at the first curve balls provided by Montana.

We were assigned to sleep at the Hilltop Motel in the hamlet of Marion. It was modest but clean and adjacent to a boisterous backwoods tavern. We laid in a supply of "Moose Drool," a dark Montana microbrew we'd discovered last summer. That evening, bathed in high-country starlight and the neon glow of the saloon sign, we lounged on the veranda of the Hilltop, sipping beer and toasting our new circumstances. The chill night air was spiced with smoke.

On the morning of August 25, we reported to our helispot at Boorman Station. By 9:00 A.M. it was already hot and dry under a clear sky. I assigned Doug and Dave to the support truck; Ray, Dallas, and Jeff primped their field packs and tools and secured them in the helicopter. While Mike and Jim performed preflight checks and Larry inspected the fuel truck, I settled into the front seat of the support truck to catch up on paperwork and monitor the radio.

At midmorning we heard a smoke report called into dispatch. Nine-Five-Mike (95M), the local Montana state helicopter based in Kalispell, was ordered to respond, along with a couple of engines. The day was off to a promising start. About twenty minutes later, the radio called our name.

"Alpha-Hotel-Romeo, Flathead Dispatch."

Despite our preparation, I was startled. I fumbled for the dashboard mike.

"Dispatch, Alpha-Hotel-Romeo. Go ahead."

"I have a fire for you."

Our testing was at hand. The dragon waited out there in the mountains. My mind crackled with the formulas of initial attack, and I didn't think of Father Pernin as I strode for the helicopter, but I needed the presence of mind he displayed so conspicuously during the trials at Peshtigo. And for him, the fire was not the only monster.

The priest and the people he inspired plunged into the Peshtigo River at about 10:00 P.M. On the nearest bank, the Factory Store, a three-level structure filled with woodenware—buckets, tubs, broom handles—was just catching fire. It occurred to the priest that if the building collapsed into the water, they'd be crushed by burning walls. But the store, stocked with dry flammables and intensely pre-heated, erupted like a kerosene-soaked bonfire. Burning tubs and broom handles flew out of the inferno and pelted the river like meteors. Mercifully, the building was consumed in fifteen minutes, reduced to a heap of blazing beams.

The heat generated by a large burning building is tremendous. As a fire department member, I once responded to fire in a structure similar to the Factory Store. It was a two-and-a-half-story log house, and flames were shooting from the roof when we arrived. In minutes it was fully engulfed. The February day was cold—about 10 degrees—with a bitter wind off Big Sturgeon Lake, and at first it was comfortable to be near the flames with a nozzle. But when the fire matured, we couldn't stand upright within fifty feet, even wear-ing full protective gear. We staffed the hoselines on our knees, and at the peak of the fire noticed a shed about seventy-five feet from the house. It was clad in old-style asphalt siding, and despite the wintry day, molten tar ran in black rivulets down the walls. We hosed down the shed to prevent ignition. A foot of snow on the roof melted so rapidly that water showered off the eaves as if in a summer rain.

So imagine the hot night at Peshtigo, the entire town essentially burning at once. At street level your throat and lungs would've been seared by simple respiration. Your hair would be singed and perhaps even smoking. No doubt Pernin was correct in observing that he and the rest hit the river in the nick of time, for "the heat was increasing. A few minutes more and no living thing could have resisted its firey breath."

Just after the priest dragged the protesting man back into the water, a pale, gasping woman arrived on the bank. A child clung to her hand, and she clutched a disheveled swaddle to her chest. She folded back the linen to inspect her infant, and it wasn't there. She screamed, "Ah! My child!" Had it slipped out on the way, or—pan-icked—had she grabbed empty bedclothes by mistake? The heat forced her into the water, and Pernin attempted to console her by suggesting that surely someone had found the baby and carried it to safety, but she didn't even look at him, wild eyes staring instead at the far shore. He learned later she died in the river.

The priest was still outside himself, in a wondrous state of calm and clarity that allowed him to perceive a focal point just beyond the horror. Like Wilfred Owen, who though subsumed in the gory quagmire of trench warfare, transformed terror into poetry, Pernin was the perfect witness. In the autumn of 1918, Owen won the Military Cross in a battle that "passed the limits of my Abhorrence. I lost all my earthly faculties and fought like an angel." Father Pernin stated that from the moment his torpor magically evaporated, he "remained in the same careless frame of mind" affording him the strength and acuity "to brave the most appalling dangers, without even seeming to remember that my life might pay the forfeit." He reminded me also of smokejumper fore-man Wag Dodge on the deadly sidehill of Mann Gulch in 1949. Clawing frantically up a 75 percent slope with a killing flame front only moments behind, Dodge possessed the remarkable presence of mind to stop, fish out a match and strike it (hoping wind and convection currents didn't snuff it), and light his famous escape fire. But then, he was charged with saving his "flock," trying to be their angel.

In cold water up to their necks, the priest and his companions thought they'd be protected from fire, but it was a vain hope. Flames arched over the river, and it seemed as if the sky itself was ablaze. Exposed heads and faces were in constant danger of being burned by radiant heat. Human skin soaks up 100 percent of radiant heat that strikes it. Even a single layer of clothing can reflect and absorb most of the energy, but exposed skin has no defense. Unlike direct contact with flame or a heated object, victims may not realize they've suffered a radiant burn until it's already happened. That's why a modern fire shelter is designed as a reflector, absorbing only about 5 percent of radiant heat impinging on it. At Grand Marais in 2000, we were issued inflatable life vests as well as fire shelters, since it was assumed that on a fuel-rich blowdown fire our only safety zones would be the lakes and rivers. In water, with a partially deployed shelter to reflect heat, a firefighter would be well armored, so long as heavy boots and other gear didn't drag him to drowning.

In the Peshtigo, they were forced to keep ducking their heads or splashing themselves to prevent burning. Quilts and clothing had been tossed into the river to preserve them—being more precious commodities for the average person than they are today—and Pernin noticed them floating by. He grabbed as many as he could. A knot of people was crowded around him, leaning and clinging, whether by accident or on purpose is unclear. But it seems likely the priest's decisive action on the bank would've naturally attracted others to his side. He lifted the sodden coverings from the water and heaved them over the heads of those near him, encouraging others to do likewise. To his amazement (and to mine) even the spongy quilts dried out in a matter of minutes and burst into flame. Continual dousing was required to prevent the makeshift fire shelters from igniting.

With literally everything in view on fire, there was not only ovenlike heat but also magnificent light, "brighter than by day," an otherworldly illumination suggesting the imagined environs of purgatory or hell. Whether or not that crossed Pernin's mind he doesn't say, but he does mention that at one point the strange spectacle of his neighbors vigorously slapping at the water, many with various fabrics draped over their heads, struck him as funny: "I actually perceived the ludicrous side of the scene at times and smiled within myself at it." This seems like more than the nervous humor of stress—for example the joking and kidding I've heard and done when dealing with a car accident or a house fire. It's nothing malicious or thoughtless, just a natural means to reduce tension. If we're chuckling, even a bit hollowly, how bad can it be? It's akin to a centering breath, positive physiological feedback. But Pernin dwelt on another plane, and he attributes the almost relaxed observations to freedom "from the fear and anxiety that might naturally have been expected to reign in my mind. . . ."

He could see everything around him clearly. Besides the light of the blaze, there was also a complete absence of smoke. The power of the convection currents had increased, further cleansing the air, and Pernin described "the terrible whirlwind . . . with its continually revolving circle of opposing winds. . . ." Looking to the zenith, he saw only leaping and rolling flames, like "masses of clouds," and too bright to comfortably stare at. The sky was a writhing aurora of fire, as if the sun had exploded, its corona violently expanding to consume the earth. Everything organic was fuel. It seems likely the priest was at or near the center of a stunning vortex. The cured, concentrated, and tightly arranged kindling that was the buildings of Peshtigo—not unlike a swath of heavy blowdown—created a particularly fierce zone of superheated atmosphere. Hot air rose in a plume to the upper reaches of the troposphere—perhaps to 30,000 feet or higher—generating a strong updraft that vacuumed surrounding flames into a rotating tornado of fire. To view that and live was remarkable, and few outside the river did.

Pernin saw several cows in the water, and one swam past him. A woman nearby was clinging to a log, and the cow bumped it. She lost her grip and submerged. The priest thought the woman was gone, but in a moment she reappeared, one hand grasping a horn of the cow, the other continuing to splash water on her face. The cow kept swimming, and Pernin lost sight of them both. A man named Coon, who successfully led his family to the river, was followed by a small white pig that jumped into the water with him. He remembered seeing little but the snout of the pig above the surface, then was distracted and lost track of it. After the fire he found the pig rooting amid the ashes.

For over three hours the priest splashed water on his head and on those around him, staving off heat, but as the fire finally ebbed, he noticed some people shuddering with cold, could hear several sets of clacking teeth. It was, after all, October, and soon there'd be ice in the river. Even in summer, a night spent in northern water would've been a trial in itself. As his own extraordinary energy waned, Pernin also felt the chill, and, suddenly fearing cramps or worse, he waded to the shore and ascended a few feet up the bank. But he'd barely left the river when someone shouted, "Father! You're on fire!"

He hurried back into the water, accompanied by a hiss. They were still trapped, and their refuge was turning deadly. It struck the priest that the warning shout was the first human speech he'd heard for hours. People had remained silent, perhaps overwhelmed by the roar of the firestorm. In several modern fire entrapments inside fire shelters, survivors report conversation among crew members (which is encouraged by training as a psychological boost) until the flame front hits, then the characteristic roar renders communication impossible, and people withdraw into their own heads.

But when Pernin retreated from the bank, a woman who'd been near him all night asked, "Father, do you not think this is the end of the world?"

"I do not think so," he said, "but if other countries are burned as ours seems to have been, the end of the world, at least for us, must be at hand."

He deflected a theological question to a practical observation, unaware that the city of Chicago, 216 miles to the south, was also burning that night, victim of an urban conflagration that destroyed 18,000 buildings and killed 300 people. About 90,000 were left homeless. Today, we'd consider the two incidents as part of a "complex," both exacerbated by the same weather conditions and fuel types.

There was no more talk, but shortly thereafter people were able to cease their splashing. The fire was running out of fuel and the temperature decreasing rapidly. Pernin approached the bank again and sat on a log, half out of the water. He began to shiver, and a young man tossed a blanket over his shoulders. A few minutes later the priest was finally able to fully emerge. It was about 3:30 A.M., and he'd been in the river for five and a half hours.

At that moment, there was another dramatic change in his mind-set. The clear-headed determination that bordered on joy collapsed almost immediately when he left the water. The heavy physical toll of the past several hours came due. He realized his throat was swollen, his chest constricted, and he was wracked by a renewed shivering that was almost convulsive. He lay down on the sand, totally enervated. He wrote later, "I can see that the moment most fraught with danger was precisely that in which danger seemed at an end." He felt literally dispirited, drained of will and motive, ready to be claimed by unconsciousness and perhaps even death.

The ground was still hot, and after lying there for a time his soggy clothes began to warm and dry. He took off his shoes and socks, pressing bare feet into the sand, and felt a small surge of energy. He was near the incandescent ash heap of the woodenware mill, where some of the larger beams were still flaming, and he saw mounds of iron hoops, the remnants of buckets and tubs. He thought to lay his socks and shoes on hoops to dry but found the metal still burning hot to the touch. Then, like a vignette from a bizarre, Dante-esque nightmare, he saw "numbers of men were lying—some face downward—across the iron circles. Whether they were dead, or rendered almost insensible from the effects of damp and cold, were seeking the warmth that the sand afforded me, I cannot say." Later the hoops would serve a grim purpose. An employee of the mill who survived the fire helped to carry charred bodies by placing one hoop under the neck of a corpse, the other under the knees.

By the time Father Pernin dried his clothes, the tightness in his chest eased, and breathing was much easier. But his eyes began to hurt, and the pain increased until Pernin, who was no whiner, called it "acute." Many survivors had a similar complaint to one degree or another. In fact, when Edward Pulaski emerged from the War Eagle mine in August 1910, he not only had difficulty breathing, he was also temporarily blind and suffered vision problems for years afterward. In both cases the eyes had been not only severely irritated by smoke and other particulates but probably also seared by radiant heat, as if gazing at the fire—which every firefighter knows is often irresistible—was akin to a glimpse of Medusa. It's also possible the priest was gripped by psychological anopia, which sometimes occurs during traumatic events; his mind had seen enough.

In any case, at dawn on October 9, some nine hours after he'd entered the river, Pernin was alive and dry, but his afflicted eyes had worsened, and he was completely blind. There'd been suffering enough, yet fresh tortures were about to grip him. And in the midst of his ordeal he'd witness "a great miracle."

EIGHT

THE FEVER OF
COMMAND

In August 2000, Montana newspapers published daily accounts of the current fires with numerous references to the comparable season of August 1910. Indeed, the forest fuels of the new century traced their lineage to the blazes ninety years before. The dominant commercial tree species in the northern Rockies before 1910 were western white pine, fir, and larch. When natural recovery began, the burned areas favored establishment of a pyrophyte, and much original forest was replaced with tracts of lodgepole pine, a tree that "likes to burn."

When I first worked fires in the Rockies, I became familiar with "dog-hair lodgepole," referring to a dense stand of young pine regeneration so thick—thousands of stems per acre—that it was like hair, or brush bristles, and almost impenetrable. In dry weather, a mountainside sprouting "dog hair" is potentially explosive. After

1910, remaining white pine was more susceptible to bark beetles, whose populations burgeoned in an environment of weakened, dying, or recently dead trees. Healthy pines, normally resistant, were overwhelmed by that infestation plus an exotic disease called blister rust that arrived around 1900. The plague created more dead and dying white pines and hence more fuel, which led to yet more fires and subsequently to more hosts for insects and disease. In many forest communities, fire begets fire in a cycle of death and rebirth. The holocaust of 1910 thus set the stage for the wildfire regime of the rest of the century and beyond. Many of the fires of 2000 were simply another installment of 1910, just as World War II can be viewed as a second round of World War I.

From personal perspective—the other important result of 1910 was that with the deaths of seventy-eight firefighters, the involvement and influence of the military, and the legendary exploits of Edward Pulaski and others—public and government attention shifted from the blazes to the people who fought them. It was the baptism of the wildland fire service as we know it. Peshtigo had been an "act of God," a disaster that humans endured. The dead were victims. The fire season of 1910 was a war, and the dead were casualties. A mass grave for firefighters in Idaho was consecrated with a rifle salute and taps. The August 1923 issue of *American Forestry* reported, "Suitable headstones with bronze tablets were created over as many of these 'heroes of peace' as could be traced, for they died as truly in the service of their country as did those on Flanders' poppy-covered fields." For worse and for better, a national wildland fire subculture rose from the ashes of the northern Rockies. Our 2000 journey west had taken us "home." Back to the ghosts of the fireground.

"I have a fire for you," said Pat at Flathead Dispatch.

It was reported by a detection aircraft, and the aerial observer had given Pat a lat-long and a legal description. I copied them down, scribbling the lat-long on a separate paper I thrust at Mike. He hurried to the ship to start the engines and punch the coordinates into the GPS. Meanwhile, Doug and Dave spread a map on the hood of the support truck and established a rough location for the fire—on the east side of Flathead Lake, about forty air miles away. Road travel was going to be twice that, if not more. They huddled with Larry to determine a route, and I strode to the helicopter.

It was a twenty-yard walk to Alpha-Hotel-Romeo—maybe twenty-five seconds—but it was sterling time. I drew in two centering breaths as I watched my three crew members buckling their seat belts and donning flight helmets. I reminded myself in a whisper to proceed deliberately. If you act calm, you will be calm. Jim was circling the ship on his last-minute rounds, peering into inspection ports, studying the rotor mast. I heard the trucks start behind me and caught a whiff of diesel exhaust. It all looked and sounded fine, and I felt a blush of affection for the people and the machines, a heady tingle akin to a wash of sweet wine. I thought: I love this. But such affection warms easily when you feel strong, when you're not defying the heat, when you're still arrogant enough to assume that fresh air is free.

The rotors whipped overhead—singing for flight—as I plucked my helmet off the seat and slipped it on, shutting out the music. That christened the moment, highlighted the inescapable present—the bold now. The past three months, the last nineteen years, were all rehearsal. Every fire is preparation for the next. Were we worthy? We'd find out. We were dispatched. We were, by god, committed.

I settled into the seat, buckled my harness, and plugged in. Mike's left hand was deftly flitting across the instrument console, as if he were playing a piano—his customary preflight concerto of checks. I switched on the FM radios and made sure Flathead Dispatch was up on FM-1. Then I opened my map and planted a finger on the fire. It was near a drainage called Boulder Creek. No lakes were indicated close by, but the map scale was 1:126,720, so smaller ponds wouldn't necessarily show.

I looked to the rear and Ray nodded.

"Ready in back," he said.

Jim appeared at the nose of the ship and raised a thumbs-up. The rotor disk chopped the late-morning sunlight into pulses that flashed across the Plexiglas bubble. Mike gripped the collective stick.

"Okay, boys," he said, "coming up."

We rose over the tops of the pines and spun to the southeast. Mike tipped the nose, and we climbed the first ridge. I keyed the radio.

"Dispatch, Alpha-Hotel-Romeo. We're off Boorman Station for the fire."

I read the lat-long for a confirmation and received it.

"Do we have a ground contact, Pat?" I asked.

"Negative. There's no one on the fire, and the detection plane is returning to base."

"Copy."

So in all likelihood we'd be first on scene. Good. That's why we'd come "home." I studied the map. There were some dashed-in roads in the area—probably logging trails—sinuous with the switchbacks denoting steep terrain. Mission Mountains, said the map. It might take ground troops a long time to get there.

We passed over U.S. Highway 2 just east of the Hilltop Motel, and at our eleven o'clock I could see Blacktail Mountain. At 6757 feet, it was our most prominent local landmark. We tracked a couple miles south of the peak, and Flathead Lake began to unfurl before us. It's twenty-seven miles long and seven to fifteen miles wide, and as we crested the Blacktail ridges above the western shore, I was struck by a sense of déjà vu. Except for the elevation, it was strongly reminiscent of descending to the North Shore of Lake Superior from above Tofte or Lutsen. The wrinkled plain of water sprawled to the north and south, and the panorama felt familiar. Wild Horse Island was at three o'clock, and directly below us a cluster of small, wooded islets that could've dotted any Boundary Waters lake. I'd already noted that our new base at Boorman was very close to the same latitude as Grand Marais.

We saw the smoke, directly across Flathead Lake. I glanced at the GPS. Twelve miles.

"Dispatch, Alpha-Hotel-Romeo. We have the smoke in sight. ETA is six minutes."

I was grateful we had a twin-engine ship, or we'd have been reluctant to traverse ten miles of open water, a stretch far exceeding our power-off gliding distance. Losing even one turbine was unlikely, but the extra security of having two wasn't trivial. The water below was frigid and deep, and despite my training in the "cage," I didn't feel confident about surviving a ditching in that high-country cousin of Superior.

The smoke was a grayish white smudge laced with black filaments, blending with haze at a ridgeline. We couldn't see the source, but it was obviously more than a single-tree smolder. The aerial observer had estimated two to three acres before breaking off for a fuel run to Kalispell. The wind was still calm, but the forecast called for afternoon breezes at 10 miles per hour, and of course the regular upslope mountain winds caused by solar heating would likely be a factor as the day matured. No doubt the fuels were dry. The relative humidity was supposed to dip to 20 percent, with a high temperature in the 80s. We might be facing a dangerous blaze.

The radio was busy. Helicopter Nine-Five-Mike (95M) was being released from its mission and returning to Kalispell, so they'd be available if needed. I was also aware that two DC-6 air tankers were on the tarmac at Glacier International, about five minutes' flight time away. I heard Doug check in with dispatch from the support truck. They'd be taking U.S. Highway 93 to Polson at the south end of the lake then heading north on U.S. Highway 83 to a forestry station at Goat Creek, which was a few miles east of the incident.

We made the east shore of the lake at Blue Bay, and two minutes later Mike tipped my side of the ship over the fire. It was about two acres, burning fiercely in a patch of deadfalls and brush beneath a canopy of large firs, about a quarter mile below the crest of a ridge. It was on the southern aspect of the slope, in full sunlight, and flanking a narrow forest road that was temporarily containing any upslope spread. The flames, three to four feet long, were backing downhill and snapping along the road edge, which was a de facto control line. No obvious spot fires, and no evidence of torched trees. It was deep backcountry with no structures in sight, but we had high potential for a large, poorly accessible forest fire. I was delighted to note that about 150 yards below the fire was an old landing for a logging operation. The opening was generous—on the rim of the cutover it had served—and except for a few scattered logs, the ground looked clear and level. In relation to the fire, we could've wished for nothing better—nearby and below.

In steep terrain, slope has the same effect on fire as wind. Flames and convection currents are closer to the fuel in front, more effectively preheating the brush and trees. For example, say we have a blaze on flat ground that runs at the rate of 8 chains (528 feet) an hour. Transfer that fire to a 50 percent slope in the same fuel, and the rate of spread leaps to 50 chains (3300 feet) per hour, a sixfold increase. Factor in the wind, which is almost always present in mountainous topography, and a fire can make explosive runs, accompanied by spotting ahead of the flame front, which ignites new fires that draw the main blaze even faster upward.

At Mann Gulch in 1949, Wag Dodge was leading his smoke-jumper crew from their landing zone to a point below the original fire, intending to put the Missouri River at their backs, when the blaze crossed a drainage and flung flames into their faces. They couldn't outrun the new fire tearing uphill. Neither did fourteen firefighters at Storm King Mountain in 1994 win their sprint. It's almost always best to approach a fire from below.

We saw no water source immediately nearby, but if all else failed there was Flathead Lake, though it would be a long haul. I figured our first priority was to get on the gravel and begin holding the fire at the road. If you have a natural barrier that's working, you beef it up as soon as possible.

I radioed dispatch with a summary of what I'd seen and informed Pat we were landing to hook up our bucket and that four helitack would be on the fire in a few minutes. As Mike eased in, kicking up dust and small bits of bark, I opened my door and leaned out to look aft. There was a small fir on the left edge of the landing, but we had room.

"Tail rotor clear," I said.

He settled in and idled down, and we began our initial attack promenade. Mike requested we attach 100 feet of longline to the bucket. It would afford him more cushion if he had to pull water out of a hover hole, and he'd also lay less rotorwash on the fire. It was important that we prevent airborne embers from crossing the road, and the helicopter had the potential to fling them across. In less than five minutes he was off, and the four of us were hiking up toward the fire. In addition to our small field packs (containing food, water, fire shelter, first-aid kit, brush coat, headlamp, and extra batteries), we carried two pulaskis, a shovel, a *combi-tool* (a cross between a shovel and a hoe), and a chain saw.

Our mood was buoyant, but we never truly believe in the tough kingdom of pain until we arrive there again. Schiller, German poet and historian, wrote, "He who is fortunate, let him learn pain." But we seldom learn it. We take it as it comes then feel abused. It's verse we cannot write or memorize. Doubt rears up. How can I endure this? But at some level firefighters must learn to welcome pain. It is, after all, inevitable.

As we approached the base of the fire I called attention to a large snag just outside the black. The fire would undoubtedly reach it before we could fell it, and the old fir might burn off and topple. We gave it a wide berth and halted briefly at the southeast corner of the fire. It was swaggering through a tangled mess of logs, limbs, stumps, and brush—fuel rich and far too hot to directly engage. Holding the road and keeping the fire below it did indeed seem the best and safest strategy. I turned to Ray, who'd spent a season on a western hot-shot crew.

"Well, Ray, I don't think we can do much with the flanks. I suggest the four of us get up to the road and kill spots until we have air support."

"I agree."

We humped along the perimeter of the fire to the road, shielding our faces from painful radiant heat with Nomex shrouds attached to our helmets. It was a narrower track than it appeared from the air, about twelve feet wide. It was still keeping the fire at bay, but even a moderate upslope wind would blow flames across it, spreading fire to the ridgeline and beyond.

"Okay," I said, "our escape route is the road itself. If this thing goes bad, follow it east and down to our helispot."

We spread out, about thirty yards apart—a thin defensive line. The road was cut deeply into the slope, so the uphill side featured a two- to six-foot embankment, ideal for catching sparks. The ground above was grassy and brushy with thick stands of small and midsize lodgepole pines and a scattering of firs, bracketed by some pockets of slash. It was crunchy and highly flammable. We'd have to jump on spots quickly to prevent a new fire we couldn't control.

"Climb up a few yards in and grid through the timber."

The crew scrambled up the embankment, and Ray found a tiny curl of smoke almost immediately. He dug out the ember and smothered it with dirt. That was the simple tactic—keep scouting the green side and snuff any ignitions at birth. It occurred to me that we were in a situation akin to our near-burnover in Ontario in 1996. We had no anchor point. Fire was bumping the road, as it had our hoselay in Canada, and we were surrounded by fuel. We could withdraw down the road quickly if necessary, but our ability to catch the spots as soon as they appeared was our only hope of containing the blaze. It was a precarious position, though not unacceptably so—at least not at that point. But the day was young, and I made no assumptions of success.

The wind was lazy and variable, and periodically the smoke column leaned over the road in a choking pall, and flames bent toward us. We pulled bandannas over our faces and snapped goggles into place. It was wickedly hot—between the sun and the fire, I figured over 100 degrees on the road. I guzzled one of my quart canteens, and the water tasted like warm sweat. The liner of my helmet was saturated, and stinging salt leaked into my eyes. Each breath stung just a little. A savage spirit seemed to possess the fireground. After all these years I'm still startled by the pain, still curiously (willfully?) naive about how swift is the break from airy blue-sky flight to grim, ground-pounding purgatory. I forget that even highly toned flesh and blood can be torpid in the crucible. I work out almost every day, year round. I'm too old to fake it. And in the afterglow of the Nordic skiing, stair climbing, power walking, canoe paddling, and simple arduous labor of woodcutting or tree planting, I forget the pain of heat, smoke, stress, and unforgiving terrain. A vigorous, heart-thumping ski jaunt over crystalline snow doesn't seem to share the same universe with the fireground, and so I usually feel potent and fit until the very moment I'm tested. Then I remember: This shit hurts. I could die out here. The fireground is unfit for human presence. We didn't evolve from smoke and embers. But as the fuel on the road edge burned up, I was hopeful the ambience would mellow.

The crew hunted spots like dogs after rabbits, and I hustled to the west end of the fire. There was a jackpot of fuel—cured slash—beneath some sixty-foot firs that flames had just reached. It burned intensely, and flames would likely ladder up the trunks and torch out the trees. That would broadcast a blizzard of sparks over the road into the flashy fuels above, probably planting the kiss of death on our plan, and definitely endangering us. That jackpot would be our first target for bucket drops.

I glanced at my watch. Almost fifteen minutes had passed since Mike left. That meant our turnaround time for water was going to be too long. I'd already figured we'd need a bucket about every ten minutes or better to hold the road. Unless . . .

"Dispatch, this is Minnesota Helitack."

No answer.

I clambered upslope a few yards and tried again. I heard the feedback squawk that indicated I'd tripped the repeater.

"Go ahead," said Pat.

"I need an air tanker on this fire."

"Stand by."

If one of the DC-6s was sent our way with 2400 gallons of retardant, it could lay one line of slurry on the upslope side of the road to mitigate the spotting then "paint" each flank to slow fire spread. That would perhaps buy us enough time to nail the rest with the helicopter.

"Minnesota Helitack, dispatch. Negative on the air tanker. You have no structures threatened. I'll send helicopter Nine-Five-Mike."

So. That altered the complexion of the day. I would've argued it was better to have the air tanker deployed and flying; you could always divert it to a higher priority incident. But I wasn't high enough on the food chain to suggest it. Okay. We'd try it with two helicopters.

Finally I heard AHR in the distance and raised Mike on the radio.

"West end of the fire, Mike. First drop in those tall firs. Be advised that Nine-Five-Mike is inbound."

He slid AHR in over the trees, and when the water crashed through the canopy and smacked the ground, I heard a loud, plosive hiss, testifying to deep-seated heat. As AHR banked away I watched the spot he'd doused, and in three or four minutes saw what I'd feared—a resurgence of flames despite 300 gallons of cold water. The fuel moisture was very low, and any active fire was going to be aggressive and stubborn. We needed the rapid, massive strike of an air tanker, and in an average season, dispatch would've given me one of the DC-6s in a heartbeat.

By then the crew had picked up two more tiny spots and snuffed them. I'd noticed no significant ratcheting up of fire behavior yet, but it was clear we'd require more people. From the briefing I'd received the day before I assumed that dispatch had also shipped ground forces to the fire, and I was about to radio Pat for an ETA when I heard voices above us. I yelled to give them a reference, and in a few moments two firefighters emerged from the woods. One caught the toe of a boot on a root and tumbled head over heels down the embankment and onto the road, crumpling at my feet. I reached down to offer him a hand, but he laughed and sprang up, unhurt. Fortunately he hadn't been clutching a pulaski or other sharpened steel. I was relieved. But it was a demonstration of the banal way a firefighter can be injured or even killed, and when I saw him fall, the scenario flashed through my mind: someone trips and sprains an ankle or fractures an arm, and suddenly we're all packing him to the helispot, and the ship halts bucketing to fly a *medevac* (medical evacuation). The spot fires escape snuffing, and soon there's energetic flames above the road, and another major incident makes the newspapers. And, more to the point, our initial attack fails. Pride was a component of our plan. Just the proper dollop of self-satisfaction is essential to the health of a fire crew, so long as it's not the kind of hubris that slays someone. Pride is one of the seven deadly sins, and the ideal dosage is relatively small and easily exceeded. Better to lose the fire than kill a colleague. Sounds like a no-brainer, but in the heat of battle, simple concepts can wander off into the smoke and be forgotten. Such would happen before the end of the day.

We introduced ourselves. Ron—the guy who hadn't tripped— was a local Bureau of Indian Affairs (BIA) crew boss, and he and his companion had driven to the fire on a road above us. I hadn't seen it from the air and chided myself for that—should've done another orbit before landing. Perhaps we'd been a bit too anxious to engage.

Ron was trying to determine if the fire was in his jurisdiction. Apparently it was close to the boundary between the Flathead Indian Reservation and Forest Service turf. In most regions of the nation, initial attack is a free-for-all, and whoever is nearby and available is expected to respond. But if a large commitment of resources and cash is anticipated, then exactly who "owns" the fire becomes important. Ron and I agreed that given the conditions we faced, a twenty-person hand crew, an engine, water tender, and one or two bulldozers would be justified. We established a tactical channel our radios had in common, and Ron disappeared into the smoke for more recon.

Meanwhile, AHR returned for another drop and 95M arrived overhead. The new ship circled the fire, and I advised the manager of our goal and that there was a decent landing zone just below the fire. They opted not to use it. Perhaps, as the fire backed downhill, that spot now looked too close. In any case, 95M banked south and settled behind the next ridge.

Between helicopter drops, I joined the crew along the embankment, peering through the smoke and coughing, our backs to the fire. It's pleasant to watch the flames, but most of our attention had to be focused on "the green." Occasionally, heat and smoke forced us to our knees, as we sought the marginally cooler, clearer air near the ground. More curls of smoke appeared, and we kept pace, but it was now afternoon, and the diurnal winds were strengthening. So far the push was mostly from the west, parallel to the road, but one errant gust could overwhelm us with spot fires. We were riding the keen edge between victory and defeat, between relative safety and potential injury.

Alpha-Hotel-Romeo returned with a bucket, and Mike reported he needed fuel. Since Larry was still en route, Mike had no choice but to scoot for Kalispell. I figured he'd be gone for at least forty-five minutes or more, so I had him lay a trail drop along the hot side of the road, temporarily cooling a scattering of burning logs that were punishing us. He could see we had a tenuous grip on the situation, and I found out later he landed in an opening a couple miles away, got out, and unhooked the longline and bucket. That allowed him to proceed to the airport at top speed.

He peeled off to the north, and a few minutes later 95M approached from the south with a first load. I directed him to hit the jackpot under the tall firs. It was still cooking in spite of 1000 gallons from AHR.

I heard dispatch hail me for an update, but I couldn't trip the repeater for a reply. The pilot of 95M stepped into the breach and told them we were "doing a good job of holding it at the road" but that helicopter turnaround times were long and an air tanker would be a big help. Again it was denied.

Nine-Five-Mike made his drop and broke away to pick another load. Ron reappeared. He still wasn't absolutely sure the fire was his, but he decided to take it on. He was now the incident commander. He'd ordered a twenty-person crew, a water tender, and two bulldozers. One of his engines—fire truck—would be on scene shortly.

"Sounds good," I said. "What do you want *us* to do?"

"Just stay with the spot-catching and direct the helicopters."

I hadn't been given the BIA's frequency, so Ron recited it and I wrote it on a notepad. I briefly gathered my crew and told them the story then quickly programmed the BIA channel into my radio. Typical. You arrive in a new locale and absorb all the information thrown your way, and on the first gig you lack a critical frequency. Such normalcy was comforting.

Ron and his partner headed downhill to hike completely around the fire for an accurate estimate of size and to scope out any potential problems for the bulldozers. Once the "heavy metal" arrived, his plan was to surround the fire with a control line, establishing an anchor point at the junction of the road and the start of the dozer trail.

When 95M returned I had him hit the tall firs again. It sounded better—no loud hiss. I pushed my way through blackened brush in ankle-deep ash to inspect the jackpot. There was still a lot of heat but little open flame, and the trees were wet. That particular threat was tempered.

The wind had picked up and was no longer strictly parallel to the road. On its slow march to the east, the fire had eaten into more slash and deadfalls, and now young pines were torching out in blasts of sparks and embers. More spots were showing up across the road, and shouts of "another one!" had become frequent. The fire was hot enough and big enough to create a favorable environment for itself. The rising convection column was drawing air upslope, and I estimated the local wind at 5 to 10 miles per hour. At eye level, some sections of the road were so hot I couldn't stand there. I scaled the embankment to join my crew and found a fresh ignition almost immediately. Instead of a smoldering bit of bark, I saw a tongue of flame. I squashed it with a boot then roughed up the soil with my pulaski. I pulled off a glove and felt the ground. Cold. But open flame was an ominous development. Watch-Out Situation #16 is: *Getting frequent spot fires across the line.* It was definitely time to watch out.

Nine-Five-Mike was back, and I requested he drop on the east end of the fire, at the road edge into a nest of jackstrawed logs and limbs. Six-foot flames were leaping from the mess, and Dallas and Jeff were scrambling in the brush and trees above it, hacking at spots. The smoke was denser and almost constantly over the road, and the pilot reported he was having trouble seeing the ground. He hovered, waiting for the smoke to shift.

He'd been keying off my blaze-orange shirt, so I jogged to the east end, hopped atop a stump, and swung my pulaski overhead in a slow arc. For a moment the smoke arched back toward the fire.

"Gotcha!" he said.

"That hot pocket just below me."

"Ten-four."

He sidled in for the drop, and smoke surged back over the road. He scored a partial hit.

"Nine-Five-Mike, Helitack. We need another one in there."

By the time he was out of sight, the doused logs were burning almost as vigorously as before the hit. It wasn't looking good. To an outside observer, say a Wall Street stockbroker or a Minneapolis housewife, our location and situation might seem crazy. We were working in dry fuel a few yards uphill from an increasingly belligerent forest fire that had grown to three or four acres—a fire roughly 400 feet on a side if it were square—and our task was to put it out. Even though 300-gallon bombs from the air were having only moderate effect. Flames were lengthening, heat was rising, and smoke was our air supply. The sun was a dull orange glow behind the pall. One reason I didn't consider any of it strange was because it was simply my job. I was normalizing risk—just another day on the payroll.

More important than the workaday momentum of employment was the zest for the game—the extreme sport of firefighting. It wasn't for nothing that Derek often called out "Game on!" as we climbed aboard the ship. Back in June, Doug and I discussed the pressures of the front seat and managing an initial attack helicopter. I told him, "You know you've arrived when it's all a game." When, that is, you've forgotten the stakes? Canadian singer-songwriter James Keelaghan wrote a haunting tune entitled "Cold Missouri Water," about the slaughter at Mann Gulch. The premise of the lyrics is that crew boss Wag Dodge is on his deathbed years later, offering a final firsthand account of what happened on August 5, 1949, "before I check out of the game." The first time I heard it, the hair rose on the back of my neck, my pulse quickened, and I wiped a tear from the corner of my right eye. When I received a recording of the song, I played it ten or twelve times in a row. Despite, or because of, the innate horror of the story, it quickly spiraled into romance. It's why exposure to the power of music and art can never really make us more humane—because even terror can be rendered beautiful, wistful, maudlin, as if mayhem were an ideal to be sought, and a burning death is somehow comely.

On another fire in Montana, Dallas and I scaled a long, steep slope to a helispot after a tough shift. We were at 7000 feet. He was packing a Stihl 044 chain saw. We were both wasted, each short step a struggle. We paused 100 yards from the top to catch our breath and gaze westward to the Swan Mountain glacier. I sensed a teaching moment. If things went bad then and there, where would we go and how would we get there? I said, "Well, Dallas, this is the big league. Imagine fire below, racing upslope. What's our status?" He glanced back down then up at me, his chest heaving. He replied, "Dead meat." We laughed. Laughed. Maybe it was the scenery or the thinness of the air. Truth was, there probably wouldn't be enough endorphins in the world to push us to the summit and over the sidehill in time. The game relies on laughter and short memories of pain.

The coda of Keelaghan's song—with Wag Dodge at the end of his "confession"—is the sweet sad strains of the American classic "Across the Wide Missouri." Cut to the thirteen crosses at Mann Gulch. Hit the replay. Why? Because maybe you're only truly alive when the hair rises on the back of your neck, your heart rate is up, and there's a tear in the corner of your right eye. Game on! In the dance of everyday life, risk eclipses routine. Is that why Father Peter Pernin inwardly chuckled at his neighbors splashing for life in the Peshtigo River? Is that why I jumped out of a Cessna 172 rather than face embarrassment? Is that why Wilfred Owen could "fight like an angel"? I know that's why we tried to hold the road against a steadily accelerating fire.

Ron and his partner appeared on the east end, giving the fire a wide berth before stomping through some particularly tangled brush and back up to the road. At that moment an engine arrived. The fire truck had a 300-gallon tank and two operators, and Ron set them to cooling down the hot pocket that 95M had tried to quell with his last drop. They parked just beyond the east end of the fire and pulled a hose back to the flames, crouching at the edge of the road. Their nozzle stream had some effect, but until a water tender arrived to resupply, they didn't have the luxury of blasting away. We needed a reserve of water in case we lost a spot above the line.

Nine-Five-Mike made two or three more sorties, temporarily knocking down flames along the road, then announced he had to leave for fuel. With accidental good timing, AHR was returning from Kalispell, and I heard Mike make radio contact with Doug at Goat Creek. Our trucks were in position, and Mike could fly there for fuel at the end of his next cycle.

We'd been on the ground for about three hours, and though the fire continued to shove eastward and downhill, we four still held the road. The west end of the fire—in lighter fuel—had cooled to the point where we could close ranks and bunch up at the hotter east end. I asked Mike to dump his bucket on the hot pocket where the engine was working, but he too was hampered by smoke and only splashed part of it. I could see that updrafts off the fire were also making it difficult for him to hover overhead with 2500 pounds of water dangling 100 feet beneath. It was tricky work to juggle a helicopter in front of a slope in squirrelly air, even for a pilot as expert as Mike.

I heard the growl and clanking of an approaching bulldozer, and Ron sent it down the west flank, gouging a six-foot-wide control line just outside the fire perimeter. I winced to hear the throaty roar. It was a necessary tool for that incident in such a merciless season, but I always consider dozers a last resort. I have a poster in my office featuring a stern-faced Smokey Bear saying, "Remember—'hit it hard' means the fire, not the land!" A bulldozer blade is a high-impact, scarring weapon and can easily do more damage than the fire itself. On the other hand, if you've decided to suppress rather than "let burn," a dozer can save time and money.

Suddenly the hot pocket flared up. Crackling and whooshing, a twenty-five-foot fir detonated in a pillar of flame and shower of sparks. The bright orange flecks whirled over the road.

"Heads up!" I yelled—unnecessarily. It wasn't a command, just a sporting cheer, like a quarterback urging "Let's go!" as the huddle breaks up. We watched the squadrons of embers drift into the trees, and we converged on the general area like moths to a light. I saw Jeff chopping at one spot and Dallas at another. I crushed a smoldering ember in my glove then felt heat on the back of my calf. I turned to see a campfire-sized blaze. Sparks had ignited a small pile of slash fifteen feet above the road. I tore into it with my pulaski, shattering the flaming sticks, but the fire had already sunk roots, burning deep into the duff. It was swelling even as I attacked it. Without looking up, I called out "Help!" Ray materialized in seconds, and together we dug it out and smothered it.

Ray shook his head. Our line wouldn't survive many more assaults like that.

Alpha-Hotel-Romeo was back.

"Yeah, Mike. Hit that same pocket below the engine."

He approached from the east, buffeted by convection currents and intermittently swallowed by smoke.

"Stay on that track, Mike. Another twenty yards."

But he lost the target in the smoke and banked away for another pass. The hot pocket was seething again, eight- to ten-foot flames lashing up and bending toward unburned ground. More conifers would be torching in a few minutes, bombarding our line with fire-brands and heat.

I watched AHR zero in on us again, appearing and disappearing in smoke, like the moon behind scudding clouds. Occasionally sun-light reflected off the bubble, beaming through the soot as if a searchlight sought us out. As he closed, I focused on the bulging bucket. It arced like a giant plumb bob, in and out of view. I tried to talk him in, but since Mike periodically lost sight of the pocket, and I often lost sight of the helicopter, it was impossible to maintain a clear reference. When he finally hovered overhead, I saw the bucket plunge out of the smoke directly over Ray and me. Mike was too far upslope. We saw the bladder open.

"Oh, shit!"

There was no time to dodge the drop. I turned my back and bent at the waist, shielding my radio. The water slammed us, and I stumbled forward to keep from falling. It was icy cold, and I gasped, my back instantly soaked.

Ray grinned, water dribbling off the brim of his hard hat. As we angled off to a new spot he said, "Well, shouldn't take long to dry off."

A twenty-person crew arrived, and Ron split them up, sending a couple squads to follow the bulldozer and secure the west line as the machine plowed to the base of the fire, then hooked around the bot-tom. The rest of the crew he deployed on the east end, several yards ahead of the flame front. With a chain saw pioneering, he had them start constructing a handline downhill, trying to cut the fire off from more fuel and ease the pressure on us above the road. Mike sup-ported that effort with his next few drops, hitting the pocket again before heading for Goat Creek to fuel.

A minute later a cluster of trees erupted into flame and billow-ing black smoke, and another wave of sparks blitzed our line. Eyes stinging, throats burning, we chased a flurry of fresh starts, savagely swinging at one and jumping to the next, then returning to the first to finish it off.

Doug radioed me from Goat Creek to establish and test our contact.

"How's it going?" he asked.

My reply was a gaffe. Precision and care should be the hallmarks of fireground communications. But without thinking, I responded to Doug's simple query with a kind of vulgar poetry:

"We're getting pounded," I said.

What did that mean, exactly? Nothing. It certainly conveyed a stark, negative image to Doug, and the natural tendency is to invest such an impression with more direness than it deserves. It was easy for him to conjure up walls of flame threatening to blow us away. Our position was iffy but not critical. Not yet. To satisfy Doug's question I should've said, "We're getting spots over the line but still holding."

I heard Mike notify Doug that he was inbound for fuel, and Doug relayed to Mike that we were "getting pounded." Repetition, of course, enhances the effect. I didn't think much about it at the time. I spouted my ill-advised "poetry" and continued to slave over spot fires. But next day I heard the rest of the story.

Understand that Mike was meticulous about helicopter mainte-nance. Yes, that's wise and unremarkable, but some pilots pay closer attention than others. Whenever he shut down for fuel, Mike expected Jim to be all over the machine, poking his fingers and eyes into every critical and not-so-critical area of the ship. And Jim was on it, scurrying atop and around AHR like a chipmunk in an oak tree.

When Mike landed at Goat Creek, Jim was at the helicopter before the rotors stopped. While Larry pumped in fuel, Mike grabbed some water and a snack, and the instant Larry removed his nozzle and secured the fuel port, Mike strode back to the ship. Jim was still at it, and normally Mike would've patiently waited for him to complete the inspection and perform any tweaking that might be advisable. But Mike surveyed the ship for a moment and called out, "Okay, Jimmy! All the big shit is there. Get out of the way!" And he climbed in and started the engines.

During my basic helicopter training nine years before, I was emphatically told, "You are now in charge of a sacred trust"—that being human life. "You must not allow undue pressure, expressed or implied, to influence your judgment during the performance of this sacred trust."

We're getting pounded was fat with implication. I'd inadvertently applied pressure to Mike. He perceived his crew to be in trouble, and he reacted accordingly. It was touching but also hazardous. I'd violated the trust we'd engendered at the Onion River.

By the time AHR returned, the engine had been refilled by a water tender, a second bulldozer was on its way in, and the first dozer had ripped a line halfway around the fire, but after four hours of battering by heat, smoke, and firebrands, our besieged line was about to crumble. Wherever an ember wafted to the ground, open flame was now the rule. The fire had roughly doubled in area since our arrival from the sky. Ron had a difficult decision: did we play offense or defense? Did he keep the engine combating the main fire, thus reducing the generation of airborne embers, or was it more efficient to drag hose uphill and kill the spots as they occurred? Ideally—with another engine or two—it would've been sweet to do both. But with only a single engine he opted for defense—directly engage new fires above the road. If even one escaped, our basic strategy would be compromised, and the fire could ramble away into the evening news. He'd have AHR concentrate on the main fire, and the engine would shuttle along the road and support us. As each of my crew called for water, the engine bumped up and down the line, reeling off just enough hose to reach the fresh flame, then retracting it like a tentacle and responding to the next call.

Up to that time we were more or less in control. Our basic plan was working, though resources were stretched thin. Sometimes when you lose a battle, it's difficult even in hindsight to pinpoint a moment when your designs unraveled. But that afternoon above Boulder Creek, two specific events shifted control from us to the fire.

First, as Mike returned with a load of water, he reported a spot fire nearly a quarter mile above the road, at the crest of the ridge. It had already burned a thirty-foot circle. Ron had him drop on it, then dispatched the second bulldozer and a squad of firefighters to attack it. But if a hot ember had sailed that far, then it seemed likely more were scattered across the high slope.

Second, at almost the same time, another burst of torching at the east end showered Ray and me with sparks. One caught beneath a small fir, and we had an instant bonfire. We tried to bust it up and knock it down, but heat drove us back. I yelled for the engine, and it was there in seconds. The operator grabbed a nozzle and yanked hose off the reel. His assistant throttled up the pump. The spot was roaring. Crouching near the base of the flames, he opened the nozzle. Water dribbled out. The tank was empty. I heard AHR returning and urged Mike to drop on the bonfire. Three hundred gallons would wipe it out or at least buy us the time and space to finish it with hand tools.

"It's a new flare-up, Mike, on the east end, just above the engine."

He tried to get a fix, but again, the viscous strata of smoke was nearly opaque. From Mike's point of view, he was hovering above—and sometimes in—a mass of cloud, punctured randomly by clots of flame. He could see the road ahead of the fire to the east, but only caught brief glimpses of the engine. He understood it was critical to score a bulls-eye, so he aborted his first pass, unsure of the target. As he swung round again, shimmied by heat and updrafts, I tried to talk him in, relying mostly on sound.

"You're getting louder, Mike, hold that track."

I saw the bucket punch through the smoke, then the belly of the helicopter. He was almost on top of us.

"Gotcha, Mike!" I waved an arm. "It's the fire in front of me— just above the road."

He opened the bucket. The salvo of water missed completely. We watched helplessly as it drenched the south edge of the road, extinguishing nothing. Visibility on the line was simply too lousy for an accurate drop.

Having dodged two bullets, the spot fire burgeoned, lunging upslope. Two more trees exploded. With what we had at that moment it was unstoppable. Our holding was over. The next natural break was Flathead Lake itself, five miles away. Just beyond the ridgeline above us was a long, sheer drop to dense forest. If the fire jumped into that, it might take hours for anyone to reach it on the ground.

If we'd only had a single air tanker at the start . . .

I gathered my three crew members to regroup, reassess, and take a break. We'd been at it nonstop since we stepped off the helicopter. We knelt on the road to eat, ingesting soot and grit with our MREs.

Ron strode up for a conference. We agreed the road was lost and that AHR should concentrate on the big spot at the top of the ridge, plus some smaller ones he'd also found. The air was clearer up there, and he'd do some real good. The first dozer would soon confine the fire below the road, and a second twenty-person crew was minutes away. The fuels were patchy near the crest, and he figured the second bulldozer could push a line from spot to spot across the top.

One reason we'd held as long as we did was because all my people had radios. We'd been able to stay in touch and focus our efforts where they were most effective.

"I need one of your guys," said Ron.

"Sure, for what?"

"My folks working that big spot at the top don't have a radio. I'd like one of you to station himself between here and there and be a relay."

For a moment I was speechless. He was asking for a firefighter to stand on a slope, in fuel, between two fires, with no good escape route to a safety zone. That person would have very little decision space. I saw Ray roll his eyes. It wasn't necessarily a suicide mission, but close. A firefighter in that position was asking to be burned over. I was stunned—not only by the request, but by the fact it had been issued from Ron. He was obviously an experienced, competent firefighter and had organized a reasonable operation under difficult circumstances. But in the fever of command he'd lost his perspective. His focus had narrowed to beating the fire. His people had become tools, weapons—chess pieces. It's not an uncommon syndrome of incident commanders under stress. It's simple and natural in the can-do meritocracy of the fire service to home in so tightly on the contest that you downplay or neglect basic safety. That's why rookies are taught to "just say no" if ordered to act in a manner that inordinately compromises their security or life. Fact is, few ever do. In the firefighting culture it's often onerous to say no.

The first time I did it was in northwest Ontario in June 1996—seven days after we'd abandoned the 5000 feet of hose. Our Minnesota hand crew was spiked out in the bush for sixteen days, supplied by air. The fire was so remote we had to string antenna wire in a tree so we could establish radio contact with base. It was a big blaze, and we often "commuted" to the line via helicopter. One morning we awoke to drizzle spattering our tents. I poked my head out and saw low overcast. I arose to help with coffee and breakfast, and in the direction of the fire I saw lightning. Thunder rumbled. Two Canadian helicopters were due in at 0800, but surely they would cancel. The weather was too ugly to fly a routine mission, and even a drizzle would dump more water on the fire in an hour than we would all day. At least that was the consensus around our sputtering campfire. After breakfast, I returned to the tent to stretch out a while longer, enjoying a respite from what had been several days of arduous labor. But in a few minutes I heard the unmistakable thumping whine of a Bell 204 Huey. Our crew boss shouted, "Squad Three! Get ready to fly!" I was astonished. I pulled on my boots, and by the time I emerged from the tent, they were boarding the ship. The sky was still wet and stormy. Another squad leader met me at the door of the tent. His face was grave.

"Do you think we should go?" he asked.

"No way! I'm not flying this morning."

It was outrageous. The fire was in the mop-up stage. It was raining. The mission was unnecessary and dangerous. But the Huey was lifting with Squad Three aboard, and a second helicopter was inbound.

Our crew boss was an excellent hand and an effective leader, but this was a bad call. I strode up to him. I suppose the urgency of the situation, coupled with the obvious folly, is what caused me to be more blunt than I should have been.

"This is fucking ridiculous!" were the first words from my mouth. True, perhaps, but not designed to initiate tactful dialogue. That was an unprofessional mistake. "I'm not getting on a ship, and neither is my squad!"

The other squad leader was gentler. "I guess I agree," he said.

More calmly, I detailed my objections as the rest of the crew gathered around us in silence, most of them grimly nodding as I spoke. It was essentially a mutiny. The tension was palpable. Thus confronted, the boss radioed the Huey and requested they return our people to camp. After they'd unloaded, the second helicopter landed and one of the Canadian commanders hopped out to meet with us. He seemed relieved. We discovered that at the helibase, several miles away, they'd taken off in sunshine. The weather deteriorated as they approached the fire and our camp, but apparently everyone was reluctant to cancel. We'd been playing another international game of chicken. I could imagine the Canadians—as mission oriented as we were—thinking, "Well, this is nuts, but if the Americans are goofy enough to fly, we'll do it." We all naturally wanted to impress each other with our pluck.

The helicopters left, and we returned to our tents to wait out the weather. On one hand, I was gratified, but I was also uncomfortable. The emotional stress of refusal and rebellion lay heavy on the camp. I was also upset that I'd lost my temper with an otherwise top-notch crew boss. An hour later he entered my tent and almost meekly inquired, "Well, when can we fly?" At that moment I was in control of the crew, and that's not what I'd desired. Fortunately, the sky cleared, and we resumed work. The tension gradually evaporated with the puddles. To his credit, the boss later admitted he was wrong and thanked us for the mutiny. I told him I'd serve with him again any time. But it could've gone another way, and when you say no you run the risk of destroying the cohesiveness of a unit or the integrity of an operation. And in the end, will your superiors side with you or with the crew boss? Careers might be at stake.

All this scrolled through my head when Ron requested that I assign one of my people to an unacceptable situation. It was out of the question, but for a brief moment I considered asking Dallas or

Jeff to do it, just to see if they had the savvy to refuse. But the fire was ripping, and it was no time for a test.

"Ron," I said, gently this time, "I can't put one of my crew in that position, and I strongly recommend that you get your people off that spot if they don't have a radio." Ray nodded his assent.

Ron was taken aback. No was not what he expected to hear. He was locked in personal combat with the Boulder Creek fire. He was in close radio contact with his BIA dispatcher and boss, who wanted him to win, who didn't want to hear about an escaped fire. But I gave him pause. He was silent for a moment, then said, "Yeah, you're right. You guys keep working this area." He turned and disappeared into the smoke.

I was instantly washed by warm elation. But not because I'd resisted authority and successfully made my point with Ron. True, it had been a kind of alpha-male face-off, albeit low-key and benign, and I'd apparently prevailed. Though that was not lost on me, I was happy simply because I'd made the observation, made the decision, and effectively conveyed it—while standing on a midslope road with fire above and below, and the eyes of my crew upon me.

I briefly flashed back ten summers, and the picture was clear: the back of Scott Hocking's flight helmet. He'd been my helitack mentor, and through a busy Idaho fire season I was in the backseat of his helicopter as we worked scores of initial attacks, medevacs, and other missions in the unforgiving aerial and fire environment of the northern Rockies. During flight, I'd listen as Scott managed the radio traffic, not seeing his face but only the helmet, decorated with a small label that read *Whiskey Bent, Hell Bound*. I studied him under pressure, as he made dozens of quick and critical decisions a day or sometimes an hour or even in a ten-minute span. I was awestruck. From whence the confidence to operate at that level, sometimes with the life and safety of others at stake? I was certain I could never do it. I didn't even want that intensity of leadership responsibility, and I was afraid it would be thrust upon me.

In the autumn of 1962, my sixth-grade teacher established a classroom council with a slate of elected officers, probably as a civics lesson. I was painfully shy then and hardly spoke to anyone besides my immediate circle of neighborhood pals. I was reticent in class and maintained—I thought—a low profile. I was therefore dumbfounded when I was nominated and decisively elected as class president. I had no clue why it happened. Though flattered, I was also embarrassed and scared. Outwardly, it was a trivial event, but it made a profound impression. I was awakened to the possibility of leadership and responsibility, realizing that individuals don't necessarily control the charges they are given—that some qualities might just be expected of you, whether you like it or not.

When I slipped under the thrall of Garner Ted Armstrong and the Worldwide Church of God, I had no thought of becoming a minister. I simply sought answers to questions of meaning and purpose, and ultimate ends. But when I arrived at Ambassador College it was assumed I would train for the pulpit—as did all male students. (Coeds were there to be groomed as our wives.) We were informed that not all were "called" to the ministry, and we spent the next four years trying to divine if God had tapped us for that role or not. By my senior year, the general assumption on campus was that I'd be chosen for ordination, and for a time I felt as if I were called. But then, on top of my doctrinal doubts, I became frightened. I did not want, and was convinced I could not handle, the responsibility of being a minister. I opted out and returned to "the world."

By 1981, Pam and I were settled into a self-built log home on forty acres of forest in northeastern Minnesota, working full-time jobs. I was a grunt at a municipal sewage plant, and after several years of newspaper reporting, Pam had a public relations business.

Our rural community of Side Lake had a volunteer fire department, and I'd driven past the modest, Quonset hut fire hall for years without giving it much thought. I did not seek the fireground. It sought me.

One afternoon a neighbor who was a fire department member invited us to join. We saw it as an opportunity for community service and that August evening signed up as volunteer firefighters. It was a laid-back, informal process of walking into the monthly meeting, shaking hands all around, and having our phone number penciled on the dispatch roster. I had no idea what I was getting into. When I responded to my first house fire a few months later, I was stunned by how dangerous and frightening it was. And how exciting.

Two years later our fire chief stepped down. He requested nominations and/or volunteers for the job. Everyone stared at the floor of the fire hall, and a long minute crawled by. It was the brand of embarrassing communal silence that seems to burden the air itself. I cracked. Surprising myself, I offered to be the new chief and was immediately and unanimously elected by acclamation. I had no idea what I was getting into.

A few weeks later I was in my doctor's office, complaining of a troubling nervous condition. I felt almost constantly on edge, with a butterfly sensation in my gut. He queried me closely about any stressful situations in my life—marital problems, job hassles, recent deaths, and so forth. No, I could think of nothing. He prescribed some beta-blockers, which I refused. Days later it finally struck me: it was the fire chief position. Two years on the department had demonstrated the seriousness of the responsibility, but a typical, male-macho presumption had delayed my acceptance of the fact that the leadership role was more of an ordeal than I imagined. An impulsive decision had plunged me in over my head, and beyond my desires. Nevertheless, I was expected to handle it.

One afternoon in April a few years later, I was playing volleyball with some friends at a public park. One of our acquaintances drove up in a cloud of dust and announced the local Department of Natural Resources Forestry station needed help with an outbreak of forest fires. It was voluntary but the class of request that makes you feel conscripted—guilty if you don't respond. I went. And never looked back—mutated into a wildfire junkie.

Four years after that I was firmly ensconced as a DNR wildland firefighter, and one June morning in 1991 our phone rang. It was Scott Hocking, calling from Grangeville, Idaho. He was a northern Minnesota native, and we'd worked some fires together. He was then a helicopter manager in the Nez Perce National Forest and was short a helitack crew member. Was I interested in coming out for the summer? But, I protested, I had no helitack qualifications or experience. No matter, he'd train me. I felt a ripple of anxiety. I hadn't aspired to helicopter operations, and though I'd been involved with fire for a decade, it scared me. But I also needed the work. I told Scott I'd think about it and call him back in three hours. After a spate of agonizing, I called him back in one. I'd be there.

I spent the summer surfing a steep learning curve, terrified of making a bad mistake and constantly impressed by Scott's skill and decisiveness. He insisted I was doing well, and he wanted to groom me as an initial attack helicopter manager. I replied I wasn't ready; I doubted I ever would be. He smiled at that, for though he was ten years younger, he'd taken on fire two years earlier—had already scouted the path to the front seat and leadership. He figured I'd come around.

Of course, in my somewhat reluctant role as fire chief I understood that sheer knowledge and experience were two of the keys because they led directly to confidence, self-respect, and the respect of others. But it was not enough. I knew several firefighters with a wealth of savvy and years on the fireground who actually avoided the leader's part, content to advise—or often criticize and complain—from the safety of the ranks.

The third key was what Father Peter Pernin so dramatically displayed on the banks of the Peshtigo River. Faced with a line of shocked people simply standing and waiting for God to kill them, the priest—who could've been expected to also believe it was Judgment Day and therefore futile to resist the Wrath of God—acted. He began pushing them into the water, immersing them in a kind of baptism. He embraced responsibility. He accepted the duty of decision. He may have reasoned: if it was indeed Judgment Day, then God's ultimate purpose couldn't be thwarted in any case, so try for survival. But I doubt that crossed his mind. He'd long before understood that taking responsibility for himself and for others was his mission as a priest. Though God was his ostensible guide, it was he who must act—and reap the consequences for good or ill.

And thus it was for me on the compromised road at Boulder Creek. When I said no—calmly, professionally, this time—and accepted the responsibility, I fulfilled my role as a fireground leader. I was in the ministry, after all. And I was aware that others now looked at the back of my flight helmet.

The water tender arrived to refill the engine, and we clambered up the embankment to engage the flames with nozzles and our hand tools. For the next three hours we slogged from spot to spot, digging, spraying, sweating like pigs. The line around our original fire was tied in to the road, and that became a sideshow. Both bulldozers advanced upslope. The second twenty-person crew fell in behind them. Alpha-Hotel-Romeo continued to drop water at the top, and a single-engine air tanker arrived to dump 500-gallon loads of retardant. A smaller helicopter—a Bell 206 LongRanger—appeared overhead to perform aerial recon. The wind died. That was the final blow to the fire. We caught it at twenty-five acres.

As the sun began to decline, Mike ran short of legal flight time. He had just enough left to ferry us back to Boorman Station.

"I'll fuel up at Goat Creek," he said, "then meet you at the original helispot."

"Copy that, Mike."

I sought out Ron. We shook hands. "Thanks for your help," he said. "This would've gotten a lot bigger without you guys." Good, no hard feelings.

We trudged down the east dozer line toward our landing zone, bushwhacking through clinging brush and crisscrossed deadfalls for the last hundred yards. My right ankle hurt like hell, inflamed with arthritis from an old fracture. My head throbbed—probably dehydration and carbon monoxide poisoning. I blew black snot into a glove. The fun was over. Ray looked older than forty-seven, Dallas was walking a little slow, and Jeff seemed pale beneath smears of soot.

I reluctantly chopped down the small fir that had been near our tail rotor when we landed, then we lay in the dirt and sucked up all remaining food and water. There wasn't much. When Mike arrived, the strong, cool wash off the rotor blades was a tonic. We flew across Flathead Lake with sunset in our eyes. We reached Boorman Station at last light, descending from luminous pink clouds into the pine-shadowed gloaming of the helispot. As the rotor blades cycled to a stop, I realized I'd already forgotten the heat. Again.

That evening, Jeff lay in bed with a vomit bucket on the floor beside him. The rest of us, with more leathery lungs and perhaps less wisdom, drank a six-pack of Moose Drool on the veranda of the Hilltop Motel. I considered it a sacrament.

NINE

A GREAT MIRACLE

On the morning of October 9, 1871, the Peshtigo River was glossed with rafts of dead fish. Whether they died there or floated in from upstream is uncertain. Perhaps they cooked in small tributaries before drifting off toward Lake Michigan. Normally fish would have little to fear from a forest fire. At Yellowstone National Park in 1988, postfire erosion of steep slopes deposited silt into trout streams. Higher sediment levels can cause a decline in aquatic insects and a rise in water temperature, both of which can negatively affect fish populations. But even during the wild, benchmark blazes of 1988, there were no reports of fish directly killed by fire. It's a strange notion, like flying birds felled by an earthquake.

Father Peter Pernin didn't see the dead fish that morning. By the time his clothes dried, his vision was gone. A stranger took his hand and led him to a spot on the bank below the dam, "a little valley" adjacent to a shallow stretch of the river. Pernin realized it was the shoreline he'd tried to reach the night before, after crossing the burning bridge. He discovered that those citizens who'd taken shelter there before being cut off by the fire had indeed fared better than he and his companions in the river. Flames leaped over the low spot, and shrubs, grass, and other vegetation in the valley hadn't ignited. It was a small oasis in the midst of black death. Those who'd weathered the fire there were mostly unhurt.

The wounded began to congregate, drawn by the patch of unburned ground. One was an elderly woman who'd taken refuge in the river, but only partially. She'd been torn between fear of the fire and dread of the water and passed the night huddled on the shore, half in, half out. She'd suffered fearsome burns, the severity of which Pernin could judge only from her "heart-rending moans and cries." She asked for the priest and he was guided to her side, but Pernin found it difficult to master his own injuries. Unable to see, barely able to speak, and so "exhausted and depressed" that his energetic courage in the river now seemed alien, he admitted he was at that moment a "poor consoler." A short time later the woman was dead.

Some of the strongest survivors mounted scouting missions and soon reported the town and its environs had been completely destroyed—approximately 2000 structures—and the only building still standing was a house under construction. The green, relatively moist lumber of the frame was burned on the side away from the fire, while the wall facing the fire was untouched. This is common in fast-moving blazes. The wind "shadow" on the opposite side of a structure or tree allows the sheltered fire to take hold. Human and animal corpses littered the town, most burned beyond recognition. But Pernin also heard that Mrs. Tyler and her family, who'd heeded his advice to flee for the river, had all survived, though six of their eight party guests had perished. The old Canadian well digger had also lived, though the church he and Pernin hoped to protect with water from the new well was gone.

At about 8:00 A.M., workmen from the company set up a large tent intended for women, children, and the injured. The priest was urged to enter, and he lay down in a corner, pushing against the canvas wall so as to take up as little room as possible. However, the company representative who was running the operation, a man Pernin didn't know, was outraged to see him in the tent. The priest later wrote that the man "was one of those coarse and brutal natures that seem inaccessible to every kindly feeling, though he manifested a remarkable interest in the welfare of the ladies, and would allow none but them under his tent." The company rep loudly cursed Pernin and ordered him out. Silently, without rising, the priest slipped under the edge of the canvas and rolled outside. One of the women protested, but to no avail.

I was reminded of a disaster I responded to in April 1998. A fearsome tornado struck southern Minnesota. The base of the funnel cloud was 1300 to 2200 yards wide and stayed on the ground for an incredible eighty miles. The havoc wreaked seemed like the vengeance of a spiteful god or the routine handiwork of a modern air force. The town of St. Peter, with its environs, was devastated. It was reminiscent of photographs of war-ravaged Berlin in 1945.

My assignment was to visit homesteads and farmsteads in the surrounding countryside, assess damage, and coordinate emergency assistance. Besides the mind-boggling destruction (a two-by-six piece of lumber driven through the engine block of an automobile, a mile of power poles snapped off and deposited on the other side of the highway), what astonished me most were the reactions of survivors.

I drove into a farm owned by a man of modest means named Ken. Most of his buildings and possessions were scattered over forty acres. His old house was a shambles. When I arrived, his wife and daughter were helping him hand-pile literally tons of debris. I told him I could have a crew, a loader, and a dump truck there next morning.

"Well," he replied, "I don't know. I'm sure there are other people who need it worse than I do."

I stared at him. I swept out an arm to encompass the ruin of all his worldly goods.

"Not many, Ken," I said. "Trust me, buddy, not many."

It took me almost five full minutes to convince him to accept free and willing help.

Then I met someone closer in postcatastrophe mind-set to Peshtigo's tent master.

Bill was a retired farmer whose obviously upscale home had suffered no damage. However, a large pole barn had collapsed on top of a wealth of high-priced tools and toys, including farm machinery, a camper, a boat and trailer, snowmobiles, and other items. Most appeared only slightly damaged or not at all. Bill's manner was gruff and demanding, and he clearly didn't esteem me in my government uniform and government truck.

As I was inspecting the site, a private contractor drove up to survey the damage. A few minutes later Bill, the contractor, and I held a conference. I told Bill I could possibly have a twenty-ton crane there in one or two days, but there was no guarantee—such machines are not plentiful. The contractor told him he could have a crane there that afternoon, but of course his wouldn't be free.

"You should go for it, Bill," I said. My thought was that not only did he seem well-to-do, but insurance would undoubtedly cover the cost, which wasn't tremendous anyway. And I could use the precious crane elsewhere.

But even in the wake of disaster, Bill lusted for the freebie.

"No," he said firmly to the contractor. "I'll wait."

I shrugged and said I'd see what I could do.

Next afternoon I returned to Bill's place leading a twenty-ton crane. I figured it was as close to being a hero as I'd ever get. I should've known better, but I expected, if not a rose-strewn path, at least a warm expression of gratitude.

Without smiling, Bill said to me, "Well, you've been cooperative."

Cooperative? Cooperative! I wanted to shout, I just brought you a twenty-ton stinking crane!

But I wished him well, bit my tongue, and drove away to the next pile of wreckage.

The first desire of many Peshtigo survivors was for a simple cup of hot tea or coffee, but few provisions of any kind remained in the ruins. At about 10:00 A.M. a handful of young men returned to the neighborhood of the tent with a few scorched cabbages they'd found in a nearby field. The blackened outer leaves were peeled off and meager slices doled out to those who could eat. It was small comfort, but there was nothing else.

That morning the city of Chicago, with a population of 300,000, was still burning. The flames wouldn't subside for another twenty-four hours, until the headfire, which ran northeast for four miles, exhausted its fuel. Blocks of buildings had been purposely blown up in a vain attempt to create a defensible break, but the fire spotted a half mile or more ahead, and control was impossible. The fire department was quickly overwhelmed by a conflagration that threatened their lives and steam engines before they had time to stage. When the City Gas-Works exploded, many thought there'd been an earthquake. Lake Michigan served the same purpose as the Peshtigo River, with hundreds of citizens plunging into the numbing water up to their necks or burrowing into sand along the shore. The attention of the state, nation, and the world was immediately focused on the city, and no one knew of Peshtigo. Official word would not reach the state capital at Madison until the morning of the tenth.

Meanwhile, news of Peshtigo and the Sugar Bush did reach Marinette, about ten miles northeast, and several wagons were dispatched, loaded with coffee, tea, and bread. They arrived at about 1:00 P.M., and the supplies were quickly consumed. The drivers offered to haul as many people as they could back to Marinette, and Father Pernin climbed aboard one of the wagons.

Marinette had partially burned, but, forewarned of Peshtigo's fate, most inhabitants fled to the shore of Green Bay a few miles away, taking refuge on three steamships, including the *Dunlap*. Some merchants buried as much of their goods as possible before heading to the lake. One man dropped dead on the wharf—perhaps from a heart attack—but otherwise there were no casualties.

Isaac Stephenson, a wealthy lumberman, dispatched a messenger to the town of Green Bay, about fifty miles southwest. It was just outside the fireground and the nearest locale with intact telegraph lines. The messenger sent a report to Wisconsin Governor Lucius Fairchild, who had already departed for Chicago accompanied by most capital officials. A clerk delivered the telegram to Frances Fairchild, the twenty-three-year-old wife of the governor, and the young woman unilaterally sprang into action, effectively acting as the governor in a time when females were not expected to fill such a niche. She diverted a boxcar of food and clothing intended for Chicago, commanding railroad officers to consider it priority traffic and route it to Peshtigo and the Sugar Bush. She mobilized the women of Madison to collect blankets, which were stuffed into the car before it left. Issuing a public appeal, Mrs. Fairchild quickly raised enough additional bedding, clothing, and other supplies to fill a second boxcar that left Madison on the night of the tenth.

The church and presbytery at Marinette had burned, and Father Pernin was taken in by the Garon family, local parishioners. He was immediately put into bed, and by Tuesday evening a measure of both his eyesight and his energy had returned. He visited several of the injured and dying but lamented that he had none of his priestly tools for "the sad occasion." He decided to return to Peshtigo that night. The clothes he'd worn in the river were tattered, and, with most of the local merchandise still buried, he ended up in workmen's overalls.

At about 10:00 P.M. on October 10, he boarded a steamboat bound for Green Bay, with a stop at Peshtigo Harbor. A storm ravaged Lake Michigan, and no landfall was attempted until daybreak. But more welcome rain fell on the area. In the wake of the cold front passage it had rained the day before, significantly cooling what heat remained.

In early afternoon Pernin joined a party of gravediggers headed for the town site—in a rail car towed by horses. The company's locomotives had been destroyed. A mile and a half from town they halted to walk the rest of the way. Heat had twisted the rails into pretzels, and the cross ties were ashes.

The town was a black desert. Aside from the partially built house, there were a scattering of charred fence posts, the boilers of the locomotives, iron wagon wheels, and the masonry portions of the factory. So little remained that Pernin had difficulty determining where the streets had been that led to his house and church. Such complete combustion over such a wide area is unusual. It's more typical for large chunks and masses of fuel to be left behind in a charred or singed state. Since wood is a poor conductor of heat, the pyrolysis reaction (the chemical decomposition of organic compounds in high temperatures) or outgassing proceeds relatively slowly, and unless high heat is maintained, the reaction dies out and stops. That's why you need kindling in a campfire or woodstove and can't ignite logs with a single match. In a "normal" wildland fire, the flame front hits, passes quickly, and much partially burned material remains. The firestorm at Peshtigo behaved more like a blast furnace.

Once on the church site, Pernin found the shovel he'd cast aside on Sunday evening. The handle was partially burned, but he used it to uncover the items he'd buried in the garden. The foot or so of soil was easily removed, and he was delighted to see that his linen vestments—still white—seemed to be in perfect condition. But as he lifted them out of the hole, the cloth disintegrated in his hands. That heat had damaged fabric a foot underground is incredible. Firefighters, of course, are taught to stay low in hot environments, and even inches can have effect. During fire shelter training students are urged to deploy while lying down, since they might avoid burns they could suffer simply by standing up. On the road above the Boulder Creek fire, the difference between standing and crouching was the difference between painful gasping and breathing free. Several years ago I entered a gutted house after we'd knocked down a structure fire. I saw a television set had melted into a plastic glob atop a dresser. I opened the drawer immediately beneath and found a box of crayons in pristine condition. The priest was justified in expecting his vestments to survive below ground. The fact they didn't testifies to the almost thermonuclear intensity of the firestorm.

The only vestiges of his house were a few crumbly bricks, some fused crystal, charred crucifixes, and the burned remains of his dog. Near the ashes of the church, the steeple bell he'd heard wildly ringing as he struggled to the river lay half melted, flared over the sand in gleaming rivulets. It was fifty feet from where it had hung.

He retraced the route he'd taken to the river the night of the fire, and among dozens of carcasses, he spied the remnants of his horse. Deeply moved, he paused over the corpse, recalling how the terrified animal had nuzzled his shoulder, shaking with fear. "There exists between the horse and his master," he wrote, "a species of friendship akin to that which unites two [human] friends. . . ."

As he roamed across the fireground he encountered several ragged, dirty men, most of them suffering to one degree or another from burns, each appearing as "a ruin among ruins." They were searching for the dead—siblings, children, parents, wives. There were no women in these grim patrols; they'd apparently been forbidden to search the killing fields of Peshtigo and its environs. One man was looking for his children but had found no sign.

"If at least," he said to Pernin, "I could find their bones, but the wind has swept away whatever the fire spared."

Some survivors were still stunned, while others wished to talk, and the priest lent a sympathetic ear to the stories. In the heap of the company boardinghouse over seventy bodies had been discovered, burned to the extent that age and gender were impossible to determine. Flames from that building had prevented Pernin from reaching the relative safety of the "little valley." Twenty dead had been pulled from a well where they'd taken cover—probably asphyxiated. A man named Towsley, who lived in the Lower Sugar Bush and who'd been helping with work on the church, was found clutching a knife, his throat slashed. He'd apparently cut the throats of his two children first. The burned body of his wife was lying nearby. It was not the only instance of suicide in face of the fire. On the road to Oconto, where many people had fled directly into the wind and the advancing conflagration, all that survived were calcined bones and the iron rims of the wagon wheels. It was difficult to distinguish the remains of horses and humans. All were temporarily interred by the side of the road.

While listening to this evil news, Pernin heard angry shouting and followed it to a lynch mob. A miserable wretch had been caught pilfering valuables from the dead. An impromptu kangaroo court had condemned him to death. But his outraged neighbors could find no rope—all had been consumed. Someone dragged up a length of logging chain, and it was slung around the thief's neck. Curiously, Pernin did not intervene, noting dryly, "Execution was difficult under the circumstances. . . ." Amid all the suffering and destruction the scene may've been just too surreal to believe. The criminal howled for mercy, and eventually the "judges" forced him to beg forgiveness from his knees then released him. The priest concluded that the mob "merely intended frightening him."

Shortly thereafter Father Pernin returned to his former church and the nearby graveyard. A funeral was scheduled for a young man who'd died of his burn injuries the night before. Presiding at the sad service in his rough overalls, with none of his priestly accouterments, Pernin could offer nothing but "prayer and a heartfelt benediction." Perhaps that's all that was required, but he did feel keenly destitute when last rites were requested for two or three of the dying and he was unable to administer the sacrament of Extreme Unction ("last anointing") because he had no holy oil. The "poverty-stricken" burial depressed him, and when it was over he headed back to the river.

The charred supports of the bridge still stood, and a rickety treadway had been cobbled together to allow passage for those willing to risk it. The priest had just crossed to the east side when one of his parishioners ran up.

"Father! Do you know what has happened to your tabernacle?"

"No, what is it?" He seems to have assumed it was lost, or he likely would've sought it out earlier. He'd only been able to shove the buggy partially into the water and was all too painfully aware of the horrendous conditions at the water's edge at the peak of the fire.

"Come quickly then and see. Oh, Father! It's a great miracle!"

He followed the man upstream to the spot. The buggy had blown over and burned to the waterline, but the tabernacle, "intact in its showy whiteness," had apparently been thrown out, landing on top of a floating log. There it still perched, two and a half days later, surrounded by blackened logs and other burned debris. When he opened it the next week he found the Host preserved and no evidence of water or heat damage, even to the silk tissue lining the interior. But for two more days, until the afternoon of Friday the thirteenth, he left the tabernacle on the log "to give all an opportunity of seeing it." He noted that many grief-stricken survivors paid no attention, but most Catholics considered the preservation of the tabernacle a miracle. The priest himself viewed it as further evidence that the holocaust was the work of God—a clear demonstration of his power to punish or bless.

He spent the next two days helping to search for bodies. Strangely, some corpses bore no burns or scars and their clothing was intact, but in their pockets were coins, watches, and other metal objects that melted. One survivor wrote in a letter, "Chickens sitting in their perches were suffocated, not burned, and fish were on top of the water from the intense heat. Father said he found a young lady beside a log—she wasn't even burned at all and had such a nice head of curly hair that he couldn't resist cutting a lock off." The man carried it in his wallet the rest of his life, frequently showing it to his children.

During this time Pernin camped in the tent that had been forbidden to him the first day. Despite an influx of some supplies, there wasn't much to go around, and those in the tent were curled up on the sand and covered with a single blanket. The priest slept little. They finally heard about Chicago in a newspaper brought by a doctor from Fond du Lac and understood why aid to them was slow.

Pernin wrote bitterly about the diversion of public attention "from the far more appalling calamities of which we had been the hapless victims."

He was being worn down by the macabre duties, and his energy was again flagging. A physician from Green Bay who arrived to treat the survivors predicted that because of the various traumas, *all* would die within ten years. It wasn't true, though the priest noted many were dying, "dropping off day by day," and suspected he might eventually be one of them. When the dam was opened, lowering the river level upstream to aid in recovery of people who'd drowned the night of the fire, the shallower water allowed him to find the chalice and paten that had been in his buggy with the tabernacle. He was overjoyed, but his mood quickly darkened again. By the afternoon of the October 13 he felt at the end of his tether, and, satisfied there were no more bodies to be found, he hitched a ride on a wagon to Oconto, where he spent two days resting in the house of a fellow priest. Eight days after the fire he traveled to Green Bay to meet with his superior, Bishop Joseph Melcher. There he learned he'd been given up for dead. The bishop had been informed that Pernin had either burned inside the Peshtigo church, died in his house, or succumbed in the river. Various sources had delivered all accounts with certainty.

"Oh! At last!" cried the bishop. "I've been so troubled about you." Then, more sternly, "Why did you not write?"

I would've loved to have seen the expression on Father Pernin's face. After barely escaping with his life, losing all he owned, then spending a brutal week tending to the dying and burying the dead, while sleeping in the dirt, he may've been forgiven at least a cocked eyebrow.

But the priest recorded only his verbal reply: "My Lord, I could not. I had neither pen, ink, nor paper. Nothing but river water."

On August 26, 2000, the day after our stand on the road at Boulder Creek, we were dispatched to two small fires that were quickly subdued. The following day Derek returned and Mike flew home to Ontario for twelve days off. Next afternoon we were sent to the Cyclone Ridge fire, just across the North Fork of the Flathead River from Glacier National Park. It started three days before and was well staffed; all they needed was the helicopter to deliver water drops from nearby Cyclone Lake. We landed at Moran Meadows down on the river flats about four miles from the fire and hooked up the bucket. Derek lifted off for the fire, and we waited for our trucks. Over the course of the afternoon, as Derek dropped almost a hundred loads on the fire, the rest of us "did time," napping, reading, and admiring the snowcapped peaks in British Columbia, only twenty miles north.

At the end of the shift we flew back to Boorman Station, cresting the Whitefish Range near the Werner Peak lookout tower. After a warm day, there was a hint of early autumn in the air, especially at 7000 feet, and Derek tried to close the sliding window in his door. But it was jammed, and he needed both hands. He looked at me with a grin in his eyes and nodded at the sticks I'd been squirming over and around for three months.

"You got it," he said—the standard command for transfer of control between a pilot and a copilot.

I hesitated a second, then carefully reached for the curved cyclic stick with my right hand, caressing it into my grasp. I knew better than to grab for it; the hydraulics made the stick sensitive to subtle inputs. We were in stable, level flight, and all I had to do was hold the "joy stick" steady.

"I got it," I said.

I tightened my fingers a little and didn't budge. Derek swiveled in his seat to jimmy the window closed. The nose of the ship began to rise. I was amazed. I would've sworn my hand and arm were solid, but obviously the stick was pulled back, because the nose continued to rise. It renewed my respect for Derek and Mike, especially for the times they were bucketing or performing longline work in variable winds, and from my view on the ground the ship was a rock.

"I got it," said Derek, and I felt the stick stabilize as he embraced the cyclic in front of him.

"Hey! You didn't let me finish my loop," I protested.

"Ah . . . Derek," piped up Doug from the backseat, "from now on we'll need to know when Leschak's going to fly, so we can be in the trucks."

August 28 was a quiet day, and we offered to construct a helipad at Boorman Station. I made the suggestion half out of courtesy and good-neighborliness and was surprised how swiftly the locals jumped on it. In a few hours the required tools and materials—form lumber, rebar, nails, a bull float—were delivered from Kalispell, along with a dump truck load of class-5, and we threw ourselves into the project. By day's end it was ready for concrete, and we ordered a batch for the next morning—early, so we'd be unlikely to be interrupted by a dispatch. But soon after the plans were laid, we were reassigned and left Boorman.

The Chipmunk Peak fire was about forty miles southeast of Kalispell, above the South Fork of the Flathead River in the Spotted Bear Ranger District near the boundary of the Bob Marshall Wilderness. We skirted Jewel Basin on our inbound flight, clearing the 7000-foot spine of the Swan Range near Tom-Tom Mountain. We landed at the Spotted Bear Airstrip, a grass runway hemmed in by steep, forested slopes and, like many such backcountry strips in the Rockies, consecrated by a scattering of nearby crash sites.

The fire was just over 3000 acres, staffed by two people. Since no human development was immediately threatened, it was awarded low priority, and local Forest Service officials told us later the blaze had been largely beneficial. But if the drought continued, there was potential for the Chipmunk to burgeon into another major, expensive incident, and it was decided suppression resources would be assigned as they became available from other fires.

That first day it was only us, augmented by three local firefighters. Derek flew us to a helispot at the summit of a ridge where the main fire had "slopped over," and while he made bucket drops, we worked hot spots with our hand tools. We labored methodically but without urgency. It was almost a picnic atmosphere; no one expected us to tame a 3000-acre fire.

Over the next two days reinforcements arrived—another helicopter, three twenty-person crews from Alaska, two Hot-Shot crews, and an overhead team that included firefighters from Manitoba and Australia. With over one hundred people on the fire, our helitack role mutated into support rather than direct suppression—organizing and managing troop and cargo shuttles up to the high helispots along the ridges.

One morning, however, the ceiling was on the deck, a damp shroud of mist wrapped around the Swan Range. The visibility was too poor to fly, but a cooler temperature and higher relative humidity rendered it an excellent day to beat up the fire. The hand crews were bused to the bottom of the Chipmunk along Bunker Creek, and I volunteered our helitack crew to hike up the ridge and resume our work on the smoldering spot fires. It was a three-mile uphill march from the end of the nearest logging road, but the weather forecast promised a late-afternoon clearing, so we'd walk in, then fly out at the end of the shift. Derek planned to pick us up at a high knob designated Helispot-6 (H-6).

After a long, bumpy drive, we assembled at a trailhead above the Larch Creek drainage at around 9:30 A.M. Besides Doug, Ray, Dallas, and Dave, our team consisted of Ted, a local firefighter who'd be our guide; Grant, one of the Manitobans who was acting as the division supervisor; and Cathy, a park service firefighter from Glacier who was a division supervisor trainee. It was a gray, mizzly morning, the brush wet with heavy dew. The temperature was in the 40s.

Ted estimated a two-hour ascent to the fireground, on a narrow, rocky trail through dense forest. I slipped a poncho over my head, hoping to avoid a soaking by the dripping foliage. On such a hike it was my practice to take the first turn packing the chain saw—an extra twenty pounds—and I slung it over my left shoulder. Our mood was upbeat—"paid backpacking," I reminded the crew.

Ted took the lead, and I fell in behind, measuring my first steps, matching breath with boot prints for the long haul. In college, I ran four marathons, and if I'd learned anything (besides pain management) it was the importance of pace. Effectively covering distance on foot is all about rhythm, and while three miles wasn't terribly far, it was all uphill, we were carrying twenty-five to forty pounds, and we'd be expected to work hard when we arrived. No doubt we'd be grateful to see AHR at the end of the day.

The air was still, the forest quiet—muffled by the quilt of mist. Ranks of lodgepole pine, as straight as their name, faded off to either side in the pleasing murk. I tuned into the familiar melody of a crew on the move—the soft squeaks of straps and buckles, the regular tread of Vibram soles on hard ground, the respiration of my colleagues. It's traveling music, like a bright bluegrass number on the radio as you motor down a rural highway.

Then Cathy started talking. Incessantly. It was, of course, a testament to her fitness and acclimation to elevation that she could expend so much breath on vocalizing and still have enough wind to sprightly traipse the ascending trail. At first Grant and Ted responded, but before long Cathy was mostly engaged in a rambling monologue. It wasn't necessarily boring—she spoke of Glacier, fire, and rescue missions—but as the mild pain of the march settled in, the unrestrained cheeriness of her prattle began to grate. Human speech can be a salve, but sometimes it's more congenial to listen to the straps, boots, and wise quiet of the woods. Still, it wasn't a major irritation, at least not then.

About forty-five minutes in, we took our first break—standing up, leaning on tools. I passed off the chain saw to Dallas. Grant pulled a candy bar from his pack. He announced he was diabetic but that he had little trouble managing it. I was surprised. Though it's possible, few diabetics take on the physical vagaries of the fireground, and it was valuable for us to know should Grant have trouble.

I peeled off the poncho. I'd soon be wet with sweat anyway, and the plastic was stifling. An intermittent light drizzle condensed out of the cloud we were hiking through, but I left the poncho in my pack. We rested five minutes, listening to Cathy, then resumed the climb. Soon we were angling along the backbone of a ridge, just below the crest. To the right, a few descending treetops poked through fog. It was a steep slope and no doubt opened on a spectacular vista down the Larch Creek drainage, but several yards off the air was opaque. I was reminded of our forced landing at Clara Lake a month before. Once again we were betting a low ceiling would lift.

At our next break we took ten minutes, and I sat down to eat an orange. We waited for Ray to catch up. A year before, when we were doing initial attack out of Dillon, Montana, I'd given Doug, Ray, and Dallas excellent performance reviews, except for physical fitness. They were adequate. I chided them for not being in superior condition. All were tougher than the average dude on the street but not sufficiently buffed for sustained combat at high elevation. All summer at Grand Marais we enjoyed an hour per day of paid work-outs, and the improvement was evident. But Ray was forty-seven and still sucking on cigarettes. Doug hung back with him so nobody hiked alone. The wet rocks were slick, and it would be easy to slip and tumble into that foggy pit.

We carried a detailed topographic map of the area, a computer-generated chart designed specifically for the Chipmunk operation and updated daily. Ever since our arrival there'd been a small circle labeled "Spot Fire on Ridge," a quarter mile outside the northeast perimeter of the fire. Derek dropped water on it the first day, and it appeared cold from the air, but one of our missions was to check it. As we approached the Chipmunk the path began to level off, and we kept an eye open for the spot. It was easy to find. A half acre of black coincided with the circle on the map, and we halted to thoroughly cold-trail it. We found no heat. That would be a relief to the over-head team, and they could delete it from the chart.

Ted's estimate of two hours to the summit was accurate. We reached the crest at about 11:30 A.M. and zigzagged downslope to the first smoke—a patch of smoldering duff near the base of a fat spruce. We were damp, chilled, and hungry. Ted and Dallas stirred the glowing duff into open flame while the rest of us collected a stash of sticks and limbs to build a welcome campfire. I felt more like a castaway than a firefighter as we huddled around the blaze and sliced open our MREs. I shivered as I spooned chicken out of foil bag, half expecting snow flurries any minute.

As we ate and warmed, Grant outlined our shift plan. We'd spread out and grid along the fire edge for spots, working our way west toward H-6, extinguishing as much heat as we could. Other than our lunch fire, we'd probably not find open flame and perhaps not much smoke either. We'd hunt with our noses and bare hands, sniffing the sky and running fingers through white ash.

Just after noon, we snuffed out the campfire and formed into a line extending downslope, five to ten yards apart. For the next four hours we contoured across the hill, ferreting out the embers. Some spots were quickly grubbed out, a few sparks crushed in a glove. Many others were several feet across—in hot duff or deeply seated in stump holes or hiding beneath deadfalls. We dug and scraped and, with the saw, bucked logs that were too big to roll over. It was a typical mop-up operation—slow and grueling. The dampness of the air was an ally, but as the afternoon wore on I began to suspect the overcast wasn't going to break. By 2:00 P.M. a light upslope breeze was stirring treetops and the fog had thinned. I grew hopeful. A shaft of sunlight briefly lanced through the cloud deck. For several minutes the high knob of H-6 was visible less than half a mile away but was soon engulfed again. A clabber of cloud spilled over it in a gray wave.

I radioed Jeff at the airstrip for a weather update. They were still socked in. It didn't look good for our prospect of a helicopter ride, but I optimistically reminded myself that sky conditions can change rapidly in the mountains. They didn't. By 4:30 we needed to decide. Did we hang out on the heights, gambling on the forecast, or did we take the murk at face value and begin the long hump down to the road?

We reassembled near the site of the lunch fire, and Grant raised the operations chief on the command repeater. Was it still supposed to clear? Affirmative. I tried Jeff again. The helibase was mired beneath a low ceiling. None of us was interested in spending the night or retracing our steps by the light of headlamps, so we opted to cancel the helicopter pickup. We fueled up on what snacks we had left and headed upslope to find the trail. Cathy, sprightly as ever, was still talking.

Back in 1972, my right ankle was severely damaged in an industrial accident. The end of the tibia was broken off, and a surgeon repaired it with a two-inch stainless steel screw. He warned me that the abused joint would likely be afflicted with arthritis in fifteen years or so. By 1989, the pain was impressive, and my doctor injected the ankle with cortisone. It was a miracle—for about a year. The pain gradually returned, and I initiated a regimen of exercises that kept the ankle just reliable enough. What I noticed over the years was that it rarely, if ever, hurt on an uphill trek. But after a long day, it almost always stabbed me on a downhill jaunt. I popped a couple aspirin and braced for the pain.

By the time we reached the trail at the crest of the ridge, I could see Ray was having a rough time. He looked pale and spent. Cathy bounced by us as we took a breather and, perhaps sensing a sudden void of silence, asked brightly of no one in particular, "Am I talking too much?"

No one replied, but from the expression on Ray's face, I suspect he might've done something regrettable with his pulaski if he'd had the pep.

At the last moment the sky lightened and another ray of sunlight pierced the roof of cloud, but we couldn't see H-6. Ted shrugged and started down the trail, and we strung out behind. Doug and I exchanged a look that told me he'd stick with Ray. Dave and Dallas were tired but good to go. My energy reserve was fine, but after a dozen steps down, a sharp, grinding jab reacquainted me with the treachery of my arthritic ankle. Besides the actual hurt, it also disrupted my cadence for the three miles ahead. From past episodes I understood the severity of the pain would soon force me into an undignified limp.

Twenty minutes brought us to the half acre of black where we'd cold-trailed on the way up. We paused. Without the morning fog we could see the valley of the South Fork of the Flathead opening up far below, with a veiled view of the Bob Marshall Wilderness on the other side. Even the attenuated vista was fabulous, and I felt that magnification of vision so common in the high places—the godlike overseeing of distance, coupled with acute awareness of human scrubbiness: *seeing the Elephant.* It's an evocative expression that gained currency as white settlers spread west into the Rockies during the nineteenth century. It's origin is obscure, but usage most often implied a kind of awestruck failure. If a disheartened family on the Oregon Trail turned tail and steered back to Missouri, it was said they'd "seen too much of the Elephant."

I first saw the Elephant in southwest Colorado in 1972. Some months after my ankle healed, I went on a solo backpack trip in the San Juan Mountains, intending to travel for five days. I hitchhiked to a trailhead outside Silverton and began walking in early afternoon. That evening I camped in a high meadow and next morning set off just after sunrise. I hiked less than a mile and stopped dead in my tracks. The trail twisted off into the distance, vanishing over the rim of a jagged saddle. The sky was an immense violet-blue dome notched by snowcapped peaks—an abyss above. A few feet from the toes of my boots the ground fell steeply into a forested valley. I was suddenly frightened by the thought of proceeding, convinced the mountains would swallow me. I felt not only small but silenced. If I shouted or sang the sounds would be absorbed into the ether and smothered. I'd spent time alone in the wild but never felt so solitary. The Elephant was just beyond that saddle. I turned around, hiked directly to the trailhead, and stuck out my thumb for the next jeep. By noon I was checked into a Silverton hotel.

I was not alone in the Flathead country, but I sensed the vulnerability, especially in the company of an old, aching ankle. What am I doing here? I thought. What hubris brought me boldly to this mountain, trusting in a pathetic paper weather forecast and my soft, mortal body? We'd marched up into the fog expecting to fly from

H-6 like golden eagles, above it all. We were like Father Pernin's neighbors, ignoring the autumn smoke and trusting our faith in human prowess and destiny. In reality, we were successfully extinguishing the Chipmunk Peak fire because cold mornings and drizzle had given us permission. In an academic way, at least, I was grateful for the pain to remind me of my place. There can be no arrogance in the shadow of the Elephant.

We resumed our hike, and I was reminded that when the arthritis was aroused it was better to keep moving. After our short break the pain was aggravated, and I sported a pronounced limp.

"You okay?" asked Ted.

"Oh, yeah, just getting old. I'll be fine."

A few minutes later I drew in a breath. A thinner, partially torn layer of cloud had drifted in from the southwest. A silken wash of sunlight, filtered by vapor, suffused the long valley 2000 feet below. The forest was a warm pastel green, dappled with velvet shadows. Below the cap of scudding cloud, which seemed to skim my head, almost close enough to touch, the air was yellow mist, every molecule emitting pale fire. For a few moments the radiance intensified, as if pure light were churning the atmosphere, and this opera for the eyes would explode into bright blue. Then abruptly it darkened. I could see the cloud rapidly sinking, the misty yellow shading to gray.

I released the breath. A surge of euphoria lightened my step, enhanced by the exertion of the hike, and I felt as I had while riding the highliner through the bog and catching a unique glimpse of Jupiter. There was a time I would've automatically praised God for such a gift and whispered a prayer of thanks—for beauty was the work of God, a prime manifestation of divine creativity. It was an innocent prayer, and I would've imbued the euphoria with sacredness and imagined myself closer to God. But like Father Pernin in the horrifying wake of the firestorm, I also had to acknowledge "the power of God in the calamity that then overwhelmed. . . ." Pernin believed good and evil ultimately emanated from the Deity, and since the universe encompassed both, the Creator must be responsible for both. You should not praise his sunsets then curse the hurricane; if you celebrate birth, then honor death; if pleasure warms you, then snuggle up to pain. After the tabernacle was discovered, Pernin contrasted that happy event with the suffering preceding it and remarked on "divine blessings or punishments." For him, the same hand that secured the tabernacle on a floating log had also slaughtered over 1200 of his neighbors—at the same time and place.

When I was a ministerial candidate, this so-called problem of evil was an important area of study. I understood that if I was to preach, comfort, and counsel, I needed a viable answer to a question like "Why did God let our little Jennifer die?" The answer I accepted was: God created both good and evil. The purpose of the latter was to be our teacher and examiner. For example, let's say the world was divinely regulated so that no one ever got hurt. Every time little Jennifer wandered from the sandbox toward the busy avenue, she was automatically halted by a guardian angel and guided back to the safety of the yard. Every time she reached out for a hot stove, her hand was redirected. If that were the case, then Jennifer was essentially a robot, not a human being. The freedom to be human demanded the freedom to suffer. We should accept pain as an indispensable nutrient for growth as a person and a child of God. The fire of suffering produced the fertility of joy. In early Jewish-Christian belief, Satan was considered Christ's older brother.

"But," someone might object, "I didn't *ask* to be born. I never volunteered for this trial. That seems unfair and evil in itself."

I'd agree, that yes, it seemed so. But since no one had complete control (did not initiate their own birth), neither could they be held completely responsible—or God was a sadistic monster. The only way that suffering, and even birth, could be justified was because the omnipotent God would ultimately right every wrong in the next life. If you were tortured and gassed at Treblinka, then God would eventually reconcile you to your torment and your tormentors and shower you with blessings and happiness. All scars, mental and physical, would be healed, and eternal life bestowed. If your children burned to death at Peshtigo, you'd eventually be reunited with them in a perfect world.

There was comfort in believing all that. And it's clear that Father Pernin derived solace from a similar faith. (Though as a Roman Catholic of that era he would also have believed that many sinful humans would burn forever in hell, and he'd glimpsed that firsthand.) But he also needed the tabernacle. He heartily welcomed its survival and readily accepted the fact as a sign from God, a signal that all the carnage and destruction had some purpose, however inscrutable. "These sacred objects [tabernacle, chalice, paten]" he wrote, "though possessing in reality little intrinsic value, are nevertheless priceless in my eyes. I prize them as most precious relics. . . . I use them with a species of religious triumph as trophies of God's exceeding mercy snatched so marvelously from destruction."

Otherwise, without divine purpose, what are we to think and feel? Some survivors of Peshtigo went mad. A postfire investigation conducted by a Colonel J. H. Leavenworth and published in 1873 maintained that "a year after the event many survivors remained partially or permanently demented as a result of their ordeal" (William C. Haygood, editor of the *Wisconsin Magazine of History*). That Pernin didn't sink into insanity was probably due not only to his religious faith, but also to the fact that he never considered himself a hapless victim. He was a player—a fighter and helper from beginning to end. He, not the God of his tabernacle, saved lives at Peshtigo.

Carl Jung wrote, "Suffering that is not understood is hard to bear, while on the other hand it is often astounding to see how much a person can endure when he understands the why and the wherefore. A philosophical or religious view of the world enables him to do this, and such views prove to be, at the very least, psychic methods of healing if not of salvation."

But on the ridge above Larch Creek, awed by the magnificent alpine light, I didn't whisper the prayer of praise. I was confronted again by the fact I'm no longer a believer. That robbed nothing from the view, but what of the pain? Not merely in my niggling ankle, but in the suffering and death of the fireground in general? I do not believe that the thirteen firefighters killed at Mann Gulch or the fourteen who expired at Storm King Mountain died for some divine purpose. In fact, some said their lives were wasted. But I don't believe that either. They were all engaged with the world, living intensely in their niche. For many, fire was a passion, and to live without passion—now that is a terrible, wasting death.

The fireground can be sacramental—in the sense of providing an outward sign of inner "grace," that is, the favor and blessings of moral strength. We are often better for having worked there. It's hostile country, quick to expose and exploit weakness. It punishes. It chastises firefighters whether they're good or bad—as it did at Peshtigo. In the ambience of fire, mere human corporeality is a sin. Almost every dispatch is an act of hubris, ignoring past warnings of pain and vulnerability. Fire can indeed be *Nemesis*, "daughter of night," eager to serve retribution upon the mortal arrogance of would-be warriors.

I flicker with restlessness when I'm too long absent from the mania of the fireground, the sacred ground. It's where happiness lives, where action removes all doubt—for better and for worse until death do us part. We most fully thrive in the arenas where we are most fully engaged. If I should vomit in the black, it will only leave me lighter. There is poetry in pain, and its verse is the seductive siren of risk. Since we were born, she ever draws us to her embrace. And if that risk should prove fatal, well, that too is inevitable.

I noted that when Christianity left me (I did not leave it) my behavior wasn't significantly changed. In that sense, God was superfluous. Will I survive and somehow transcend physical death? I don't know. In the hurly-burly of the present it hardly matters. Life rumbles on in any case. Whatever we believe, we do our best—or should. Father Pernin was saved by action, by "doing" life. Whether our trials and tests are presented by God or by an impersonal cosmos, they shape us nevertheless and possess value in themselves. Jung also wrote, "The most intense conflicts, if overcome, leave behind a sense of security and calm which is not easily disturbed, or else a brokenness that can hardly be healed. Conversely, it is just these intense conflicts and their conflagration which are needed in order to produce valuable and lasting results."

And those results have more to do with the struggle itself than with its resolution. In the psychological sense it was less important that we "lost" the Boulder Creek fire than the fact we were there. As Woody Allen quipped, "Eighty percent of life is just showing up." Day after day. Now when I confront the problem of evil, I have no religious dogma to justify or explain. God is not testing me with suffering, disappointment, or loss. Those maladies are endemic to life, and it's essentially pointless to ask why. In the midst of suffering you have two choices: either seek comfort and healing by whatever means you have available, or just give up. Healing requires action—of mind and body—and even when I professed to trust in God's mercy, I was mindful of the admonition of the apostle Paul: "Work out your own salvation with fear and trembling." It's hard as hell but still the straightest path.

And though I'm no longer a churchgoer, I'm still a member of a congregation. I didn't despair when I saw the Elephant above Larch Creek because I wasn't alone. I was part of a crew, and we fight and suffer together. It covers a multitude of sins. The foundation of life is experience, and that experience is enhanced by sharing it.

There's a pyrophilic insect, the Melanophilia beetle, that's equipped with powerful infrared sensors on its thorax and smoke detectors on its antennae—a true fire bug. The small black (what else?) beetles can detect a wildfire from miles away. They flock there to meet, mate, and lay eggs on scorched wood, sometimes so eagerly that they burn off their legs on smoldering fuel. The fireground is the locus of their rejuvenation, their link to the fundamentals of life. I belong to a community of fire bugs.

And after two decades in that community I possess the privilege and responsibility of leadership. I'm a secular priest ordained by training, experience, and, most important, the willingness to accept the mantle of command. That willingness encompasses the realization that failure is easy, and such failure could kill me or, worse, kill someone else. It's the nature of our society that I'm considered unworthy of huge financial reward for that risk. But what can be earned is a certain nobility—not in the sense of aristocratic status but in the sense of striving for quality and dignity of behavior and living. Better to be noble than rich; better to hurt than be arrogant; better to see the Elephant than be deluded by small victories; better to arrive at the Peshtigo River with a tabernacle than empty-handed.

An hour later the path leveled out as it neared the trailhead, and the pain in my ankle subsided. We gathered at the trucks and, when Ray and Doug arrived, drove back to the airstrip.

"You know," said Derek, "I could've safely snuck into H-6 to pick you up."

"That's okay," I replied. "It was an excellent path."

TEN

A SINGLE LOVELY ACTION

Over the next three days the weather and one hundred firefighters finished off the Chipmunk. One morning we watched the high ridges around Spotted Bear gradually turn white with snowfall. We shuttled two crews to the fire and Derek did some bucket work, but the sky turned ugly, and we advised the operations chief that the helicopters would shut down because of high wind and imminent rain. By late afternoon the sky partially cleared, and we were gathered around the helicopter, shooting the breeze and waiting for supper. Our shift was almost over.

Then Dave shouted, "Look at that!" and pointed up.

I looked. At first I could make no sense of what I was seeing; it was too far out of context. A strange object was floating into the airstrip from the direction of the fire camp across the road. It was about 100 feet up and just beginning to descend. The crew was hooting and hollering. It was a tent! But not somebody's backpack model. It was a kitchen tent from the camp—a twenty-five-by-eighteen-by-eight-foot canvas pavilion with a hefty aluminum tubing frame, and it probably weighed a couple hundred pounds. It had been staked down. And it was flying a quarter to a half mile from camp, perfectly shaped in the air as if it was still on the ground sheltering the salad bar. It settled quickly, just missing the other parked helicopter, then landed upright on the airstrip. A gust lifted it again, and the tent tipped sideways in slow motion and rolled onto its top. By then several of us were running across the field, and a truck from the camp was pulling in. Those guys had watched as a sudden cyclonic wind gust swelled the pavilion, ripping out its ropes and stakes, then spun it up and over a stand of fifty-foot pines. Three people had been knocked over, and one suffered a head injury requiring transport to a hospital. A wind like that is most often associated with a passing thunder cell.

We stormed the tent, yanking apart the sections of tubing to collapse the canvas before it could be wafted away again. The bizarre episode triggered a recollection for Derek.

"I saw a crashed airplane today," he said. "It's old and probably known, but . . . "

While he'd been doing bucket work, a glint of metal caught his eye. He banked and hovered over the wreck of a small aircraft, obviously old. Such a sight is not all that unusual near a mountain airstrip, and in the course of his fire mission Derek forgot it. I passed the information to the local Forest Service office, and their first reaction was that it was indeed a known site. But as they questioned Derek more closely about the location—far up the Larch Creek drainage—a couple of folks became excited and requested a flight to the scene. There'd been a missing Cessna a decade before that, despite an extensive search, had never been found. Apparently a doctor and his mistress took off from Spotted Bear and disappeared. It was a prominent regional news story at the time.

Next morning, September 9, we ran our final mission in Montana. We flew a Forest Service law enforcement officer with extensive knowledge of the local geography and a memory of the original search. Derek tracked a few miles east then turned up the drainage, slowly climbing toward the ridge. We weren't far from the trail we'd hiked.

"I remember the switchback in that road," said Derek. "We're close. It was on the east side of the creek."

He swung the nose east, and we ascended "sidestep," peering through the lodgepole canopy a hundred feet below. It was another gray morning, and the lighting was flat, no reflections.

"There was a small opening near that rock outcrop . . . we're very close . . . there it is!"

We were hovering over a white tail section crumpling forward into a nondescript heap of blackened, tangled metal. It appeared to have burned after violently smashing into the slope. Any fragments of human remains were invisible from our height. It was sobering to view a destroyed aircraft while sitting in a helicopter. The irony was that the bones of this plane were only a few hundred yards from a road. Now that we saw the wreck it was obvious, but it's rarely easy to find a small airplane in remote forest. Our Forest Service passenger snapped several photos, and I recorded the lat-long from the GPS.

We returned to Spotted Bear, and I drove to the ranger station to phone Boise regarding our demobilization plans. At first I was informed that AHR and crew were reassigned to Texas, but the order was canceled a few minutes later. We were released back to Minnesota. I heaved a sigh of relief. Though I delight in Texans and their easygoing hospitality, and lived in the state for four years, when it comes to wildfire there—oppressive heat, vicious fire ants—I agree with General Philip H. Sheridan, who said in 1858, "If I owned Texas and hell, I'd rent out Texas and live in hell."

That afternoon we flew to Kalispell, and Mike met us at the airport. He'd returned from his twelve days off in time for the long ferry back to Grand Marais. Derek caught a flight to British Columbia. Next morning our circus hit the road, heading east. The trucks left early, and we waited to fly, checking the weather. Once we traversed the mountains it appeared to be clear sailing. Mike decided we had enough ceiling to negotiate the Middle Fork of the Flathead and Marias Pass, and once we gained some altitude over the high plains, we might find a significant tailwind.

We followed U.S. Highway 2 over the pass, our windscreen peppered with drizzle and the slopes above sheathed with fresh snow. At East Glacier the overcast began to lift, and on the horizon we saw a band of blue sky. From that point the forecast promised fair weather all the way to Minnesota and beyond. Mike climbed to 7500 feet, and we picked up a 40- to 45-knot tailwind. The GPS clocked our ground speed at 160 knots. It would be a fast ride home.

Our first fuel stop was at Shelby, a small town on Interstate 15 southwest of the prominent East Butte. The airport looked deserted, but as soon as our engines died a man strode out of a hangar to pump Jet-A.

"Hey!" he called out. "You must be the helicopter that found the crashed plane."

It was barely twenty-four hours since we'd hovered over the wreck.

"It was on the news," he said.

We zipped across central Montana at 7000 to 9000 feet, Mike keeping us in the grip of the powerful westerly airflow. We landed at

Glendive in early afternoon, hoping to scam another round of cus-tom-grilled hamburgers. Instead we were jovially invited to a beau-tiful potluck buffet spread out on sawhorses in the hangar. It was part of a radio-controlled model airplane derby, and after heaping paper plates with home-cooked fried chicken, baked beans, and other delights, we passed an hour watching an impressive air show. An added attraction was two full-sized aircraft dropping bowling balls. They were trying to hit a 55-gallon drum set upright in a field—without success. One of our hosts informed us the "bombers" were practicing for a demonstration at an upcoming parade in Glendive. Mike shook his head in disbelief.

"The only safe spot at the parade," he said, "will be inside that drum."

We reluctantly left the air show and buffet and in late afternoon landed at Grand Rapids, Minnesota.

Next morning, I took the same walk to the Minnesota Interagency Fire Center that I'd taken three weeks before. I met with Sheldon, and we finalized an invoice for our services to Montana: $169,000. We arrived back at our base in Grand Marais around noon and quickly prepared for northern Minnesota initial attack, reprogramming our radios and tying in with the local dis-patchers. I'd decided that after three and a half months I was fried and needed to go home, and a replacement helicopter manager was there to transition into command. I spent the afternoon briefing him on the ship, the base, and the crew.

That night I went alone to the Gunflint Tavern for dinner. Over a tall glass of Belgian ale, I gazed out the window at Lake Superior and considered the rest of the season. I had six weeks of fire work ahead back home in Side Lake, then layoff and the clois-tering of the coming winter. I slipped into a contemplative reverie. One evening in Montana I'd scribbled some notes in my journal, comparing the experiences of Father Pernin with my own. I played a mind game I'm fond of: what were the "critical moments"? In the midst of the Great Peshtigo Fire, what was the defining event for the priest, the transcendent thought or action? In my view it was clear: when he pushed two people into the river. Perhaps he thought it *was* Judgment Day. Maybe the grim prophecies of the book of Revelation were indeed unfolding. But Pernin didn't hesitate. He leaped into service. He ministered to the flock. He was not content to passively submit to an "act of God." It isn't piety, dogma, or brilliant apologetics that denotes a worthy religious life. It's deeds. "Every man feels instinctively," wrote poet James Lowell, "that all the beautiful sentiments in the world weigh less than a single lovely action." On the banks of the Peshtigo River, on the verge of bursting into a human torch, Father Pernin was lovely and magnificent.

I recalled my fear at the beginning of the Assignment—the doubts about my abilities, the dread of making a bad mistake that jeopardized my crew. I had not achieved perfection and had a raven as witness. But in surveying the season and our own trials, one moment focused in front of all others: on the hot, lost road at Boulder Creek, bracketed by flames, the soot-stained flock gathered round; and the word I offered to my commander was no.

But I am not the equal of Father Peter Pernin. Perhaps I would've been fit to be his altar boy, his acolyte. I see us leaving the churchyard in the face of the conflagration. The maid has run off screaming, and the dog is trembling beneath the bed. Though almost sick with fear, I offer to pull the buggy. "No," he says, understanding his duty, "but grab hold and help." He doesn't need my assistance any more than he does at mass, but he knows that I also require a mission. We head for the river, knocked about by the hurricane and stumbling over the dead. My temples are pounding, my throat is seared. At one point I smell the breath of a horse. All I see clearly are the priest's hands on the tongue of the wagon.

The burning bridge is a nightmare of slow-motion jostling, thick with smoke and acrid terror. I gag and choke, dropping to my knees, then feel his grip on my collar as he jerks me upright. We're literally pushed off the span on the east bank. The heat is a merciless weight, like hot gravity pressing down from above. I hear a jumble of prayer in my brain, convinced I'm mumbling the Act of Contrition, but my mouth is merely open to frantically suck at poisoned air.

Pernin suddenly halts, and I fall to the heated sand.

"Up! Up!" he shouts, as he spins the buggy on its wheels and shoves it into the river.

I struggle to all fours and think, This is the end. I see Father Pernin push two men into the water, and it seems violent and strange. I crawl toward him as one sloshes out and the priest drags him back in.

He turns, and our eyes meet. He sees I cannot rise, tears streaming down my cheeks. He surges out and grabs my arms. His hair is smoking, an image to haunt my dreams for the rest of my life. He yanks me into the cold water.

It's more than I ever could have done.

The morning of September 12, 2000, was crisp and blue, the maples beginning to turn red and orange. I arrived early at the helibase to tidy up my final paperwork. Alpha-Hotel-Romeo had a transport mission back to Grand Rapids, and the new helicopter manager climbed into the left front seat. I stood in the grass in front of the ship as Mike spooled up. The rising sun laid a bright sheen on the fuselage. Goldenrod had sprouted on the fringe of our helipad, and the rotorwash pressed it flat like a yellow carpet. I scanned the sky for traffic, and just before he raised the collective, Mike caught my eye. I flashed him a last thumbs-up, keenly aware it was no longer my ship. He nodded a farewell, lifted off the pad, and spun to the west. I watched until Alpha-Hotel-Romeo disappeared, then walked to my car and drove away.

EPILOGUE

After the fire at Peshtigo, Father Peter Pernin was offered a change of venue by Bishop Melcher, who decided the priest had endured enough "suffering and hard toil," but Pernin declined, preferring—not surprisingly—to help rebuild the parishes in the Peshtigo-Marinette region. The bishop, Pernin reported, thought "my brain was severely injured by the firey ordeal through which I had passed." Feeling "feeble," the priest did rest for a few months. He desired to travel to Louisiana, but made it only as far as St. Louis before being overtaken by a tenacious fever that compelled him to sojourn there.

He fulfilled the goal of reestablishing his northeast Wisconsin churches and remained in the area until the mid-1870s. He transferred to Wisconsin Rapids from 1876 to 1878 and in 1879 moved to La Crescent, Minnesota, in the southeastern part of the state. He staffed several parishes in that region, the last one on record being at Rushmore, Minnesota, in 1898.

The town of Peshtigo was rebuilt and by 1881 had largely recovered from the fire. Actual losses were never determined since so much was totally consumed, and an accurate prefire accounting didn't exist. An 1873 edition of the *Wisconsin Assembly Journal of Proceedings* listed the following destroyed: "27 schoolhouses, 9 churches, 959 dwellings, 1028 barns and stables, 116 horses, 157 working cattle, 266 cows and heifers, 201 sheep, and 306 hogs." A tally of human deaths ranged from 1152 to as high as 1500, and many of the dead were never identified. The *Assembly Journal* listed only 383 names. Despite the uncertainty, no other North American fire's casualty list even approaches the low-end estimate. In October 1951, an official state marker was unveiled on the eightieth anniversary of the fire, and nineteen survivors were there to see it, the oldest being ninety-six.

Logging, land clearing, and fire practices that contributed to the Peshtigo disaster didn't immediately change in the Great Lakes states, and similar fires wreaked havoc into the twentieth century. In 1894, the Hinkley, Minnesota, fire killed 418 people, and the 1918 Cloquet, Minnesota, fire claimed 551. My hometown of Chisholm, Minnesota, was burned to the ground by a wildfire in 1908, with the tragic loss of fifty saloons.

During 2000, over 92,000 fires nationwide burned 7.4 million acres—almost twice the annual average acreage for the past forty years, though it's startling to note that Peshtigo alone equaled about 15 percent of that, and it happened in a matter of hours. In 2000, 850 homes were lost to wildfire, and twenty wildland firefighters died in the line of duty—four of them in helicopter crashes. I and my crew were pleased not to be among them.

I did find out later that the crashed airplane Derek found in Montana was not the one piloted by the missing doctor. A Forest Service investigation and a consultation with an ex–Flathead County sheriff revealed the plane went down circa 1950, killing four elk hunters. Horses were used to pack out the bodies.

Despite a dry autumn in Minnesota, the Blowdown didn't burn. However, a few prescribed fires were ignited in swaths outside the Boundary Waters Wilderness, offering a hint of the potential. In a patch of downed aspen—a tree species not generally associated with extreme fire behavior—Forest Service personnel observed 75- to 100-foot flame lengths, and spot fires a half-mile away.

On the evening of October 19, just after a pleasant dinner with Pam and some friends, I was ordered to the Carlos Edge fire in Anoka County, Minnesota, just a few miles north of the Twin Cities. It was a huge (8500 acres), fast-moving blaze that originated in a private yard and burned four houses. Given the human density in the area, it was astonishing to all concerned that more buildings weren't lost. I was assigned to manage helicopter Nine-Five-Whiskey, a Bell 206 Jet Ranger, and the first time we lifted off and flew over the fire I snickered at the irony. After all the hoopla and preparation for the big wilderness blowdown blaze, the largest fire of the season in Minnesota encompassed suburban sprawl. From the front seat of my helicopter I saw not the forested palisades of the Ontario border, but the skyscrapers of Minneapolis.

SOURCES

BOOKS

Carrier, Jim. *Summer of Fire.* Salt Lake City: Gibbs-Smith, 1989.

Heinselman, Miron. *The Boundary Waters Wilderness Ecosystem.* Minneapolis: University of Minnesota Press, 1996.

Leschak, Peter M. *Hellroaring: The Life and Times of a Fire Bum.* St. Cloud: North Star Press, 1994.

Maclean, John N. *Fire on the Mountain: The True Story of the South Canyon Fire.* New York: Washington Square Press, 1999.

Maclean, Norman. *Young Men and Fire: A True Story of the Mann Gulch Fire.* Chicago: University of Chicago Press, 1992.

National Wildfire Coordinating Group. *Intermediate Fire Behavior.* Boise: National Interagency Fire Center, 1994.

Pernin, Reverend Peter. *The Great Peshtigo Fire: An Eyewitness Account.* 2nd ed. Madison: State Historical Society of Wisconsin, 1999.

Putnam, Ted. *Your Fire Shelter: Beyond the Basics*. Boise: National Wildfire Coordinating Group, 1996.

Pyne, Stephen J. *America's Fires: Management on Wildlands and Forests*. Durham: Forest History Society, 1997.

———. *Fire in America: A Cultural History of Wildland and Rural Fire*. Princeton: Princeton University Press, 1982.

———. *World Fire: The Culture of Fire on Earth*. Seattle: University of Washington Press, 1995.

Sewell, Alfred L. *The Great Chicago Fire*. Chicago: Alfred L. Sewell, 1871.

Wuerther, George. *Yellowstone and the Fires of Change*. Salt Lake City: Haggis House Publications, 1988.

ARTICLES

Baltic, Scott. "When Safety Efforts Can Backfire." *Fire Chief* (October 2000), 4.

Barrett, Stephen W. "Fire History Along the Ancient Lolo Trail." *Fire Management Today* 60, no. 3 (Summer 2000): 21–28.

Brown, Hutch. "Wildland Burning by American Indians in Virginia." *Fire Management Today* 60, no. 3 (Summer 2000): 29–39.

Milius, Susan. "Why Fly into a Forest Fire?" *Science News* 159, no. 9 (March 3, 2001): 140–41.

Perkins, Sid. "A Nation Aflame." *Science News* 159, no. 8 (February 24, 2001): 120–22.

Pyne, Stephen J. "Where Have All the Fires Gone?" *Fire Management Today* 60, no. 3 (Summer 2000): 4–6.

Titus, Stephen. "Spontaneous Combustion: Dispatches from the Field." *Outside* 25, no. 9 (September 2000): 36–44.

U.S. Forest Service. "Boundary Waters Canoe Area Wilderness Fuel Treatment Impact Statement Update." Superior National Forest (December 2000).

Williams, Gerald W. "Early Fire Use in Oregon." *Fire Management Today* 60, no. 3 (Summer 2000): 13–19.

———. "Introduction to Aboriginal Fire Use in North America." *Fire Management Today* 60, no. 3 (Summer 2000): 8–10.

———. "Reintroducing Indian-Type Fire: Implications for Land Managers." *Fire Management Today* 60, no. 3 (Summer 2000): 40–48.

ACKNOWLEDGMENTS

I'm grateful to Joe Durepos, my agent, whose phone call out of the blue took us down an unexpected but enriching path; and to editor Gideon Weil, who manifests the rare talent of knowing more about the book than the author does and who is more relentless than a crown fire. Thanks also to Ellen Bogardus-Szymaniak, U.S. Forest Service fuels specialist at the Minnesota Interagency Fire Center, who provided valuable insight into a 130-year-old fire, and to Priscilla Stuckey for her deft tweaking of the manuscript.